WING
to
WING

WING to WING

AIR COMBAT IN CHINA, 1943–45

Carl Molesworth
and
Steve Moseley

ORION BOOKS / NEW YORK

Copyright © 1990 by Carl Molesworth
All rights reserved. No part of this book may be reproduced or transmit-
ted in any form or by any means, electronic or mechanical, including pho-
tocopying, recording, or by any information storage and retrieval system,
without permission in writing from the publisher.
Published by Orion Books, a division of Crown Publishers, Inc., 201 East
50th Street, New York, New York 10022
ORION and colophon are trademarks of Crown Publishers, Inc.
Manufactured in the United States of America
Library of Congress Cataloging-in-Publication Data
Molesworth, Carl.
    Wing to Wing air combat in China, 1943-45 / by Carl Molesworth and
  Steve Mosely.
        p.   cm.
      1. World War, 1939–1945—Aerial operations, American.   2. United
  States. Army Air Forces. China Air Task Force—History.   3. World
  War, 1939–1945—China.   1. Title.
  D790.M56   1990
  940.54'4973—dc20
  89-38609
  CIP
  ISBN 0-517-57568-X
  10 9 8 7 6 5 4 3 2 1
  First Edition

To the officers and men of
the Chinese-American Composite Wing.

Acknowledgments

I didn't set out to write a book about the Chinese-American Composite Wing. I just wanted to write an article for the *American Aviation Historical Society Journal*, because I'd never seen anything specific about the CACW. Then Steve Moseley signed on to help with the research, and pretty soon we had far more material than I could fit in the AAHS article. By the time it was published in the journal (Winter 1982), this book was well under way.

Writing a book isn't easy work, but my task was eased tremendously by the contributions of some seventy-five men who served in the CACW. Their outpouring of letters, photographs, documents, diaries, and other materials gave life to the project. The following men are due special thanks in this regard: Dick Frye, John Hanrahan, Jim Kinder, and Al Sweeney, 1st Bomb Group; the late Bob Gardner, Jim Kidd, Liu Shaio-Yao, the late Charles Lovett, Bob Riley, and Wilbur Walton, 3d Fighter Group; Bob Kruidenier, Mac McCullough, and Glyn Ramsey, 5th Fighter Group.

I also would like to thank some other people who contributed to this book—some with material and others with moral support. They are: Jane Dahlberg (John Dunning's widow), Tony Garra, the late Tom Holcomb, Mrs. Darrell King, Jeff Lindell, Paul Ludwig, Clay Mc-Cutchan, Milt Miller, Van Moad III, Rachel Perkins, William R. Reed, Kenn Rust, and Nick Williams. My wife, Kris, and daughter, Claire, were patient and encouraging throughout this long process.

Official documents provided the framework for this book. The folks at the Albert F. Simpson Historical Research Center USAF, at Maxwell Air Force Base, provided the vital microfilms that made it possible for us to review the records on our own schedule.

If I have one disappointment with *Wing to Wing*, it is that the book is heavily weighted toward the stories of the Americans who served in the CACW. This is only natural, given the barriers of access and language that separated us from most of the Chinese, especially those who served in the enlisted ranks.

My goal for *Wing to Wing* was that it would fill a gap in the recorded history of military aviation. The more I learned about the CACW, the more impressed I became with its accomplishments. This in turn made me more determined to write a book that would bring recognition and honor to the men who served in this unique organization. I hope I have succeeded.

Carl Molesworth
Mount Vernon, Washington

Contributing CACW Veterans

Forrest G. Ashmead, CACW headquarters
Albert Awana, 1st Bomb Squadron
Bennett M. Bennett, 17th Fighter Squadron
James Bennie, 17th Fighter Squadron
Richard C. Boward, CACW headquarters
Ferdinand Buechele, 32d Fighter Squadron
Glenn Burnham, 17th Fighter Squadron
Raymond L. Callaway, 8th and 32d fighter squadrons
Donald Campbell, 28th Fighter Squadron
Lee K. Chadwick, 3d Fighter Group
Chow Lai Pin, 7th Fighter Squadron
Clifford L. Condit, 5th Fighter Group
Richard C. Daggett, 28th Fighter Squadron
Eugene H. Dorr, Jr., 1st Bomb Group
Harry R. Drebbin, 3d Fighter Group
William A. Elmore, 8th Fighter Squadron
Frank K. Everest, 17th and 29th fighter squadrons
Jack W. Fetzer, 27th Fighter Squadron
Mount E. Frantz, 28th Fighter Squadron
Richard C. Frye, 4th Bomb Squadron
Robert L. Gardner, 8th Fighter Squadron
Robert F. Garriott, 26th Fighter Squadron
James B. Gibson, CACW headquarters
Warren E. Girton, 17th and 27th fighter squadrons
John C. Hamre, 8th Fighter Squadron

John P. Hanrahan, 2d and 3d bomb squadrons
John Henderson, 1st Bomb Squadron
William Hill, 29th Fighter Squadron
William T. Hull, 29th Fighter Squadron
William H. Joyner, 27th Fighter Squadron
Anthony H. Kao, 5th Fighter Group
Kenneth E. Kay, 3d Fighter Group
Charles J. Kidd, 32d Fighter Squadron
Hundley B. Kimbel, 17th Fighter Squadron
James A. Kinder, M.D., 1st Bomb Group
William J. King, 26th Fighter Squadron
Robert Kruidenier, 29th Fighter Squadron
Kuo Ju-Lin, 28th Fighter Squadron
Liu Shiao-Yao, 28th Fighter Squadron
Charles Lovett, 7th Fighter Squadron, 3d Fighter Group
Edward J. Lydon, 7th Fighter Squadron
Armit W. Lewis, 7th Fighter Squadron
Marvin A. Marx, 26th Fighter Squadron
Winton E. Matthews, 27th Fighter Squadron
William E. McCullough, 29th Fighter Squadron
Robert C. McNeil, 3d Bomb Squadron
Howard M. Means, 5th Fighter Group
Walter F. Michaels, 8th Fighter Squadron
Joe Millington, 5th Fighter Group
William R. Mustill, 27th Fighter Squadron
Lonnie Neal, 7th Fighter Squadron
Charles R. Norberg, 29th Fighter Squadron
Joe L. Page, 28th Fighter Squadron
Sol Panush, 5th Fighter Group
Charles F. Parker, 28th Fighter Squadron
Ernest J. Phillips, Jr., 8th Fighter Squadron
Richard J. Pontrich, 8th Fighter Squadron
Hoyt C. Powell, 17th Fighter Squadron
Glyn W. Ramsey, 17th and 26th fighter squadrons
Thomas A. Reynolds, 7th, 17th, and 26th fighter squadrons
Robert G. Riley, 32d Fighter Squadron
Roger W. Roberts, 32d Fighter Squadron
Sidney Rosenthal, 5th Fighter Group

Albert C. Rudert, 26th Fighter Squadron
Santo J. Savoca, 29th Fighter Squadron
Wayne Senecal, 3d Bomb Squadron
Burr Shafer, 32d Fighter Squadron
Melvin M. Simmons, M.D., CACW headquarters
Eugene L. Strickland, 28th Fighter Squadron, 3d Fighter Group, CACW
    headquarters
Allen H. Sweeney, 1st Bomb Group
William C. Thomas, 17th Fighter Squadron
Richard A. Usher, CACW headquarters
Robert L. Van Ausdall, 26th Fighter Squadron
Joseph J. Walsh, 2d Bomb Squadron
Wilbur W. Walton, 7th Fighter Squadron
Wang Kuang-Fu, 7th Fighter Squadron
C. F. Zimmerman, 17th Fighter Squadron

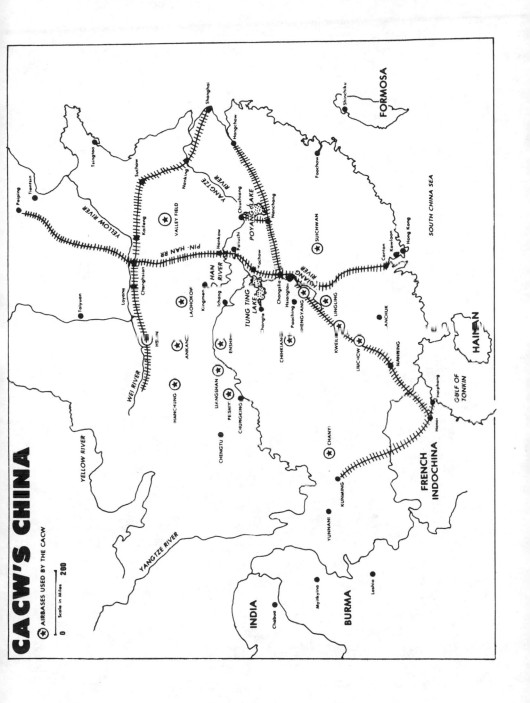

CACW'S CHINA

⊛ AIRBASES USED BY THE CACW

Scale in Miles
0 ——— 200

FORMOSA
Shinchiku

SOUTH CHINA SEA

Peiping
Tientsin
Tsingtao
Taiyuan
YELLOW RIVER
Suchow
Kaifeng
⊛ VALLEY FIELD
Nanking
Shanghai
Hangchow
Foochow
Loyang
Changhsien
⊛ HSIN
PIN-HAN RR
Hankow
YANGTZE RIVER
Chuchiang
Nanchang
⊛ SUICHWAN
Kweilin
Ichang
Kingmen
Paiushi
Fuchow
POYANG LAKE
HAN RIVER
⊛ LAOHOKOW
⊛ ANKANG
⊛ ENSHI
TUNG TING LAKE
Changte
Changsha
Hsiangtan
Hengyang ⊛
HSIANG RIVER
⊛ HENGYANG
⊛ LINGLING
Lingling
Nanching
Canton
Kowloon
Hong Kong
⊛ HANCHUNG
⊛ LIANGSHAN
⊛ PESHIY
⊛ CHUNGKING
CHENGTU
⊛ CHIHKIANG
Paoching
⊛ KWEIYANG
⊛ LIUCHOW
Liuchow
Nanning
ANCHUK
HAINAN
GULF OF TONKIN
⊛ CHANYI
KUNMING
YUNNANI
Haiphong
Hanoi
FRENCH INDOCHINA
WEI RIVER
YELLOW RIVER
YANGTZE RIVER
INDIA
Chabua
Myitkyina
BURMA
Lashio

WING
to
WING

1

The old P-40 was in trouble. It glided silently over the desert, its once fearsome shark mouth now grinning helplessly as the young pilot in the cockpit struggled to drag the fighter back to the field at Malir.

When the engine quit out over the Sind Desert just inland from Karachi, India, it was the beginning of the end for the P-40. Once it had roared to battle against the Japanese over Burma and China as part of the famous American Volunteer Group—the "Flying Tigers." Once it had been flown by the great AVG aces like Bob Neale, Tex Hill, and Jack Newkirk; now, eighteen months later, a young USAAF captain named Charlie Wilder—who had never even seen a Japanese airplane—was at the controls.

Wilder was flying one of the six rickety ex-AVG P-40s that had been supplied to the fledgling 3d Fighter Group at Malir for operational training. The old fighter's once natty camouflage paint scheme had long since faded to a dull khaki color; the wings that once had carried four machine guns and enough ammunition to blow apart several enemy airplanes were now stripped of their sting; its tires were bald, its brakes were spongy, and now its engine was dead.

From his vantage point in the cockpit, Wilder could have gazed out across the desert to the sprawling air base at Malir if he hadn't been so busy trying to save his life. Given a few moments to sightsee, Wilder could have marveled at the 6,000-foot concrete runway and the five-mile gravel extension, the sandbag revetments, the gun emplacements, and the big tin hangar. Beyond them were the concrete and tile barracks, the U.S. Army hospital and—even more incongruous than the air base itself—a Polish refugee camp.

This was the great base at Malir, built by the British in the dark days of 1942 when it was feared that Rommel would drive the British Army all the way out of the Mideast and to the gates of India.

Now it was September 1943, and instead of being a base bristling with British desert fighters ready to defend the last bastion of their colonial empire against the Germans, the base contained only a few hundred men preparing to take their B-25s and P-40s to China and join Gen. Claire Chennault's 14th Air Force.

Down on the field below Wilder's barely flying tiger, men of his fighter group and the 1st Bomb Group were finishing the long training that would prepare them to do battle against the Japanese. If their meager equipment and desolate surroundings weren't enough to set them apart from most outfits, the makeup of their personnel certainly was. Working side by side on an aircraft or flying in formation might be men who called home Canton, Ohio, or Canton, China.[1] These were the men of the Chinese-American Composite Wing.

In the hot, dusty wind their voices carried an explanation of overhauling a B-25's Wright Cyclone engine or the fine points of air-to-air gunnery in a flat Yankee twang or slow southern drawl, the interpretation in a quick jumble of guttural Chinese.

In all, the CACW eventually would consist of two fighter groups, the 3d and the 5th, of four squadrons each, plus the four squadrons of the 1st Bomb Group. All were units of the Chinese Air Force.

While it was a wing for organizational purposes, the CACW would never fly together as one. Men of the same group often spent months on bases hundreds of miles apart, and at one time a squadron of bombers operated out of Moran, India, while fighters of the 3d Fighter Group were flying from Hsian in North China, nearly 1,000 miles away.

If the organizational problems faced by the CACW were formidable, the logistics were even worse. China was at the end of the longest supply line in the world, and the CACW would find itself at the bottom of the 14th Air Force's list for supplies once they arrived in China. Captain Wilder's dying P-40 was symbolic of all the patched up airframes, rebuilt engines, and ill-supplied airfields that would mark the history of the CACW.

But that is getting ahead of the story. More important for now is the understanding of how and why the CACW was born in the first place.

The CACW can't be explained simply by facts and figures, missions and campaigns, or men and machines. It was the child of immense political and social pressures that marked relations between the United States and Chiang Kai-shek's Nationalist Chinese government throughout World War II.

By September 1943 the never very effective Chinese Air Force had deteriorated to the point that it could no longer be considered a combat force. Its rocky history contained only a few proud moments among the various beatings it had taken from the Japanese since the Marco Polo Bridge incident of July 7, 1937, when Japanese and Chinese ground forces clashed near Peking, touching off full-scale war between their nations

American and Italian missions to China from 1932–37 had failed to build an efficient force of Chinese pilots and aircraft to combat the Japanese in the air, and this failure became all too obvious in the first aerial skirmishes over the Yangtze Valley in 1937.

Enter ex-Capt. Claire Chennault, 47, recently retired from the U.S. Army Air Corps after a turbulent career largely spent defending pursuit aviation against those who considered fighter planes and pilots obsolete. Chennault, hired by the Chinese government to survey the combat effectiveness of its Italian-trained air force, found China totally unprepared to defend itself against Japanese aerial attacks.

Chennault rarely left China over the next eight years and earned his place in history there. From his frustrating start training Chinese pilots and organizing the ragtag International Squadron, he built air power in China largely through his own persistence and brilliance, until he literally had swept the Chinese skies clean of Japanese aircraft by early 1945. It was in those early days of 1937–38 that the idea of a Chinese-American combat unit first was tried in China. Its failure taught Chennault the lessons he would need to make the concept work when the time came to try it again.

In October 1937, with the Chinese Air Force nearly wiped out after the Battle of Shanghai, Chennault quickly threw together a group of

foreign pilots to fly combat while a force sent from Russia set up operations and established training programs for a new generation of Chinese
pilots. The Russians would provide the bulk of the opposition to the
Japanese in China skies until they pulled out in 1940.

The International Squadron, made up primarily of American, British,
and Dutch soldier-of-fortune types, proved unruly and only marginally
effective. Flying a motley collection of U.S., Italian, and Russian aircraft, they flew only a few successful missions.

Late in 1938, Chennault tried to reorganize the International Squadron by using selected foreign pilots for flight leaders and filling in the
other slots with Chinese pilots. Though not terribly confident of success,
Chennault tried the idea in order to use a group of new Vultee bombers
China had just purchased.

One of the most ancient and constant of Chinese considerations immediately arose, that of "face." Nothing was as important to the Chinese
as saving face, or pride. Losing face was to be avoided at all costs, and the
Chinese pilots considered flying under foreign leaders to be a great blow
to their pride. The Chinese pilots went on strike, and the bombardiers,
who were also officers, walked out in sympathy. Only the aerial gunners,
enlisted men who had no desire to return to the starving, corrupt Chinese Army, remained on duty.

Eventually the strike was resolved after a pep talk by Chennault, but
the squadron didn't last long. After flying a few missions, the Vultees
were caught on the ground by the Japanese at Hankow and bombed into
junk. With that, the squadron was disbanded, and Chennault went west
to Kunming, deep in Central China, to begin building an all-new Chinese Air Force.

Madame Chiang Kai-shek had set Chennault a two-pronged task.
While the schools at Kunming were teaching Chinese how to operate a
modern air force, other Chinese all over Free China were busy building
airfields that would eventually become vital to the nation's survival.

After the fall of Hankow on October 25, 1938, the Japanese advance
in China stopped. With all routes to the sea cut off, the Japanese felt
they could rely on aerial bombardment to keep the Chinese at bay and
plunder their resources while they continued their military buildup on
the home islands. Kunming was bombed for the first time by the Japanese
in January 1939, and for the next two years Japanese would range back
and forth across Free China, bombing every major city.

As Chennault's Kunming operation struggled to train new Chinese pilots, the old guard of the CAF continued to put up sporadic defense alongside the Russians. More modern Japanese fighters took ever-heavier tolls on them, but the crowning blow came at Kunming on September 13, 1940, when Japanese naval pilots in their prototype A6M "Zero-Sens" first caught up with a formation of Chinese fighters. Minutes later twenty-seven Curtiss Hawks and Russian I-15s and I-16s lay in smoking rubble while the Japanese returned to their base unharmed. This drubbing left a lasting impression on Chinese pilots and became another important impetus for the formation of the CACW.

A month later Chennault was on his way to Washington, D.C., for the visit that would result in the formation of the American Volunteer Group. The appearance of the Zero-Sen and the weakness of the CAF made it obvious to all that the Chinese had no hope of defending themselves in the air for the foreseeable future.

The AVG began to take shape in the summer of 1941 at a steamy jungle air base in Burma, where ninety-nine Curtiss P-40s were delivered to the ex-Army, -Navy, and -Marine pilots Chennault had recruited in the United States.

While the AVG was learning its lessons, Lend-Lease was having an effect on the CAF. Export fighters—108 Republic P-43A Lancers and 129 Vultee P-66 Vanguards—were sent to Chinese squadrons in the second half of 1941, and arrangements were made to give Chinese cadets flight training at the USAAF's Luke and Thunderbird fields in Arizona. Many of those cadets would return to China as combat-ready pilots of the CACW.

For almost two years after Pearl Harbor the China air war would be fought primarily by American pilots. In its six months of combat from December 1941 until July 1942, the AVG piled up one of the most impressive records in aviation history while firmly establishing Chennault's reputation as a brilliant tactician and leader.

When the AVG was disbanded on July 4, 1942, its score stood at 297 Japanese aircraft destroyed, and it numbered twenty-six aces among its pilots. The Burma Road had been lost, but the Japanese could no longer bomb Free Chinese cities at will.

The AVG was replaced in China by the China Air Task Force of the USAAF, with now-Brig. Gen. Claire Chennault in command. Chennault had been reinducted into the USAAF the previous spring.

The CATF, which consisted of the four P-40 squadrons of the 23d Fighter Group plus the B-25s of the 11th Bomb Squadron, carried on the fight in China until it was expanded to become the 14th Air Force in March 1943.

Despite the infusion of American-built aircraft, the CAF remained largely dormant during this period. Apparently no missions were flown until October 1942. From then through the end of the year the CAF flew eight missions, the first being an intercept at Nancheng on October 24, when two P-43s shot down a Japanese recon aircraft. Only two of the other seven could be considered offensive strikes.

The CATF was a mobile, hard-hitting outfit, but its five squadrons simply weren't enough to wage aerial war on the scope envisioned by Chennault and Chiang Kai-shek. As a result, the generalissimo began pressuring Washington in late 1942 to establish a numbered air force in China, with Chennault as commander. The heavy lobbying brought action, and in February 1943 Gen. H. H. "Hap" Arnold, chief of the USAAF, flew to China for a five-day conference with Chiang, Chennault, and Lt. Gen. Joseph Stilwell. Arnold came away convinced that a buildup of air power in China could be beneficial, but he also wanted the Chinese to begin bearing more of the load. In Washington, meanwhile, President Roosevelt was hearing Chiang's plea for a separate American air force in China.

Arnold's desire to get more Chinese into the air war was in line with the U.S. war policy of "Europe First." It was easier to provide combat-ready aircraft than combat-ready aircrews to the remote theater.

Chennault and Stilwell knew that Chinese fliers—both those on duty in China and also the ones training in the United States—would be available if they could get aircraft for them. Their major concern was how to make sure that once equipped the Chinese would actually fight, for thus far in the war the air force and particularly the army had shown a persistent reluctance to do so. Many Americans believed Chiang was hoarding his forces, looking past the present conflict to the day when he would face the Chinese Communists in a civil war.

Their solution was to devise a way to place these Chinese under Chennault's command. The first idea, as shown in the following correspondence, was to incorporate Chinese pilots into American squadrons. This was done, but the numbers involved were too small to accomplish their goals.

Chennault, however, was already looking ahead. On January 21, 1943, he had written to Stilwell:

". . . I have given careful consideration to the matter of supervising and commanding Chinese Air Force units in China. As a result of more than five years' experience in training and controlling Chinese air units, I herewith submit the following suggestions:

"The supervision and control of Chinese air units by foreigners in an advisory capacity never produces the best results.

"Chinese air units will be effective in combat only if provided with flying equipment equal to or superior in performance to that of the enemy.

"While there is a considerable number of experienced aircrews, both bombardment and pursuit, available in China, the majority of those crews will need carefully planned refresher courses. For several years the Chinese have not had a sufficient number of airplanes to maintain pilot And crew efficiency. Nearly all the older pilots will require special training in the tactics considered most suitable for the new types of airplanes which will be furnished them.

"Special attention will have to be given to the organization of tactical units and to other necessary features such as communications, supply, housing, mess, and transportation.

"While it is believed that supervision and control by foreigners acting in an advisory capacity cannot produce the best results, it is believed that excellent results could be commanded by a foreign officer assisted by a staff composed of officers from all the nationalities having combat units operating in China. In this way, the facilities, supplies, and personnel now available in China would be made available equally to all operating units. Plans for the offensive and defensive employment of combat units could be coordinated and put into execution with the least delay and greatest effectiveness." [2]

With a little fine tuning, that last paragraph can be considered the birth of the CACW. The aircraft and training needed to bring it to maturity, however, were still many months away. In the meantime Chennault—after his meeting with Arnold—wanted to get some of the Chinese fliers into action with his USAAF units, so he wrote to General Chow, director of the Commission on Aeronautical Affairs, in Chungking on March 4:

"I am informed that many Chinese pilots in both bombardment and pursuit classes find it difficult to maintain pilot proficiency due to the shortage of combat-type airplanes in the Chinese Air Force. In order to correct this situation, it is suggested that selected Chinese pilots be assigned to American air units for flying duties.

"At present the CATF has the following units in China: four fighter squadrons; one medium-bombardment squadron. In addition to the above, it is anticipated that four heavy-bombardment squadrons will arrive in the near future. It is believed that four selected Chinese pilots could be given sufficient flying time on combat missions to maintain their efficiency. Chinese pilots assigned to bombardment units would be required to fly as copilot for the usual period of time before qualifying as first pilots. Chinese pilots assigned to fighter units, regardless of rank, would be required to fly as wingmen for the usual period of time. [Note here how Chennault has carefully sidestepped the issue of "face," as only an old China hand would know how to do.]

"In the selection of Chinese pilots for these duties, it is suggested that junior officers who completed their flying training and who understand and speak English should be selected. These pilots were trained in American tactics and tactical methods and should be able to understand orders and instructions issued in English without the need of interpreters. However, pilots who understand and speak English, but who did not train in the United States, should be given second priority for these assignments.

"If desired by the Commission on Aeronautical Affairs, these pilots could be rotated at intervals of approximately three months so as to afford all qualified pilots in the CAF an opportunity to serve with American combat units.

"In addition to maintaining pilot proficiency in combat aircraft, this plan would offer the following advantages: A. Training of Chinese pilots in American tactics and tactical methods. B. Acquainting Chinese pilots with the latest technical equipment received by American Air Units in China. C. Promoting closer spirit of cooperation and comradeship between American and Chinese flying personnel."[3]

On the same day he wrote his letter to General Chow, Chennault also wrote to an old friend, Lt. Henry C.Y. Lee of the CAF, who was then stationed at Chengtu with the 23d Fighter Squadron of the 4th Fighter Group:

"For a long time I have been considering the use of Chinese pilots with

American air units and your letter confirmed my decision to submit the matter to General Chow. I have just suggested to him that he permit selected Chinese pilots, both bombardment and pursuit, to serve with appropriate American air units. If approved, this plan will allow all of you to receive more flying time, keep abreast of modern tactics, and to take a part in more combat missions. Naturally, such service will assure better cooperation between American and Chinese personnel in the future. As soon as a decision is rendered, I will advise you.

"I often recall your service with me from 1937 and in my recollections, you will always be an outstanding figure because of the excellent cooperation and the faithful service which you rendered.

"It is my earnest wish that you and other Chinese pilots who desire to serve fully in this war should be given every opportunity to do so."[4]

Lee was one of five young CAF members assigned to Chennault when he first arrived in China, serving as his radioman and interpreter. He recalls:

"When the AVG was formed, General Chennault told me to go get flying training. One hundred of us Chinese cadets went to United States in 1941. We graduated in Luke Air Advanced School 42E at Phoenix, Arizona. One of our instructors (ground school) was Capt. Barry Goldwater.

"I never became a member of the CACW. The general had me in his headquarters, and I also worked in Fighter Control until the war ended."[5]

The 14th Air Force was activated on March 10, 1943, but at that time it amounted to little more than a name change for the CATF. In May Chennault flew with Stilwell to Washington to attend the Trident Conference. At the conference, among other things, plans for the future of the 14th Air Force were made.

More U.S. bomber and fighter groups were slated for service in China, but the plans also called for a force of eighty fighters and forty bombers of the CAF to be commanded by Chennault. This force would become the CACW.

The Karachi American Air Base Command, which had been training Chinese pilots since early that year, was replaced by the China-Burma-India Air Forces Training Unit (Provisional). This new organization was given the responsibility for training the Chinese-American units.

On June 30, Chennault sent the following cable to Arnold:

"An OTU [Operational Training Unit] for Chinese Air Force at Karachi has been staffed with American and Chinese personnel and is now prepared to train Chinese personnel from the states commencing August 5, 1943. Imperative that commitments to the Generalissimo be kept and that following plan be adhered to: organize and train two Chinese fighter groups, one Chinese medium-bombardment group of four squadrons each. Two fighter squadrons and one medium-bombardment squadron may train simultaneously; training period six weeks, first class starts August 5th.

"In order that these Chinese units operate efficiently and be employed to advantage tactically, organization of groups and squadrons necessitate the assignment of American officers and enlisted supervisory personnel as an integral part of each unit. This requires that American personnel reach Karachi at the same time, or prior to arrival of Chinese personnel.

". . . All personnel referred to . . . must be furnished as same are not available Fourteenth Air Force."

"First contingent requires forty U.S.-trained Chinese P-40 pilots plus American personnel as outlined. First contingent for one medium-bombardment squadron requires twelve U.S.-trained Chinese B-25 pilots plus American personnel. All thirty-six Chinese pilots now available can be utilized to advantage. . . ."

"Best interest will be served if Chinese B-25 pilots ferry aircraft to Karachi utilizing ATC flight leaders. Plans call for twelve B-25s [to] arrive Karachi by July 25 for maintenance before start of training. All other personnel, both Chinese and American, arrive prior to August 5. Immediate attention should be given to meeting the requirements of the above plan."[6]

Brig. Gen. Howard Davidson, who was later to command the 10th Air Force in India and Burma, was given the job of organizing the CACW under the code name "Lotus." In a July 5 cable to his boss, Maj. Gen. George Statemeyer, USAAF commander in India and Burma, Davidson reported satisfactory progress on Lotus.

While Davidson was busy in India, the group of pilots and technicians Chennault had requested were on their way to Miami, Florida, from bases around the United States to organize for their shipment to the Far East. Lt. Col. T. Alan Bennett, who had been busy at Mitchel Field,

New York, forming a P-47 fighter group to serve in Europe, was chosen to command the first CACW fighter group.

In all, sixteen American fighter pilots and eight bomber pilots were in the first contingent of CACW fliers.

Bennett was a burly, balding man of 32. He had joined the Air Corps in 1933 as an aviation cadet and served in fighter squadrons prior to the outbreak of the war. In February 1942 he was sent to Brazil to train fighter pilots on the new aircraft they were getting from the United States. With the war came long-awaited promotions. He advanced from first lieutenant to lieutenant colonel in six months and returned to the United States to command the 50th Fighter Group. His next stop was the 1st Fighter Command Operational Training Unit. He finally got his combat assignment when he convinced General Davidson to include him in the Lotus project.

The first two fighter squadron commanders were to be Maj. Eugene Strickland and Capt. Bill Turner. Strickland had been training one of Bennett's squadrons when the CACW assignment arose, but had not flown any combat. Turner, on the other hand, was a combat veteran who was credited with two kills in the Java campaign of early 1942 with the 17th F.S. and another with the 41st F.S. in August of that year. Both eventually would command the fighter group.

These men, with the help of flight leaders like Charlie Wilder, would lead the first CACW pilots into battle and can be credited with a great deal of the success of the wing.

The fighter pilots congregated at Grand Central Station in New York City on July 18 to board the Silver Meteor, bound for Boca Raton. Using pennies collected by pilots Jim Bush and Keith Lindell during their days at West Point for chips, the men played poker all the way to Florida. A break was taken occasionally when Bennett, a big bluffer, would blow his top after losing a pot.

The group was processed for shipment at the Floridian Hotel in Miami, trucked to the Thirty-sixth Street Airport for weighing and tagging, then trucked again to the Battle Creek Hotel in Miami Springs to spend the night.

At 3 A.M. on July 22, 1943, the first elements of what would become the CACW flew out of Miami in a collection of Air Transport Command C-46s, C-87s, and C-54s. They arrived at Karachi Air Base on July 31, after the flight from Florida to Natal, Brazil, over the Atlantic with a stop at Ascension Island, across Africa and the Middle East to India.

The 1st Bomb Group (Provisional) and the 3d Fighter Group (Provisional), Chinese Air Force, were formed on July 31, 1943, the day they arrived in Malir. The bomb group was partially made up of American officers and enlisted men reassigned from the 402d Bomb Group, USAAF.

If the U.S. officers of the fighter group were largely untested in combat, the bomb group could at least boast an illustrious commander. Col. John A. Hilger had been one of the pilots who flew B-25s off the deck of the U.S.S. *Hornet* on April 18, 1942, with Jimmy Doolittle on his famous raid on Japan. Ironically, this very mission, during which he crashed behind Japanese lines, would preclude Hilger from ever flying combat with the CACW.

Chosen to command the bomb squadron—designated the 2d Training Squadron for the time being—was Capt. Thomas F. Foley. By the time he left China after finishing his tour, Foley was the top bombardment pilot in the CACW, credited with having sunk 28,900 tons of Japanese shipping.

As the Americans settled into their new desert home, they met the Chinese with whom they would serve. The pilots were a mixed bag: some were veterans of the earliest fighting against the Japanese, while others were fresh from flight training in the United States. The Americans were pleasantly surprised to find that some of the CAF technicians, especially those assigned to the fighter group, were already familiar with much of their work.

Many of the technicians had worked on early Curtiss Hawks, which were similar to the 3d F.G.'s P-40s in most respects except the engines and radios. The B-25s were another matter: even many of the U.S. personnel were unfamiliar with the sophisticated twin-engine bombers.

The command system that would be used throughout the history of the CACW was set up immediately. It called for duplicate U.S. and Chinese commands all the way from wing command down to individual flight leaders in the squadrons. Most of the staff functions, such as intelligence, also were duplicated.

The Chinese named Maj. Li Hsueh-Yen[7] their 1st B.G. commander and Maj. Yuan Chin-Han as 3d F.G. commander. Major Yuan would prove a particularly capable officer, commanding the 3d F.G. throughout the war and flying missions as late as May 1945. He was described by group historian Ken Kay as "a smiling, taciturn soldier with an ear half shot away from some earlier battle; hospitable, a speech-making party man and a fine tactician."[8]

Training began with a tawdry collection of war-weary fighters and bombers. Of the six B-25s retired from service with the 11th B.S. in China, only two were operational at first. There were also six P-40s— actually export Curtiss Hawk 81-A2s—that had been flown by the AVG and later the CATF. These fighters, referred to as "P-40Bs" by the CACW, were later supplemented with a number of worn P-40Es and -Ks that had been flown in combat over North Africa by the 57th Fighter Group. During the early days the two fighter squadrons had to take turns flying the P-40s because there weren't enough for both squadrons to fly at once.

Training actually started on August 5, when a morning meeting was held in the big hangar at Malir for all bomber and fighter personnel. Lt. Col. Louis Hughes, commander of the Operational Training Unit at Malir that was responsible for preparing them for combat, spoke first, followed by Lt. Col. Lee C.S. of the Chinese detachment.

Hughes set the tone of the meeting by reading a telegram from General Chennault welcoming the newcomers to the war. Then he explained the purpose of the organization: "to train Chinese personnel in the American methods of aerial warfare and to place a real meaning to the phrase 'United Nations.'" Also speaking were Hilger, Bennett, and Yuan.

The first order of business was to acquaint the U.S. personnel with something of Chinese customs and language, and a plan was devised to begin classes. Meanwhile the aircraft were being worked on; some were set aside for ground-crew training while others were fixed up for flight.

The language barrier would dog the CACW throughout its existence. From the beginning interpreters were used extensively, both in classroom training and also in the air. An extreme example of this problem arose during training, when a Chinese tail gunner in a B-25 misunderstood an order over the intercom and bailed out of the plane, only to sheepishly walk into Malir after a night on the desert.

It was also discovered early in the history of the CACW that the

Chinese technicians, while adept enough at assembly, were very poor at troubleshooting mechanical problems. It was thought that this was due to the fact that China was a much more primitive country in the 1940s than was the United States, so the average Chinese simply didn't have the technological experience needed to work on complicated aircraft systems.

These problems would ease in time, but they were never completely solved.

From the beginning at Malir, it was determined that CAF and American personnel would have segregated living and dining areas. This varied in China among squadrons and bases, but the wing was Chinese-American primarily during duty hours only. CAF officers and enlisted men had separate quarters and mess facilities in Malir, just as the U.S. personnel did.

Flight training on the B-25s was strictly transitional for the first two weeks, as the Chinese pilots were familiarized with the powerful Mitchell bombers. The first bombs were dropped August 20: 100-pound demolitions from 1,500 feet altitude using the D-8 bombsights.

Meanwhile, Capt. Derward Harper, operations officer of the bomb squadron, organized ground school for the U.S. pilots, navigators, bombardiers, radio operators, gunners, and ground personnel. A skip-bombing range was set up later, as well as a firing range on the beach near Malir to practice with the B-25s' flexible .50-caliber guns and their fixed .50s and 75mm cannon.

The fighter squadrons were going strong, too. Ground school for pilots consisted of about sixty hours of instruction in emergency procedures, navigation, maintenance, air tactics, gunnery, and bombing.

Flight-training requirements were as follows: ten hours transition; eleven hours formation; seven hours ground gunnery; eleven hours shadow gunnery; six hours aerial gunnery; two hours bomber escort; seven and a half hours navigation; and dive bombing as was practical.

As training progressed, more U.S. and Chinese personnel arrived at Malir. Lt. Col. Irving L. Branch was assigned deputy commander of the 1st B.G. Capt. James T. Bull was assistant operations officer of the 3d F.G., helping out Maj. Tom Summers, operations and executive officer of the group.

Two more fighter squadron commanders arrived to form the final two squadrons of the 3d when the first two completed training. They were Majors Howard Cords and William Reed. Reed's assignment was made interesting by the fact that he had formerly served in the AVG. Originally, Chennault had hoped to draw many ex-AVG fliers into the CACW; as it turned out, only Reed and Lt. Col. Gil Bright were ever assigned.

As the Americans and Chinese spent more time together, they began to understand each other. If the technical abilities of some Chinese were frustrating, the courage and spirit of others were inspiring.

Perhaps the best example came on October 1, during a practice bombing mission. Sgt. Lo Te-Hsiu was riding in a B-25 when he noticed that a bomb had fallen from a faulty rack and was lying on the closed bomb bay doors. It wasn't possible to simply open the doors and drop the bomb because its arming spinner was turning in the draft, so the bomb could explode with the slightest concussion.

Sergeant Lo dropped down through the bomb bay and grabbed the whirling spinner, cutting his hands and arms while he removed the vanes. After he finished disarming the bomb, the sergeant climbed back up into the aircraft, the bomb bay doors were opened, and the bomb dropped out harmlessly onto the desert below.

On another occasion, Lieutenant Colonel Bennett had to put his foot down after a CAF sublieutenant of Turner's squadron got a little carried away on a strafing pass over the offshore flats.

"Now yesterday," said Bennett solemnly, "someone got three camels and two probables on a strafing mission. I don't know whether it was one of the Chinese boys or the Americans, and I don't care, but it will have to stop. Furthermore, these camels were pregnant, according to the letter we got."

The Chinese-American Composite Wing (Provisional) itself was formally activated on October 1 at Malir, with Col. Winslow C. Morse as commander. Morse had been commander at the AAF's proving ground at Eglin Field, Florida, before coming overseas. As the months passed he was able to bring many of his Eglin people over to China to serve with him, especially in the 5th F.G.

Colonel Morse was a big, athletic man in his midthirties. He grew up in Long Beach, California, and graduated from the University of Redlands after majoring in physical education and playing on the football and baseball teams. He joined the Air Corps after graduation, completed flying school in 1929, and was commissioned a second lieutenant in January 1930.

Morse served in various pursuit squadrons during the early 1930s and won the national aerial gunnery championship in 1932. He flew in the National Air Races twice and also flew the mail during 1935 on the Salt Lake City–Oakland run. He traveled to China and Japan in 1936 while assigned to the Philippines, and then in May 1940 was appointed commander of the 1st Pursuit Squadron of the 23d Composite Group at Orlando, Florida.

Morse's squadron moved to Eglin Field, Florida, in June 1941, and the following September Morse was named deputy commander of the 23d Composite Group and deputy chief of the Proof Department, Proving Ground Command, at Eglin. January 1942 saw Morse named commander of the AAF Proving Ground detachment, and in April 1943 he became chief of staff for the AAF Proving Ground Command. He left that post to come to India and his first combat command, the CACW.

Training continued on the old fighters and bombers, which would remain behind at Malir for the next squadrons after the first three departed for China. New P-40Ns and B-25Ds and -Hs were slated for the squadrons to take into combat.

At this time it was thought that the Americans eventually would leave the wing to the Chinese when the time was right. The CACW headquarters history recorded: "The mission of the CACW(P) will be complete when Chinese personnel are capable of officially operating the fighter and bomber groups and squadrons without further supervision on the part of USAAF personnel. At this time all American personnel will be withdrawn from the entire wing, and the composite units welded into a smooth-working organization will be turned over entirely to the Chinese Air Force."[9]

As it turned out, this goal was never attained. As late as May 8, 1945, top U.S. command discussed the issue, but the war ended before any action was taken on it.

And what became of Charlie Wilder, whom we left gliding along in his P-40 trying to get back to Malir with a dead Allison engine underneath the shark's grin on his old fighter? Wilder proved equal to his task. The young captain got his plane back to Malir, all right, but he couldn't put it down on that big runway. The fighter landed in a nearby field and skidded along in a cloud of dust until it collided with a gun emplacement left by the British and tore itself to pieces.

Wilder was quickly pulled from the wreck, his face a mass of blood after he banged into the P-40's instrument panel. The injury was more dramatic than serious, however, and he soon returned to his job as 28th F.S. operations officer.

Wilder, a quiet, serious man from Georgia, became one of the CACW's longest-serving American officers. He transferred to the 5th F.G. in early 1944 to command the 17th Fighter Squadron, became group operations officer later that year, and finally commanded the entire 5th group briefly before he returned to the United States in July 1945.

2

Operational training of the first three CACW squadrons stretched on beyond the planned six weeks and into October 1943. The initial shortages of aircraft and organizational growing pains had conspired against the eager fighter and bomber squadrons, but they need not have fretted: it was raining in China anyway.

At Malir, it was dusty and hot as ever as the pilots and crewmen finished their training. Finally the squadrons were activated on October 9. Major Strickland's outfit was designated the 28th Fighter Squadron (Provisional); Captain Turner's was called the 32d; and Captain Foley's command was designated the 2d Bomb Squadron (Provisional).

The Chinese squadron commanders were: 28th F.S., Capt. Cheng Sung-Ting; the 32d F.S., Capt. Hung Chi-Wei; 2d B.S., Capt. Hu Chao-Tung. Captain Cheng had replaced Capt. Tseng Pei-Fu, who was killed in a flying accident at Malir on August 26.

Graduation ceremonies were conducted on October 15. Brig. Gen. Julian Haddon, commander of the China-Burma-India Air Forces Training Unit at Karachi, spoke to the first graduates of his school.

The same day, twenty-four new P-40N-5s began to arrive for the 28th and 32d and twelve B-25Ds and -Hs for the 2d B.S. The fighters were a handsome lot, carrying the twelve-pointed Kuomintang stars, blue-and-white striped rudders, and fearsome shark mouths on their noses. The

B-25s, on the other hand, were practically devoid of markings, with the USAAF stars and serial numbers painted out and only tiny Chinese serials on their rudders.

The Curtiss P-40 fighter has practically become synonymous with the China air war. Gradually improved from the early models flown by the AVG, the P-40 reached its peak with the N series that equipped the CACW fighter squadrons. By late 1943 it was considered obsolete for use in the European theaters, but it was still capable of doing the job over China. The P-40N was rugged, reasonably fast, and capable of carrying heavy and diverse armament under its wings and belly. While not as maneuverable or fast-climbing as the Japanese fighters used in China during that period, the P-40N's speed and diving ability made it a formidable opponent for the Japanese Ki-43 Oscar and Ki-44 Tojo fighters it would most often face.

This was especially true when the "Sharks"—the preferred nickname for the P-40 in the 14th Air Force—were flown by well-trained, heads-up pilots.

Lt. Keith Lindell of the 32d F.S. was the first U.S. officer of the CACW to cross the Himalayas—the infamous "Hump'"—into China. He led an advance party out of Malir on October 17 in a transport plane. Six B-25s, led by newly promoted Maj. Tom Foley, left Malir on October 24 and became the first CACW aircraft to reach China.

On October 27 Lieutenant Colonel Branch led the other six B-25s out of Malir. Branch had replaced Hilger as commander of the 1st B.G. on September 21. A 14th Air Force policy stated that airmen who had escaped from behind Japanese lines were not allowed to fly any more combat in China for fear that if they went down again and were captured, the Japanese might learn how they had escaped the first time and make reprisals against the Chinese who had helped them.

Hilger couldn't very well command the group without flying combat, so he was reassigned and Branch took over.

Flying with Branch's B-25s were the nineteen P-40s of the 28th and 32d. They flew first across India to Chabua, then spent a few days preparing for the flight across the Himalayas into Kunming. Bennett had occasion to unleash his impressive temper several times along the way as Lieutenants Tien, Martin, Kuo, Hung, and Meng damaged their fighters in various landing and taxiing mishaps.

The CACW suffered its first taste of war on October 28. On that day a transport carrying sixteen U.S. and Chinese ground crewmen, mostly of the 28th F.S., crashed over the Himalayas, killing everyone on board. The wreckage was never found. Finally, on November 3 the formation of B-25s and P-40s led by Branch and Bennett climbed away from the jungle strip at Chabua and headed east for China. The flight over the Hump was uneventful, and they landed at the air base at Chanyi, just northeast of Kunming. Because of the slight possibility that they might meet Japanese fighters while crossing the Hump, this flight was considered the first combat mission for each of the crews. This rule meant that the crossing of B-25s led by Major Foley on October 25 was the first official combat mission in the history of the CACW.

Meanwhile, training began back at Malir for the next three squadrons of the CACW. Maj. Bill Reed was named commander of the 7th F.S., Maj. Howard "Snatch" Cords commanded the 8th F.S., and Capt. John Washington commanded the 1st B.S. The Chinese commanders were: 7th, Capt. Hsu Chi-Hsiang; 8th, Capt. Szutu Fu (he would be replaced before the squadron went into action by Capt. Liu Meng-Jinn); 1st B.S., Capt. Lee Yien-Luo.

The 28th and 32d fighter squadrons were left on alert at Chanyi after they arrived, and the 1st B.G. personnel moved on to Yangkai and established headquarters there. The B-25 crews of the 2d B.S., however, flew east to Erh Tong Airfield at Kweilin and began combat operations almost immediately.

Finally, after having cooled their heels for two weeks, the fighter squadrons were ordered on November 17 to move up to Kweilin. The weather turned bad before the fighters could make the move, and it wasn't until November 23 that the 3d F.G. fliers arrived at Erh Tong. For the time being the CACW squadrons would be part of the 14th's Forward Echelon, commanded by Col. Casey Vincent.

The 2d B.S. had been busy in the interim. The CACW's 21½-month combat history began at the famous air base snuggled among the ice-cream-cone mountains in Kwangsi Province on November 4, 1943, when three 2d B.S. B-25s accompanied other Mitchells of the 11th B.S. (USAAF) on a sea sweep against Japanese shipping.

The mission was flown by Major Foley, Capt. William Carson, and Lieutenant Kao with an all-Chinese crew. The formation found cargo boats at Swatow Harbor and swept in for the attack. Guns and bomb releases malfunctioned on Foley's and Kao's aircraft, so they turned around and came back across the harbor to try again. In the repeat attack Lieutenant Kao became separated from the others, but Major Foley's bombs hit a cargo boat and sunk it. This was the first damage done by the CACW to the Japanese, but there was a price to pay. It is believed that Lieutenant Kao's bomber was damaged by return fire during one of his attacks. Two hours later the plane crashed near Wuchow, Kao apparently having become lost while trying to find the way home. All aboard were killed.

That was not the only bomber lost on that first day. Captain Carson went out on a second mission later in the day, flying another sea sweep along the China coast. This time Carson had trouble with his bomb release and was hit by antiaircraft fire that severed the gas line in the bomb bay while he was attacking an enemy vessel. On the return flight to Kweilin, Carson and his 11th B.S. flight leader became separated in bad weather. When the B-25 lost its right engine at 12,000 feet, Carson decided it was time to drop down out of the overcast and find out where he was.

He tried to contact his Chinese radioman, but found that the airman had already bailed out of the plane. Then the other engine began to lose power, so at 1430 Carson crash-landed the plane near a railroad line at Ishan. No one was injured, and the plane was considered salvageable. The radioman rejoined his crew later on their way back to base.

A sea sweep flown by Foley's crew followed on November 7, but no targets were found. The next day Carson was out again. He found no shipping targets, but he attacked the airfield at Kiungshan on Hainan Island and was credited with probably destroying three or four parked Japanese aircraft.

Action continued through the month as Foley and Carson flew the CACW's first high-altitude mission, a strike against targets at Yochow, near Tungting Lake, on the 11th. Then on the 16th Lieutenant Colonel Branch flew his first mission, sinking a 200-foot freighter and probably sinking a 150-footer. Bombardier-navigator Lt. Louis Graves was wounded by flying Plexiglas when the nose of the bomber was hit by flak. Later that day Major Foley sank a 300-foot tanker. That same day the headquarters of the 1st B.G. began its move from Yangkai to Kweilin. This movement, like that of the fighter squadrons, was delayed by weather.

The weather broke just before Thanksgiving, and when it did Casey Vincent didn't intend to waste the opportunity to strike. A long-planned mission to Shinchiku airfield on the island of Formosa was set, and six CACW bombers were slated to take part. They left Kweilin at 0600 and staged through Suichwan, where they picked up eight B-25s of the 11th B.S. and a fighter escort of P-38s and P-51s of the 23d F.G. after they refueled.

The formation crossed the Formosa Straits at minimum altitude and caught the Japanese completely unprepared. A few Japanese planes in the landing pattern were quickly shot down by the P-38s as the bombers climbed to 1,000 feet to release their fragmentation bombs, which were armed with instant fuses. Seeing that there were no opposing interceptors and only minimum antiaircraft defense, Branch led his flight down for a strafing pass before they headed for home. Even the turret gunners got into the act, firing into a barracks area as the bombers swept low over the field. For this action Branch was awarded a Distinguished Flying Cross.

Vincent, the charismatic young commander of the Forward Echelon who would soon become a general at age 29, recorded in his diary that night: ". . . Cleaned house—shot down fourteen Japanese planes over their own field and destroyed or damaged 50 to 60 more on the ground. We lost not a plane! The Chinese-American bomber outfit got in it with six of their B-25s and did admirably. I'm thinking they're going to be a damned good outfit . . . a very lovely Thanksgiving Day!"[1]

The Shinchiku raid was the most successful thus far in the history of the 14th Air Force, and the 2d B.S. received commendations from Colonel Vincent and Lord Mountbatten for its part in the attack.

The 1st B.G. lost two bombers on the 29th when Major Foley and 1st Lt. William Daniels attacked shipping at Amoy Harbor. They encountered heavy antiaircraft fire over the harbor installations. A radio station and a power station were hit by bombs, but both B-25s also sustained damage. Foley's ship was hit in an oil line of the left engine, while Daniels's plane was hit in the hydraulic system, causing the wheels to partially extend.

As the B-25s left the target area, the drag from Daniels's wheels hanging out in the breeze caused him to fall behind Foley. Finally, Foley circled back, even though his left engine was now running very rough.

Foley pulled in behind Daniels, then radioed a message about the bad motor that Daniels only partially received.

Four minutes later Foley ordered his crew to bail out. The radioman, Lt. Yang C.C., and turret gunner, Sgt. Lo K.C., bailed out first. Then Foley and Lieutenants Wilbur Taxis, the navigator, and Tsao K.K., the copilot, jumped out.

In the meantime, Daniels proceeded with his crew to the base at Namyung and circled there until his fuel supply had been used up. Finally, Daniels brought in the B-25 on its defective landing gear and made a crash landing. Three days later the damaged bomber was shot up by strafing Japanese fighters on the field at Namyung.

Foley's crew landed near Engteng and were contacted by Chinese army forces, who escorted them to Kukong. There on December 8 they boarded a train for Hengyang, and on the next day they flew out of Hengyang to their base at Kweilin.

The first CACW fighter mission was flown on December 1, 1943, a week after the 28th and 32d squadrons reached Kweilin.

The December 1 mission wouldn't prove particularly exciting, but it was notable for a number of reasons. In all, nine B-25s, five from the 2d B.S., were assigned to strike the docks at Kowloon on the coast near Hong Kong, and seventeen P-40s of the 3d F.G. contributed to the fighter escort, providing close support.

The formation joined up over Erh Tong, then headed south toward the target. CACW bombers were flown by Branch, Captains Chester Conrad, Derward Harper, William Carson, Winston Churchill, and 1st Lt. Mark Seacrest. Majors Yuan, Summers, and Strickland, plus Captains Turner and Bull, led the fighters. Also in the formation was Lt. Col. Frank Rouse, who was in China to get some combat experience prior to forming the 5th Fighter Group at Malir the following month. The other USAAF fliers were Lieutenants James Bush and Frank Smiley of the 28th F.S. and Lieutenants John DeHaven and Clifford "Tip" Boyle of the 32d.

Rounding out the fighter pilots were the Chinese squadron commanders, Captains Cheng and Hung, plus Capt. Wang S.C., and Lt. Wu S.L. of the 32d and Lieutenants Meng C.Y., Chang C.M., and Cheng T. of the 28th.

The bombers crossed their target on a heading of 160 degrees, then turned sharply back north toward home. The bombing appeared to be accurate, with only three bombs falling outside the target area. The flak was medium in intensity and accurate for altitude, but it trailed the formation.

Five Ki-44 Tojo interceptors approached the formation but were driven off near Kowloon. During this exchange one of the B-25 gunners, Sgt. Wei C.C. in Branch's plane, claimed a Tojo probably destroyed, the first air-to-air damage claim made by the CACW.

All aircraft returned to base, and the bomber crews reported that the escort provided by the fledgling fighter squadrons was "very satisfactory."

The first big air battles involving the CACW came on December 6, when an ambitious dual mission was laid on for the Changteh area west of Tungting Lake. A mission against the same target on the 4th had not been opposed, but the Japanese were ready when the formations returned.

The plan was for the CACW fighters and bombers to stage through Lingling, fly the mission to Changteh, then land at Hengyang to refuel and rearm. Then they would return to Changteh for another strike and continue home to Kweilin.

The first attack was made at 10,000 feet, the four CACW B-25s carrying twelve 100-pound bombs each. As the formation reached the target a flight of six silver Ki-44s attacked individually from head-on. They bore in and fired, then pulled up over the formation. The bomber of Lt. Lin C.Y. took a hit in the leading edge of the left wing, and Lieutenant Seacrest's aircraft was hit in the top turret, but neither B-25 was seriously damaged.

The escorts, which were above and behind the bombers, jumped on the Tojos as they pulled off the bombers, and Lieutenant Boyle scored what was to become the first CACW fighter kill, plus a probable. The victory was not confirmed until the following month. Captain Bull and Lieutenants Wu Yuen and John DeHaven also scored probable kills during the scrap.

All aircraft landed at Hengyang at 1130, the B-25s were repaired as needed, and the second mission took off at 1345.

Again the bombers struck Changteh at 10,000 feet, but this time the bombing was more accurate than during the morning mission. A formation of about ten Ki-44s and Ki-43 Oscars attacked over the target, wading head-on into the escort fighters.

The Japanese got the best of the afternoon scrap. Lt. Tan S.Y. of the 32d was shot down in P-40N No. 632. He was wounded and bailed out, then was captured near Changteh and interned in Hankow. The irrepressible lieutenant escaped fourteen months later and returned to his squadron in April 1945.

Another P-40 went down on the mission, but its pilot wasn't so lucky. Lieutenant Boyle, who had proven to be masterful at handling the Chinese pilots of his flight, was killed in his P-40 No. 652, "Quincy Queen," named for his hometown in Illinois. He was credited with a probable kill on the mission before being shot down.

Branch's gunner, the deadeye Sergeant Wei, was credited with destroying one Tojo that he had spotted chasing a P-40 and saw dive into the ground after he fired at it. The P-40 of Lieutenant DeHaven was damaged by one of the attackers, and two bullets hit Lieutenant Seacrest's B-25 in the windshield during the attack, but they didn't pierce the glass.

On December 16 Bennett, who had just been promoted to full colonel, piled up No. 655 after he had engine trouble on takeoff for a mission. Fortunately, he wasn't hurt in the wreck. Meanwhile, the B-25s made several five-plane strikes, then began a series of two-aircraft antishipping sweeps that netted considerable tonnage destroyed.

The 2d B.S. also took the aerial scoring lead temporarily on December 16, when Lieutenant Colonel Branch and Captain Harper flew single-plane shipping sweeps along the China coast. Branch found no targets and returned, but Harper found plenty of action.

About thirty miles northeast of Canton four Ki-44s attacked Harper's aircraft, two head-on and two from astern. The gunners were able to fight off the Tojos without Harper's aircraft being hit, then Harper proceeded to bomb river docks at Tung-Wan and head for home.

Just then, a twin-engine Japanese plane identified by the crew as a Ki-46 Dinah was spotted, and a twenty-five-minute dogfight ensued. Considering the capabilities of the Ki-46, a fast and maneuverable recon aircraft, it is more likely that the Japanese plane involved was a bomber, perhaps a Ki-48 Lily or Ki-21 Sally, because the top speed reported for the enemy craft was 200 mph.

At any rate, three passes were made at it from behind, and all members of the crew took shots at the Japanese plane. Finally one crewman bailed out, though only his small parachute opened, and Harper's crew watched the enemy plane crash into the ground.

Credit for the victory was shared by the crew, since it was impossible to determine whose gunfire had caused the fatal damage. Later it was reported that Chinese troops recovered important documents from the wreckage, and Captain Harper was awarded a Distinguished Flying Cross for the action.

The fighters got their next taste of action on December 23, when the 32d participated in an escort mission for B-24s of the 308th B.G. that were hitting Canton. Captain Turner scored the first victory of his tour, bringing his total to four, and Lieutenants Lindell and Chen scored their first kills of the war. Lindell also scored a probable victory, as did Captains Hung, Tom Maloney, and Jim Dale. Two Chinese lieutenants, Hwang S.Y. and Wang K.C., were shot down and listed as missing in action. Both were flying P-40s assigned to the 28th, Nos. 631 and 635, on the mission. Lieutenant Wang had been something of an artist, having designed the 3d F.G. insignia only a few weeks before his death.

The next day it was the 28th's turn to get on the scoreboard. On a strike against Tien Ho airfield by the same 308th B-24s, the 28th scored three kills, two probables, and four damaged. The kills were registered by Lieutenants Meng C.Y., Chao Y.H., and Chow S.L. Lieutenant Chow also had a probable kill, and Chao added a damaged claim. Lieutenant Smiley racked up a probable and damaged two others, and Lieutenant Art Skidmore damaged one Japanese fighter.

Major Strickland led his fighters and gave this detailed account of the mission:

"Eight B-24s were staging at Erh Tong and had to take off prior to our takeoff. As soon as their last ship cleared the field, my squadron started taking off. In approximately ten minutes we were all airborne and assembled in formation. By that time the B-24s had already set course for Canton and were out of sight. I headed for the course and increased my throttle setting to thirty-five inches of manifold pressure. We finally caught up with them about fifty miles from Canton.

"A flight of about five Zeroes hit the bombers from twelve o'clock. It is believed that in this initial pass they shot down a B-24. I saw one parachute open at the tail end of the bomber formation immediately after the first pass. Whether this was a Jap or an American I do not know.

"As the Zeroes would come into the bombers from the front, they would do a half-roll through the bombers and break away down and to the side.

"I was leading the first flight of fighters and I pulled them up slightly ahead of the bombers and did some long-range shooting at subsequent Zeroes coming in at twelve o'clock. This helped to some extent, for when they saw tracers coming across their nose they immediately flipped over on their backs and dived out. We did not try at any time to follow them down but maintained our position on the bombers.

"In the meantime several Zeroes were stunting off to the side and out of range of our fighters. Captain Cheng, our Chinese squadron commander, was in command of the second flight and occasionally would turn into them and chase them off.

"I got in several ninety- to sixty-degree deflection shots, but each time the Zero would flip on his back and do two or three turns and a spin and keep going down. Only once did I have a chance to follow a Zero in a climb. I was forced to break off because my airspeed was down to 150 mph. Following the Zero to my left, I broke sharply down and to the right. Looking back I did not at any time see the Zero again.

"The bombers pulled off the target to the left and headed north again. The enemy continued to make attacks, which persisted until we were about eighty miles out from the target.

"When we were about twenty miles on our way home I was on the right side even with the lead bomber and trying to reassemble the formation when I noticed a Zero on the tail of a lagging P-40. Immediately I pulled up and back. Lieutenant Smiley was on my wing all the time, a fact I was not aware of. I started firing slightly out of range to make the Zero quit firing as soon as possible. He immediately flipped over on his back and did about three turns of a spin. I continued firing while he was in the spin, with unobserved results. Pulling back up, I rejoined the formation.

"The last Zero I saw was about five minutes later, about a thousand yards behind the last bomber and shooting at the formation. Shortly afterwards he broke off into diving turn. The bombers were left about ten minutes later and we came back to our base without further mishap."[2]

The mission had lasted three hours and fifteen minutes, with the fighters landing at Erh Tong at 1450.

The three CACW squadrons soldiered on through the end of the year, but the weather was deteriorating and no further claims were made. The 32d did manage to lose another pilot, however, Lt. Wong K.C.

Christmas celebrations began with a chicken dinner at the Erh Tong hostel mess hall, followed by the first movie the CACW boys had seen in China, a doubtful tale entitled *The Crystal Ball*. Many officers attended a Chinese-hosted party at the Luchan Hotel in downtown Kweilin, and others attended midnight religious services in town.

All squadrons were busy on Christmas, so the holiday wasn't celebrated until the following day, when a huge party was staged at Casey's bar in Kweilin.

New Year's eve found some of the officers invited to a big party hosted by the Chinese provincial governor, while the rest were on their own to make merry in Kweilin.

On January 1, 1944, Generalissimo Chiang Kai-shek arrived at Erh Tong to look over his new squadrons and present all the men with diaries. A big party was laid on by the 32d that night to celebrate Bill Turner's promotion to major, and the next day "Twig" Branch was promoted to full colonel. He had led four pilots with new B-25s for the 1st B.G. in from India the previous day.

While all this activity was going on in China, three more CACW squadrons were wrapping up training at Malir and preparing to make their own trip across the Hump.

The 7th F.S. had lost its first operations officer, Captain Hackleman, in a flying accident on November 29 at Malir. Otherwise, the training had gone reasonably well for the squadrons. Besides Major Reed's 7th and Major Cords's 8th F.S., the 1st B.S. had been preparing under Capt. John Washington.

These three squadrons left for China in mid-January and arrived at Kweilin—after the now customary and frustrating stopover at Chanyi— a month later.

In the meantime, the first elements of the 5th Fighter Group and the final two bomb squadrons were arriving at Malir to begin training. They had been less fortunate, having been shipped to India from the United States by sea.

The trip had not been uneventful.

3

While the 3d Fighter Group had been rushed to India via air transport to begin its training, the 5th group proceeded, beginning in early October 1943, in the more traditional "hurry up and wait" military style.

Before leaving his assignment at Eglin Field for India to command the CACW, Colonel Morse had made arrangements to draw on the tremendous pool of trained technicians there to form the core of his second fighter group, the 5th, and round out the bomb squadrons. Col. William E. "Mac" McCullough, USAF retired, then a chief warrant officer assigned to the Proof Department of the Air Proving Ground Command, got the job of selecting 152 enlisted specialists and then was ordered with them to Goldsboro, North Carolina, for further processing.

After a three-week delay at Camp Patrick Henry, Virginia, the group was joined by a cadre of officers from Eglin and others from a casual pool of recent Officer Candidate School graduates to form Air Force Shipment No. 6404. They were sent to Hampton Roads, Virginia, to board the liberty ship *Andrew Hamilton.* The disappointed men, who had expected to fly to India, sailed out on October 2 and arrived in Oran, Algeria, twenty-three days later after a cramped, uncomfortable trip.

It was another month before the shipment of 152 enlisted men and 82 officers got any closer to their destination, which they knew to be Karachi. During that time the officers were left largely at loose ends, but the technicians were put to work for the 19th Air Depot Wing, cannibalizing crashed and force-landed aircraft from the surrounding countryside. McCullough recalls that many of the spare parts that they recovered were shipped to the 5th Air Force in the South Pacific, where spare parts were sorely needed.

During this time some of the officers to be assigned to the 5th F.G. decided to jump the gun and hop a ride to India. Lt. Col. John Dunning; Majors William Hull, Rex Barber (of the Yamamoto intercept mission fame) and George MacMillan (who had served with Bill Reed in the AVG); Captains Fred Ploetz and Fred Scudday (a veteran of the Eagle Squadrons) were all reported AWOL during their trip but quickly were forgiven when they showed up at Karachi. Barber, Scudday, and MacMillan, because of their combat experience, were soon transferred to the 449th F.S. in China to fly P-38s.

The men of Shipment No. 6404 took their next step closer to the Orient on November 23, when they boarded three ships—the *Rohna, Egra,* and *Karoa*—in Oran Harbor, bound for India. The officers were split alphabetically among the three ships because of the limited quarters for them, but the bulk of the enlisted men were assigned to the *Rohna.*

The HMS *Rohna,* a British ship of 8,602 tons, had been built in 1926 and already had a distinguished war record. The officers found their quarters a vast improvement over the *Andrew Hamilton,* though the enlisted quarters were hardly better than those on the liberty ship had been. The *Rohna* was crewed by Indian sailors with British officers, and it left Oran carrying 96 officers and about 1,800 enlisted men.

The three ships waited until the evening of November 24 to steam out of Oran and join a convoy that included about fifteen troop ships headed east toward the Suez Canal and on to India.

The next day was Thanksgiving, and some of the enlisted men groused because they heard that the officers had been served fresh turkey for dinner while they had been given canned turkey.

By the following day, November 26, 1943, some of the men were beginning to wonder about the lack of air cover over the convoy, but the nine escorting destroyers seemed to add some security with their heavy antiaircraft armament. Over across the Mediterranean at Marseilles, France, members of the Luftwaffe's KG 100 bomb wing were also aware of the destroyers' antiaircraft guns, but they were preparing to attack the convoy nevertheless. They were equipped, they figured, with just the weapon to do it: the Henschel radio-controlled flying bomb.

The Luftwaffe began attacking the convoy at about 4 P.M. on the 26th. The German bombers, Dornier Do-217s, were able to make continued attacks because they launched the flying bombs outside the range of the convoy's antiaircraft defenses. Despite this, the attacks were almost totally ineffective, possibly because the radio control signals were being jammed by a radar-equipped U.S. destroyer in the convoy.

The Dorniers approached the convoy from dead astern, released their flying bombs, ignited the rocket motors in them, then guided them on into the convoy and tried to ram them into one of the ships. It seems fairly obvious why most of the bombs missed, when it is considered that the flying bomb was being controlled by someone riding in a bomber far behind it while the bomber was trying to avoid being shot down by return fire from the convoy. If the signals were being jammed as well, that made the likelihood of getting a hit even slimmer. Nevertheless, one flying bomb succeeded.

The memory of the *Rohna* attack is something that time can dull only slightly for the CACW members who survived it. One of them is Col. Glyn Ramsey, USAF retired, who was a young fighter pilot aboard the HMS *Karoa* on the day of the attack. He recalls:

"They were Dornier bombers, and they were carrying under their wings these glide bombs which were used on us. Rather than getting within the convoy they stayed outside the curtain of fire our defense was able to throw up and they flew racetrack patterns with impunity just outside the range of our guns. They would release the bombs when they were flying parallel to the convoy. I watched some of them released. The bombs seemed to be so slow. Of course, they were on course directly toward us and we didn't have much of a concept of movement. . . .

"The alert was called around four o'clock in the afternoon . . . and it continued until dark.

"One [destroyer] in particular was a powerful vessel that had a rooster tail out behind it during this engagement that seemed to be almost as high as the conning tower. Finally one of the bombers broke away and dropped down and ran the risk of the ship's fire and made a run from the stern of the destroyer. I watched as the destroyer raced under full power with the bomber catching up, but not too fast since the bomber was only flying 140 to 150 mph and the destroyer was going some forty knots. I thought to myself, 'That bomber is not more than 300 feet above the water and he can't hardly miss unless they knock him down first.' But he continued, and lo and behold, just as I thought it was time to release bombs the captain of that destroyer threw everything in reverse, and that destroyer literally popped up like a cork and stopped dead in the water.

"That's the way it appeared to us. I mean a ship moving that fast; it took some time to stop, but it actually appeared to stop, and the bombs went over the destroyer and landed in front. When that bomber got out in front of that destroyer, the stuff they threw up was murderous. I know they must have torn him apart with shrapnel. However, he did fly off; I didn't see him crash.

"Finally, after about twenty minutes of repeated attacks, they hit the *Rohna,* which was directly behind us about a quarter mile. It was the next ship in line behind the *Karoa.*

"They blew that ship almost in half. I was looking at it when it was hit, and all kinds of deck cargo it had just flipped end over end up in the air, and that ship was immediately cut out of formation because you could see it was fatally hit."[1]

Two men aboard the *Rohna* who lived to tell the tale were Capt. Robert D. Kruidenier, a fighter pilot, and S. Sgt. Marvin A. Marx, a supply specialist. Their accounts are remarkably similar, considering the panic and confusion of the situation.

Kruidenier wrote an outline of his experiences overseas after he returned home in 1944. This is his report of the *Rohna* attack:

"All of our well-armed transports plus our nine escorting destroyers were firing everything they had as bombs began falling much too close for our peace of mind. Several of us picked up our tin hats and went up on deck, the better to see the action.

"The attack kept up for about twenty minutes with some very near misses until one German bomber let go a radio-controlled glide bomb, and as I stood rooted to the spot I knew that this was the one with our number on it.

"Our boat was moving under forced draft, and I did not know which way to move but just stood and watched the bomb come rushing toward us at terrific speed. It struck amidships just above the water line, and it must have had a delayed-action fuse as it did not explode until just after it had entered the hull of our boat. Then it let go with a gigantic explosion which shook the ship violently. The engines and boilers blew sky high, and great fires immediately started roaring below deck.

"With the initial explosion we lost hundreds of lives as there were troops packed in the very decks where the bomb exploded. Our ship, of course, lost headway, and the rest of the convoy raced ahead pursued by the bombers.

"As soon as the bomb struck, every sign of order vanished, and it became a fight of survival in which many lives were lost needlessly. As the men recovered from the shock of the explosion sufficiently to move into action, panic spread like wildfire, fanned on by the terrifying screams of the dying and the horrible sight of frantic men clawing their way to the upper decks with clothes on fire and skin hanging loose from their faces and bodies. The only alternative was to jump over the side into the cold salt water, which many of them did even though they did not have on their life belts, and their chances of survival in the heavy seas running at the time were one in a million.

"The situation was made worse by the desertion of the Indian crewmen from their posts. They raced for the lifeboats and rafts. These they cut loose before any of the troops had a chance to get aboard and be lowered to safety.

"The boat started to list heavily to one side, and we knew she could not last long. I went back to see if the other boys had gotten out all right, but the cabin had been demolished, and some fine boys had left this world for a more peaceful one.

"On returning to the open deck I found Brown [his friend, bomber pilot Sam Brown], and we decided it was high time we left our present position and started swimming. We inflated our life belts, which we had worn all the time, and climbed down a rope net hanging over the side.

"The water was cold, and we stayed together as we rode up and down on the big waves, trying not to drink any of the salt water. After what seemed like hours we found a submerged lifeboat and climbed into it. In the boat we found a couple of tin buckets and started to bail.

"As fast as we bailed water so that the boat would hold a little more cargo we reached out and pulled in half-drowned soldiers. After much bailing we had around sixty men packed into our little rescue craft.

"Darkness had moved in, and our flaming transport had gone down beneath the waves. Along toward midnight we found a large British ship standing by in the darkness trying to pick up as many men as could reach her. She, of course, could show no light, but as we came drifting alongside we found a rope net that had been let down over the side. All the able-bodied men went swarming up the net to the security the *Clan Campbell* offered.

"However, we had many horribly injured men in our boat with third-degree burns and broken limbs who could not climb to safety. The hours spent in which Brown and I worked getting these men up the side of that big British ship still seem like a bad dream to me, but at least it was done."[2]

Marvin Marx was in a line of men waiting to march through the engine room to another room to eat dinner when the German bomb hit the *Rohna*. He wrote an article titled "The Real Thing" that graphically describes what happened next:

"Orders to march into the 'mess hall' were never given. One bomb rocked the ship more violently than any of the others, and we concluded that we had been hit. We were ordered up the companionway to the main deck; then ordered back down again; then up again.

"What met our eyes and ears here was mass confusion!

"The crew of this ship were natives of India; the officers were British. Members of the crew were in lifeboats, pleading with the GIs (who were strictly passengers) to operate the mechanism that would lower them into the Mediterranean. Someone tried to lower a lifeboat, but due to faulty equipment, only one end was lowered, and the Indians tumbled haphazardly into the sea. Later observation showed that the mechanism for some of the lifeboats was rusted to the deck.

"Some members of the crew were crouched on the deck, praying to Allah, and there was an animal on the deck that I identified as an ibex, but it was said by another American soldier to be a sacred cow.

"NO ONE SEEMED TO BE IN CHARGE! No one was giving orders. We observed the captain of the ship at his post, smoking his pipe and saying nothing.

"I saw an American soldier climbing up through a burning hold from below, his face bloody, no doubt from being thrown against a portion of the ship. Of course, he was not the only one injured in this manner. And no doubt some were so severely injured that they couldn't climb up. Others probably were killed instantly by the explosion.

"An American lieutenant ordered a group of us to throw overboard life rafts, wooden planks, and anything that would float, as a large number of GIs had jumped into the sea, some of whom could not swim.

"We began rushing to the rail, dropping everything overboard without looking to see where it was landing.

"'It's not Thanksgiving—it's the Fourth of July!' we shouted, hoping to boost the morale of some of the others. Soon we were told to look first, as some of this material was landing on the heads of the men who were close to the side of the ship.

"We learned later that some of these men, panic-stricken, had jumped overboard fully clothed with helmets in place, straps under chins, a full pack on their backs, and/or rifles in their hands!

"Their chances for survival was nil. All this while the fire below deck was raging.

"Finally there was only about fifteen of us left on deck; the guys who had been throwing floatable stuff overboard. Collectively and individually we decided it was time for us, too, to unofficially abandon ship.

"I swam to the nearest life raft, already occupied by several Americans, and we all held on, literally, for our dear lives. I was determined that no telegram from the War Department would be sent to my bride of twenty months.

"We could see a hole in the side of the ship, large enough for an automobile or truck to drive through. Later, some of us saw the *Rohna* sink, stern first.

"Just like the *Lusitania* in the movies, I thought.

"I do not know for how long we clung to the life raft, but during that period the sun sank and the moon and stars came out. At that geographic location and at that time of year, 6 P.M. was like broad daylight in the U.S. in July. Some survivors later claimed to have been in the water up to twelve hours."

"The rescue ship that picked me up had only two rope ladders. When a crewman lowered a length of rope I grabbed it eagerly, but I was so exhausted I did not have the strength to pull myself up hand over hand as some of the younger men did. I just held on to the rope and two sailors pulled me up.

"It was later I learned that the bomb—or aerial torpedo—that finally sank the *Rohna* had struck in the engine room, next to the 'mess hall' in which we guards were to have eaten our dinner."[3]

Probably the most courageous action during the *Rohna* tragedy was taken by Maj. Edward A. Kelly, a physician who would become the 5th F.G. flight surgeon. He was awarded the Silver Star on May 14, 1944, for the bravery he showed in treating the *Rohna*'s wounded, but unfortunately no account of his actions has surfaced.

The *Rohna* survivors were put ashore the following day at Phillipsville, about sixty miles east of Algiers on the coast of North Africa. The number of men lost on the *Rohna* has been listed variously from 1,170 to 1,283, and hundreds more were wounded. McCullough and Ramsey recall that of the 152 enlisted technicians bound for the CACW, only 48 survived. Of those, says McCullough, only 28 actually were fit for duty. It was an excruciating baptism of fire for the 5th Fighter Group, a blow that the Japanese were never able to duplicate in the sixteen months of combat the group would spend in China.

Meanwhile, the rest of the convoy continued on its way toward the Suez Canal. About three days after the *Rohna* went down, the ships were attacked again, this time by German Ju-88 bombers. They were south of Crete, about a day and a half out of Port Said, when the bombers struck.

Another CACW-bound officer aboard the convoy was Lt. Charles Lovett, who later became intelligence officer of the 3d Fighter Group. He recalled the second attack during an interview in his law office in Portland, Oregon.

"We were hit again right off of Alexandria, and these planes came from Crete. They just dropped straight bombs. They would fly over and make a bomb run and drop them down. They didn't hit anything. In Egypt were some RAF boys, and the Germans made one pass on the convoy before the RAF showed, and then that was the end of the bombing right there. The RAF chased them out of there. We never saw any of them shot down, but they didn't hit anything in our convoy. We went through the Suez Canal and across the Arabian Sea, and we landed in Bombay."[4]

Ramsey recalled that during the second attack, his ship, the *Karoa*, was covered with water several times from near misses by the Ju-88s. The ship was later found to have a bent rudder, which was fixed at Port Said before the convoy continued on to Bombay.

The shipment was held up in Bombay for a week before the men departed by train for Karachi. They boarded the Frontier Mail, a crack express train to New Delhi, and found that Colonel Morse had had all the mail that had been collecting for them at Karachi shipped down to Bombay and loaded aboard the train for them to read on the trip.

McCullough picks up the tale of the trip:

"The Frontier Mail ran 125 miles in 100 minutes. It was too good to be true, and then it happened. We were shunted onto another branch line, and for the next four days we chugged along at twenty miles an hour.

"Christmas day we stopped for lunch, which consisted of chili, dehydrated carrots, a piece of bread, and a half peach. After mess kit drill (we used the engine as a source of hot water) we found that the driver was 'stoned out' and was asleep in the coal tender. The conductor was fit to be tied and after frantic telephone calls and telegraph messages was advised to wait until the following day for a replacement engine driver. Since the food had been exhausted, it looked like we would have nothing except a bit of tea for supper and breakfast.

"A big decision was made. I became the driver and successfully 'drove' the train eighty-seven miles in nine hours. That was forty-five minutes under the regular schedule. I might add that the poor conductor and fireman were 'basket cases' when we reached the division point. The fireman, who spoke no English, did a magnificent job in holding up his side of the cab and also kept me out of trouble.

"We finally reached Karachi on the 27th of December, 1943."

The 5th Fighter Group was activated at Malir on January 13, 1944, with Col. Frank E. Rouse as commander and Lt. Col. John Dunning deputy commander. Maj. Shiang Kuan-Cheng was named Chinese group commander.

The training cycle began again as the first two squadrons of the 5th took shape. Commanding the 26th was Maj. Robert Van Ausdall, with Ramsey as operations officer. Maj. Hull and Capt. Ploetz, who had jumped the gun and avoided the *Rohna* tragedy, were assigned commander and operations officer, respectively, of the 29th F.S.

4

The opening months of 1944 were far busier for the weathermen in China than they were for the flight crews of the CACW. The fighters of the 3d F.G. flew only two missions in January, and the 1st B.G. was able to fly only fourteen missions in ten days during the month, mostly two-plane sea sweeps.

The bomb squadron used its USAAF pilots almost exclusively during January, though many Chinese were in the aircrews. Captains Derward Harper and Winston Churchill flew the first mission of 1944 on January 1. Then, on the 12th, Harper and Capt. Chester Conrad, who later would command the 3d B.S., took off from Erh Tong headed south toward the coast to look for enemy shipping.

About 100 miles out the B-25s became separated in bad weather, and Harper turned back. Conrad pressed on south for the coast, and as they neared Maoming the weather improved to a scattered cloud condition.

Conrad's bomber was flying northeast up the coast at about 1,500 feet altitude when the crew spotted a Japanese Ki-21 "Sally" Mk. II bomber about 1,000 feet above them at one o'clock on a reciprocal course to their own. Conrad immediately made a 180-degree climbing turn to the right and began chasing the enemy aircraft, which was out of sight by the time he got his bomber turned around.

The brownish-black Sally was overtaken in about five minutes, and it was now about 500 feet lower than the pursuing B-25. Conrad dove and approached from the left rear quarter, firing the four forward .50-caliber nose guns of his B-25H from a range of about 500 yards. The burst missed, and the top gunner in the Japanese bomber returned the favor when Conrad had closed to about 200 yards.

The B-25 continued to close, and it passed over the top and to the right, with only about ten yards separating the two bombers. Conrad took up "formation" about thirty yards off the Sally's right wing. The top turret guns, operated by T. Sgt. J. Hanrahan, jammed on approach, but he was able to charge one of them and open fire, knocking out the Sally's top turret on the first burst.

Hanrahan's next burst drew a line from the Sally's wing root through the cockpit, and the copilot was seen to slump over in his seat.

At that point the Japanese pilot nosed his craft over into a dive and Conrad followed. The B-25, however, accelerated too fast, and Conrad found himself sitting out in front of the Sally. He pulled up and banked to the left while Hanrahan continued to fire. Then return fire from the Sally hit Conrad's left wing and knocked the B-25 beyond vertical.

As Conrad leveled the B-25, his tail gunner, T. Sgt. P. Dodge, got in another long burst at the Sally. By the time Conrad completed leveling out the B-25, the Sally had disappeared from view. Since tracers from both turrets had been seen to hit the Sally, and it apparently never pulled out of its dive, the crew claimed it as probably destroyed when they returned to base. Conrad never had found any shipping targets, so the entire combat had taken place while the B-25 carried four 600-pound demolition bombs in its belly.

Captain Harper had his second crack at air-to-air combat on the 24th, when he took part in a six-plane coastal shipping sweep led by Major Foley. The B-25s staged at Suichwan took off at 0645. They found their first target, a 300-foot freighter, at 0915, and Captain Carson sank it with a near miss.

Next they flew to Lichanoa Bay, where they found six vessels and immediately swung to the attack. When it was all over Foley was credited with sinking two 250-foot freighters; Carson, with a 300-foot freighter and a 175-foot freighter sunk; 1st Lt. Charles Miles, with a 225-foot freighter damaged; Harper and First Lieutenants William Daniels and Mark Seacrest, with a 300-foot passenger-freighter sunk; Harper, a 100-foot seagoing tug damaged.

As Harper made a diving run toward the oceangoing tug, the Plexiglas blew off the top turret of his B-25H, No. 608. He fired at the tug with the 75mm cannon in the bomber's belly, dropped his bomb, and then was pulling out over the bay at 2,000 feet when a Japanese E-13 "Jake" seaplane approached head-on.

The Jake opened fire, and Harper returned the favor with his four nose guns. The Jake began to smoke, but its pilot made a tight turn over the harbor and attempted to attack the B-25 from behind. The Jake and Harper turned together, and the Japanese aircraft pulled in on the tail of the B-25, but by now its engine was smoking badly. Before the Japanese pilot could open fire, the Jake's engine quit and the pilot made a hasty water landing.

Seeing the Jake land, Harper brought the B-25 in for a bomb run and dropped two 500-pounders on the helpless Japanese aircraft, sinking it and confirming the second victory for his crew.

The glory of Harper's crew was short-lived. Two days later, as they were returning from Suichwan to Kweilin, their B-25 got trapped in bad weather and crashed into the side of a mountain, killing them all.

Lost, besides Harper, were Capt. Charles Waugh, Master Sgt. Albert Danovitz, Technical Sergeants Sanford Carhart and Frank Leimer, and the Chinese copilot, Lieutenant Chow. These were the first Americans of the 1st B.G. to be killed in action. A final note came on April 1, when Captain Harper was posthumously awarded the first Silver Star in the CACW for bravery in aerial combat.

The bombers may have been keeping busy, but the 28th and 32d fighter squadrons could do little but play softball and wait for a break in the overcast.

The first fighter mission of the year was an escort of B-25s against Mon Kay, down in Indochina, on January 19. The fighters strafed after the bombers finished, and Capt. Jim Dale of the 32d was hit by ground fire in his P-40, No. 651. He was forced to crash-land on the way home and walked into Kweilin two days later.

The first fighter kill of the year was recorded on January 23 during a mission against Kai Tak airfield at Hong Kong. Maj. J. T. Bull, group assistant operations officer, flying Major Turner's No. 646 P-40, knocked down an Oscar over the field for the only score of the month.

Weather continued to hinder fighter operations, but an especially significant mission was flown on February 11, when the P-40s returned to Kai Tak. This time there were twenty Japanese fighters in the air to intercept the formations, and the 3d F.G. lost two fighters while scoring four confirmed kills and a probable, as well as holding the Japanese fighters off the B-25s.

Most notable of the kills was that of Maj. Bill Turner. His victory gave him a total of five kills and made him the first ace of the CACW.

The two pilots shot down on the mission were Lieutenants Yang Y.C. and Don Kerr, both of the 32d. Yang was killed, but Kerr survived the first of many epic escapes from behind enemy lines that CACW aircrews would experience in the months to come.

Kerr and Lieutenant Teng were attached to the top cover, which was provided primarily by the 23d F.G. for the mission.

Over the target, about twenty Japanese fighters bounced the formation. Kerr got in a three-second burst on one of them and saw it begin to flame. He lost sight of it after seeing the pilot jettison the canopy, and Teng reported seeing it crash.

In the meantime, three more enemy fighters jumped Kerr while he was in the midst of rejoining his flight with a dive-and-zoom maneuver. One of them followed his dive, and he took a 20mm hit in his left-wing tank. Fire quickly spread from the wing to the cockpit, and Kerr bailed out at 16,000 feet, directly over the Japanese air base.

He landed on a low hill on the northern perimeter of the base, and a small Chinese boy immediately appeared. The boy led the burned pilot through the nearby mountains, with Japanese soldiers in hot pursuit. Once they approached so close that Kerr had to stop and exchange gunfire with them. The boy stayed with Kerr until near evening, when the Japanese appeared to be closing in. Finally, he ran off, and Kerr was left alone.

Kerr found a shallow cave and covered himself with leaves and brush until darkness fell, then treated his burns and moved on. He eluded his trackers for several days, until they gave up the search. Finally, he met four Chinese who led him to a guerrilla group. They took over and transported Kerr by sedan chair, boat, and foot through enemy lines. At times he had to stop and rest because his leg burns had become infected.

Eventually the guerrillas contacted British forces, who provided escort to lead Kerr the rest of the way home. He rode into Kweilin on a bicycle March 29, more than a month and a half after he had been shot down.

On February 12, the aircraft of the 1st B.S. and 7th and 8th F.S. arrived at Erh Tong. With the arrival of the new squadrons, there were now some forty fighters and twenty bombers flying from the base, and it was getting pretty crowded. On February 21, the first of many moves for the squadrons took place, when the 28th was sent to Lingling. The 7th and 32d moved to Li Chia Chen Airfield, across the valley from Erh Tong at Kweilin, on March 14. Finally the 8th followed the 28th to Lingling on March 17, leaving Erh Tong entirely to the 1st B.G.

Other changes were in personnel: Captains Jim Dale and John De-Haven of the 32d and Captains Charlie Wilder and Charlie Martin of the 28th were sent back to India on February 25 to join the 5th F.G. Wilder and Dale would command the last two fighter squadrons of the CACW, the 17th and 27th respectively, while DeHaven and Martin became operations officers for the squadrons.

Over in the 1st B.G., Capt. Chester Conrad, the group operations officer, was assigned to the 3d B.S. as commander, and Maj. Tom Foley replaced him in the group command. Also going to India to join the 3d B.S. were Captains John Hinrichs and Thomas Simpson, and Lieutenants Eugene Dorr, Louis Graves, George Cunningham, Mark Seacrest, William Daniels, and Charles Miles.

The 26th and 29th fighter squadrons of the 5th F.G., plus the 4th B.S. under Maj. Bill Dick, had been busy training at Malir since their arrival in India. The fighter squadrons' task had been complicated in January, when it was decided to transfer the remaining technicians who hadn't gone down with the *Rohna* to the 3d F.G.

The job fell to Mac McCullough and Lt. Wildy Stiles, who became engineering officers of the 29th and 26th, respectively, to train a new group of mechanics, radiomen, armorers, sheet-metal men, and propeller specialists from the only men available at Malir, mostly general clerks.

Stiles took over the training. He was a five-year veteran who had been a line chief in a bomber squadron before going to Officer Candidate School. By late February, he was able to report that his American mechanics "are the best damned bunch of men I've ever had. The Chinese are, also, progressing rapidly despite the language difficulties."

While training of the ground crews progressed, flight training began. Of the twelve P-40s now at Malir, four were set aside for use as training aids and the other eight were used for flight training. McCullough recalls that the Chinese technicians were surprisingly able, most with considerable experience in all areas except the liquid-cooled Allison engines of the P-40s.

Soon training operations depleted the 5th's tiny air fleet, so Mc-

Cullough was sent with about sixty Chinese and eight American mechanics over to Karachi Base Command, which was responsible for assembling aircraft for the China-Burma-India theater. The intention was for the CACW men to help out constructing the 5th's allotment of new P-40Ns, but they boosted production so much (from one P-40 every seven hours to one each fifty-five minutes) that they spent a month building 120 P-40s before they got their own thirty-six fighters starting about March 1.

The first twelve P-40s were quickly thrown into the training effort, but the remaining twenty-four got special treatment from McCullough, Stiles, and company. McCullough recalls:

"After the assembly job we were given twenty-four P-40s, which we promptly took to Malir. We stripped them down, re-trimmed the engines and valves, pumiced the fuselages and wings, modified the propeller governors, installed a fine British ranging gun sight, and gave them a special 'haze' paint job. (See appendix.)

"Of course, the 'haze' paint was one of the things that was tried at Eglin with various results. . . . I had gotten enough paint shipped from Eglin by sea, and it arrived about the same time we did. We had no proper authorization for this camouflage and spent much time in justifying our actions." [1]

One of the pilots who test-flew the hot-rodded P-40s was Glyn Ramsey, who said:

"We showed a great deal of interest in our airplanes. We painted the leading edge of the wings white and a part of the vertical stabilizer was painted white. And then we sandpapered those airplanes. I remember flying my airplane before it was sandpapered and after, and at the same power setting I got from fifteen to twenty miles per hour faster with the sandpapered and polished airplane. It made that much difference in the airstream." [2]

One amusing incident at Malir is recorded in the 26th F.S. diary on February 11, 1944. It seems that jackal hunting had become a popular night sport among some of the officers, who would pile into a Jeep and pursue the animals out across the desert, firing wildly with their .45-caliber pistols.

During one wild chase close to base, a stray shot "whistled through the quarters of Lt. Col. Charles A. Miller, commanding officer of the Chinese-American Operational Training Unit," the diary recorded. [3]

The immediate result was an order banning the use of firearms on the Malir reservation as well as "indiscriminate use of firearms after dark."

After that, the diarist reported, the jackal hunters moved farther afield out into the desert for their sport.

Finally, on March 17, 1944, the 26th and 29th fighter squadrons, led by Lieutenant Colonel Dunning, flew out of Malir with the 4th B.S.— destination, China. Because of the limited number of aircraft, the pilots were mostly Americans.

Flight leader Bob Kruidenier of the 29th gave this account of the trip:

"On the afternoon of the 17th we landed at Agra, where we were to remain overnight. We all made a quick trip out to see the wonderful Taj Mahal, which is truly one of the seven wonders of the world.

"The next morning we took off for Gaya, which was our second stopping place, landing there about noon. So far all was going well; we had no planes drop out for any reason, and we were in hopes we would be able to get them all to China without an accident of any sort. On the following morning we took off for Chabua, where we landed shortly after noon. This was the jumping off place for our flight over the Hump. Here we had to wait for eight days for weather suitable for fighters to make the trip over the most rugged country in the world.

"On March 28th the bomber squadron took off first as we were to follow them to China. The bombers were all carrying terrific loads, and they gained altitude slowly. We took off behind the bombers and started running into bad weather. It became apparent that the bombers would not be able to reach sufficient height to get on top of the stormy stuff, so they decided to return to the field at Chabua and wait for the weather to clear.

"We in our fighter planes went on up to 23,000 feet and were able to get across the Hump and break into clear weather over China. We landed in a small field with a gravel runway near the town of Chanyi, located about eighty miles above Kunming. We were proud that all of our fighter planes had made the trip from Karachi without an accident, except for one that ground-looped on landing at Chanyi."[4]

Glyn Ramsey of the 26th also was in that flight over the Hump. He recalls an amusing sidelight to the trip:

"I had a Chinese guy flying with me who was a good pilot, but he got to falling behind, and I kept calling him. I was real worried about him because I could tell something was wrong, and I couldn't figure out what it was.

"Finally when we got over the divide, the highest mountains, and started dropping down he began to respond normally. By the time we got over into China he was back in formation.

"When we landed we found out that he still had a full tank of oxygen, so we checked the system and it was OK, and we found out that he had purposely saved his oxygen for combat. That kid flew across there at 23,000 feet without any oxygen at all. It was amazing what some of these guys would do."[5]

Meanwhile, Major Dick's ten B-25s of the 4th B.S., plus two others flown by Major Foley and Captain Sheldon of the 2d B.S., got a break in the weather and made the hop over the Hump to Chanyi. They waited there only briefly, then flew on to Kweilin on April 6 to join the rest of the 1st B.G. at Erh Tong Airfield.

This mass movement of fighters and bombers over the Hump without mechanical failure or mishap was the largest of the war, and it was a genuine indication that the fledgling mechanics of the 4th, 26th, and 29th had learned their lessons well.

The arrivals at Chanyi had brought with them a quick introduction to the human condition in China for the pilots of the 26th and 29th. Again, Glyn Ramsey recalling his first landing at Chanyi:

"They came down and picked us up in an American-made 'six-by' truck, and we started up through the village, which was right at the edge of the field, up toward the hostel which was a couple of miles away. The first thing I remember seeing was a grown Chinese woman squatting in the rice paddy taking care of body functions, and all the guys were so shocked that they waved at her, and she sat there and waved back.

"Then we got up the road maybe 100 yards or 200 yards and I saw something sitting beside the road. It was a raven, sitting on something beside the road and feeding on it. When we got up there close to it I thought it looked like a man, and then I could see it was a corpse. It had no eyes and no skin on its rib cage. It had been there a couple of weeks or more, and that raven was eating on him.

"Quite an introduction to China, and I had a lot of others as time went on."[6]

While the recent arrivals were getting their first tastes of life in China, the final contingent of men bound for the CACW from the U.S. were just arriving at Malir to form the 17th and 27th fighter squadrons. One of those men was Glenn "Red" Burnham, a crew chief in the 17th:

"A bunch of us were alerted in February of 1944 at Goldsboro, North Carolina, loaded quickly on a train, and sent to Fort Hamilton, New York, for several days. At 4 A.M. February 19 we transferred to the baby aircraft carrier U.S.S. *Mission Bay,* moored at Staten Island.

"Shortly thereafter, accompanied by the carrier *Wake Island* and several destroyer escorts, we left for Recife, Brazil. The carriers were being used for transport only: the flight and hangar decks were loaded with P-47s.

"After further stops at Capetown, South Africa, and Madagascar and the lapse of thirty-eight days, we finally arrived at Karachi. We later were informed we were replacing the CACW lost in the Mediterranean."[7]

The CACW had marked a milestone of sorts on March 1, when the first all-Chinese mission was flown from Kweilin. Major Yuan led the 3d F.G. fighter escort for B-25s of the 1st B.G. that were hitting Nanchang. There was no opposition from the Japanese, and all aircraft returned home safely. The bombing accuracy, however, was disappointing.

The 7th and 8th fighter squadrons, which had been itching for action since their arrival at Kweilin three weeks earlier, finally flew their first mission on March 4, when they accompanied six B-25s of the American 11th B.S. and 23d F.G. in a surprise attack against Kiungshan Airfield on Hainan Island.

The low-level strike against the Japanese air base caught the defenders unprepared, and the CACW fighters had a field day. Aerial kills were scored by Capt. Liu M.J., Chinese commander of the 8th F.S., and by Capt. Harvey Davis and Lt. Coyd Yost, also of the 8th. Ground kills reported by the 8th F.S. were as follows: Liu, one; Major Cords, two and a half; Lt. Lung C.J., one and a half; Lt. Chang S.S., one, plus a fighter damaged in the air. Scoring ground kills in the 7th were: Capt. Hsu C.H. (Chinese commander), one; Lt. Wilbur Walton, three; Lt. Tan Kun, one.

The only other 3d F.G. mission of interest during the first four months of 1944 was flown on March 9, when twenty-four P-40s escorted B-25s to Shihweiyao. The bombs missed their target, a foundry, but the CACW fighters tallied three aerial kills. Lieutenants Don Burch and Chang Y.K., both of the 7th, scored their squadron's first aerial victories, and

Lt. Liao T.C. of the 32d added another. Liao was forced to land on the short emergency strip at Chaling after his fighter, No. 653, was damaged. The fighter's brakes failed on landing and Liao dumped the P-40 into the river at the end of the runway, causing slight damage to the ship. Lt. Lin S.C. of the 7th was shot down and listed as missing in action.

With all the CACW aircraft at Erh Tong during March, the Japanese night bombers began paying the base some attention. One P-40, No. 648 of the 32d, was destroyed by a fragmentation bomb on March 11. On the 14th another raid came in after flares were fired off by "fifth columnists" to mark the field, but no damage was done . . . except to the nerves of the CACW personnel.

The bad weather of March only worsened in April, but the 26th and 29th fighter squadrons were finally able to move up to Kweilin from Chanyi, again following the earlier squadrons by taking up residence at Erh Tong. The squadrons flew in on April 7, but flew only a few uneventful local alerts during the next three weeks.

Likewise, the 3d F.G. and 1st B.G. squadrons were largely earthbound during April because of the weather, but the month was far from uneventful for them. More moving plans were being made, because it was clear that the Japanese were preparing to mount a major offensive in the interior of China.

The Japanese plan was to drive southwest from the Hankow-Tungting Lake area all the way to Indochina. This would provide them with an overland rail link to move raw materials for the war effort north to the great East China ports of Shanghai, Tientsin, and Nanking, then on to Japan, while avoiding the costly shipping losses they were suffering in the South China Sea. At the same time, the Japanese could capture all the important 14th Air Force bases that lay along the route: Hengyang, Paoching, Lingling, Kweilin, Liuchow, Nanning, and others. If enough damage was done, the Japanese hoped Chiang Kai-shek would be forced to sue for peace. This drive would be called the ICHIGO offensive.

Before the drive could build up much strength, however, the Japanese needed to close the last gap in the Peking-Hankow rail line, improving their routes of supply and communication. When they began this effort in the famine-ravaged province of Honan, the 3d F.G. and 2d B.S. were sent hundreds of miles north from Kweilin to some of the most remote air bases in China to oppose them. This deployment, named Mission A, would have a lasting effect on the history of the CACW.

5

On March 8, 1944, Colonel Morse, CACW commander, received urgent orders from Chennault to proceed at once with his staff for a meeting at 14th Air Force Headquarters at Kunming. Out of the ensuing meeting came the plans for Mission A, code name "Fateful."

For the past sixty days, according to Chinese intelligence, the Japanese had been transporting supplies and troops south from Peking and Manchuria via railroad to the Yellow River Bridge near Chenghsien. When it was determined that the Japanese were going to use this buildup for a push south to take the portion of the rail line from the Yellow River to Sinyang—the last section of track between Peking and Hankow held by the Chinese—Mission A was conceived to help oppose the offensive.

It was easy to see, though the Chinese failed to recognize it at the time, that completing that rail link to Hankow would ease Japanese dependence on the Yangtze River for moving supplies and ultimately threaten the entire network of 14th Air Force bases in eastern China. And even as Mission A was being planned, the Japanese were building up their forces in the Hankow area via the Yangtze for what would become the famous ICHIGO offensive.

The plan behind Mission A was simple: let the Japanese concentrate their Honan forces, then smash them by air attack just before the offensive begins and continue to strike until the drive is halted. Weather and poor communications, however, conspired against Mission A before it

Maj. Gen. Claire Chennault, commander of the 14th Air Force, watches a track meet, probably at Kunming, October 13, 1944. (Glenn Burnham)

Sgt. John Hamre, a mechanic in the 8th Fighter Squadron, poses with one of the CACW's original P-40 trainers at Malir, India, fall 1943. The aircraft had flown originally with the American Volunteer Group and was passed on to the 23d Fighter Group before being ferried to India in early 1943 at the end of its operational days. The CACW was assigned six ex-AVG P-40s at Malir. (E. J. Phillips)

A Chinese armorer of the 8th Fighter Squadron practices servicing the guns of one of his squadron's P-40s as several Chinese and American ground crewmen look on, probably at Malir, India, 1943. Training was a continuous process for the Chinese technicians of the CACW. (E. J. Phillips)

A Chinese pilot of the 8th Fighter Squadron prepares for a training flight in a war-weary P-40K at Malir, India, fall 1943. (E. J. Phillips)

The CACW's American "wheels" meet, probably at Kweilin in late 1943. They are, from left, Col. Irving "Twig" Branch, commander of the 1st Bomb Group; Col. Frank Rouse, future commander of the 5th Fighter Group when it formed in January 1944; Col. Winslow Morse, commander of the CACW; and Col. T. Alan Bennett, commander of the 3d Fighter Group. (Jane Dahlberg)

The original commander of the 2d Bomb Squadron was Maj. Tom Foley, shown here in front of a well-armed B-25D. Foley led the first contingent of CACW aircraft over the Hump into China, and he flew the CACW's first combat mission on November 4, 1943. (John Hanrahan)

Brig. Gen. Winslow Morse (left), and Col. Chiang I-fu were co-commanders of the Chinese-American Composite Wing during 1943 and '44. Note that Morse's uniform includes a pair of Chinese Air Force wings, which were presented to many of the American fliers in the CACW. (Glenn Burnham)

M. Sgt. John Hanrahan poses next to his B-25 top turret after the mission of January 12, 1944, when he shot up a Japanese Ki-21 "Sally" bomber near the coast of China at Maoming. Capt. Chester Conrad, who assumed command of the 3d Bomb Squadron two months later, was the pilot on the mission. (John Hanrahan)

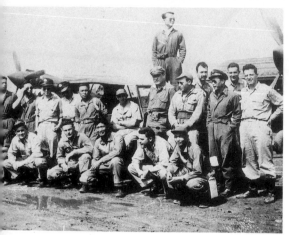

Chinese and American officers of the 3d Fighter Group pose at Kweilin during the spring of 1944. Kneeling from left, are: Maj. Yuan Chin-han, vice-commander of the group; Maj. Bill Reed, commander of the 7th Fighter Squadron; Lt. Herman Byrd, pilot of the 32d Fighter Squadron; Lt. Yu Wei, 32d pilot; Maj. Tom Summers, group headquarters; unknown. Standing: first six unknown; Col. T. Alan Bennett, group commander; Maj. Bill Turner, 32d commander; Capt. Tom Maloney, 32d pilot; Capt. Hung Chi-Wei, 32d vice-commander; Capt. Mike Hitchko, 32d flight surgeon; Lt. Roger Roberts, 32d intelligence officer. Standing on Jeep's hood, Lt. Liu Po Wen, 32d pilot. (Jim Kidd)

Generalissimo Chiang Kai-shek (wearing cossack-style hat) and Madame Chiang inspect the 2d Bomb Squadron at Kweilin, February 5, 1944, under the close scrutiny of the press (foreground). The tall American officer at right is Col. Tex Hill, commander of the 23d Fighter Group. (John Hanrahan)

This P-40N of the 32d Fighter Squadron was destroyed at Erh Tong Air Base, Kweilin, by a Japanese bomber on the night of March 11, 1944. It carried the squadron number, 648, and Chinese Air Force serial, P-11139, on its fin. (Richard Usher)

This accident occurred on May 7, 1944, when Capt. John Hancock and Lt. Wang Kuang-Fu collided during landing at Liang-shan. Hancock, in the plane on the bottom, suffered an injured arm and was transferred out of the squadron. Wang's P-40, serial no. 663, was repaired; he went on to become the CACW's last ace of the war. (Wilbur Walton)

Three pilots of the 29th Fighter Squadron take a break from training at Malir, India, in early 1944. They are, from left, Lieutenants Liang T.S., Bob Kruidenier, and Chiao W.O. All would fly in combat in China later that year. (Jane Dahlberg)

1st Lt. Bill Stiles, in cockpit, and W. E. ("Mac") McCullough inspect a 5th Fighter Group P-40N that has belly-landed at Chihkiang. (Jane Dahlberg)

Like an army of ants, Chinese coolies by the thousands contributed to the war effort by constructing an extension on the runway at Chihkiang in 1944. (Jim Bennie)

A two-ball air-raid alert goes up at Kweilin, 1944. Claire Chennault devised a complex system of air-raid warning for use in China that depended on ground observers reporting to a control center, which relayed information to the appropriate airfields. One ball on the pole indicated enemy aircraft had taken off from their base; two balls meant enemy aircraft were approaching; three balls meant attack was imminent. A standing joke was that no one ever saw three balls, because everyone had taken cover before it went up. (Bob Kruidenier)

B-25H No. 607 of the 2d Bomb Squadron suffered structural damage in a wheels-up landing, probably at Hanchung in 1944. Note that a band of color has been painted on the front of the engine cowlings, and the serial number has been painted out on the tail. (Wayne Senecal)

This B-25 suffered a direct hit on its cockpit by a Japanese fragmentation bomb while it was parked on the line at Liangshan in August 1944. Note how the bomber is equipped with a folding shade and a ring and bead gun sight. (Jim Kinder)

B-25II 43-4903 of the 1st Bomb Group turns away from its target after bombing the railroad yards at Wuhu; date and squadron unknown (Allen Sweeney)

A B-25H is gassed up for a mission at Kweilin, just before the squadron pulled out on September 14, 1944. The bomber carries the 4th Squadron patch on its nose and the name "Butch" on the cockpit armor plating. (Dick Frye)

Eight P-40Ns of the 7th and 8th fighter squadrons sit on the field at Liangshan during the summer of 1944. The fighters carry full CACW fighter markings, with roundels on the fuselage and on the undersides of both wings. The first two P-40s at left are M1, tail number 682, and P, number 687, of the 8th F.S.; the third, I3, number 663, belongs to the 7th squadron. (Ray Callaway)

Capt. Ray Callaway of the 8th Fighter Squadron sits in the cockpit of his fighter after scoring his fifth victory, late August 1944. The P-40N was coded 03 and carried the tail number 681. Its name was "Shirley II." Barely visible is a strap of reinforcement metal installed over the sliding portion of the canopy. (Ray Callaway)

Below: A Japanese Ki-57 "Topsy" transport begins to smoke after being hit by gunfire from a 7th Fighter Squadron fighter in this print made from gun camera film. The pilot and location are unknown. (Charles Lovett)

could get off the ground. What was to have been a bold countermove became instead a defensive struggle, and the Japanese could not be prevented from achieving their goals in Honan Province.

The air power assigned to Mission A included the four squadrons of the 3d F.G., one squadron of B-25s from the 1st B.G., and two P-40 squadrons from the 4th F.G. of the Chinese Air Force. This small force (84 aircraft during the rare times when all squadrons were at full strength) was to operate over Honan and the areas immediately west, with the following assignments:

1. Defend Chinese-held airfields and cities from Japanese aerial attacks;
2. Destroy the Yellow River bridges;
3. Destroy rail junctions at Sinsiang and Kaifeng, the key supply centers for the Japanese drive;
4. Destroy the railroad line from Hankow north to Sinyang, and interdict the Hankow railroad yards;
5. Bomb the railroad bed in the Chinese-held portion of the rail line;
6. Attack Japanese aircraft and airfields and traffic on the Yangtze and Yellow rivers;
7. Provide close air support for defending Chinese ground forces.

It was decided that Chinese intelligence would alert the 14th Air Force to move its squadrons into position four days prior to the date when they estimated the Japanese were ready to begin their offensive. From their new bases, the CACW aircraft would attack the Japanese at Sinyang and Kaifeng, then continue flying from their bases for about a month until the Japanese were halted. It was estimated that after the thirty-day battle, the CACW squadrons would no longer be needed in North China and could move to Southwest China to fly in support of the Chinese troops in Burma.

With his objectives for Mission A in hand, Morse returned to Kweilin, then set out for North China on March 19, 1944, to inspect his new bases. His seven-day tour quickly revealed the shortcomings of the airfields at Liangshan, Hanchung, and Ankang. The wing historian noted that the fields were "decidedly inadequate and of a capacity more suited to an air force of World War I."

The 2d B.S. and the 7th and 8th fighter squadrons were to be based at Liangshan, along with 3d F.G. headquarters. The base consisted of an established grass runway and another one under construction. There were six revetments big enough for B-25s and fifteen more being built for P-40s. There was a 100,000-gallon gasoline dump (less than half-full when Morse inspected the base) and very primitive radio equipment. Hostels and mess halls for the men were under construction, but they were not finished when the CACW arrived, so personnel had to be housed and fed in the ramshackle Kuomintang hostel in downtown Liangshan.

The town of Liangshan was typical of those in the interior of China that the CACW would come to know so well. Much less cosmopolitan even than Kweilin, the town boasted no streetlights, no modern buildings, and a single, narrow street that twisted along and sprouted alleys at random intervals. There were only seven trucks on the base initially, and when they rolled through town carrying personnel back and forth, the Chinese citizens would line the streets and cheer. The trucks had no brakes and were driven by Chinese speedsters who would shut off the engines to save gas and coast downhill into town at high speed over the often slick, muddy road. The effects of Japanese bombing earlier in the war were obvious in Liangshan, where wrecked buildings had been left as piles of rubble by the Chinese inhabitants.

On base there was an odd assortment of Russian bombs and Belgian ammunition left over from the early days of the war, as were two gasoline trucks and a station wagon that probably had been used by the AVG in 1942. For aircraft, there were two rickety, leaking P-43 Lancers of the Chinese Air Force, apparently used for air defense.

The Hanchung base had two unpaved runways in place and was big enough to handle B-25s, but it had no revetments, and the gasoline dump's capacity was only 60,000 gallons. There was housing on base for 210 men, as well as an operations building and alert shack; transportation was seven trucks and two cars in fair condition plus three disreputable gasoline trucks. More Russian bombs were stored at Hanchung, but there was no .50-caliber ammunition. The 32d F.S. would be based there.

John Henderson, who flew from Hanchung with the 1st B.S. later in the war, recalls the town of Hanchung:

"Hanchung was a walled city in the northern part of China, about halfway between Chengtu and Hsian. Normal population was about 50,000 people, but with the refugees from the east it was nearer 100,000 while we were there."[1]

Bad weather during the trip prevented Morse from getting to his easternmost base, Enshih, which the 28th F.S. would call home. The wing commander did, however, get to Ankang. It would be used as a staging base and was located north of Liangshan, about halfway to Hsian. Ankang had a single runway, no revetments, and the only building was an open-air alert shack. The fuel-dump capacity was only 5,000 gallons, and there was but one ancient truck and one telephone. Ankang was capable of handling only P-40s—and not too many of them.

Other bases to be used for staging were at Hsian, the major northern outpost of the Kuomintang forces on the Wei River, and an isolated strip at Laohokow, about 150 miles east of Ankang and suitable only for emergency use at that time.

After completing his trip, Morse flew to Chungking for a session on March 26 with Gen. Chow Chi-Jou, CAF commander. The general promised support for Mission A in the form of a Beechcraft airplane for liaison, more trucks for the bases, a squadron of CAF P-40s at Liangshan for air defense, and movement of excess P-40s from India to Chengtu to speed replacements. He also promised to furnish intelligence and target information on Japanese military facilities, storage areas, means of communication, and troop dispositions.

When he returned again to Kweilin, Morse got busy with his staff planning the actual move north for Mission A. Intelligence, photo processing, and communications centers had to be established at Liangshan; five radio stations had to be established at the bases, and a fighter control net for air defense had to be rushed to completion to protect the bases from Japanese bombers. The work was done at a feverish pace, and the first transports carrying equipment and supplies from Kunming touched down on the Liangshan runway April 1. By April 21, radio stations were operating at Liangshan, Ankang, Enshih, Laohokow, and Hanchung. In addition, five liaison teams, including one behind Japanese lines at Chenghsien, were on the air and transmitting valuable intelligence from their locations to the east.

The CACW units assigned to Mission A were busy as well during

April. Capt. Bill Black of the Eglin AFB proving grounds in Florida had visited Kweilin in March to demonstrate the use of bazooka-styled rocket launchers that could be hung under the wings of P-40s, and since then the squadrons had been busy installing racks to carry the bulky affairs on their fighters. In the 1st B.G., plans were made to split the group between the Mission A assignment and an East China Task Force that would fly missions out of Suichwan against the familiar coastal targets.

The carefully laid plans involving notification by the Chinese four days prior to the peak of the Japanese buildup were quickly discarded when the Japanese crossed the Yellow River in force on April 19, 1944—with no warning from the Chinese. As the Japanese, spearheading their attack with tanks and cavalry, moved south from Chenghsien, it was clear that an early opportunity to cripple the offensive had been lost. Mission A, and the course of the war in China, had been altered dramatically.

On April 20, the squadron commanders who would be participating in Mission A were called to Kweilin to get their final instructions for the move north and the action that would follow. It was planned that the units would fly out as soon as the weather permitted—which, unfortunately, proved to be more than a week later.

Late that afternoon, after the meeting, Maj. Howard Cords, the high-spirited and popular young commander of the 8th F.S., climbed into his P-40 and headed back to Lingling. It was nearly dark when he reached the field and buzzed the hostel area. Then, in one of those unexplainable flying tragedies, Cords misjudged his landing.

As the P-40 lined up on final approach, it faltered and mushed into the top of a tree off the end of the runway. The fighter's left wing broke in half, and the aircraft carried about another 100 yards before it crashed into the side of a hill and exploded. Cords was thrown 200 feet from the P-40 in the explosion and was killed instantly. His stunned squadron mates shipped his body by train to Kweilin, then on to Kunming. Capt. Harvey Davis assumed command of the 8th, with Capt. Ray Callaway taking his place as operations officer.

The next blow came to the newly arrived 26th and 29th squadrons, who were itching to get their souped-up P-40s into action at Kweilin, and it was taken only slightly less personally than was Cords's death. A day or two after the April 20 conference at Kweilin, the squadrons were ordered to turn over half their fighters (six from each squadron) to the 3d F.G. to fill out the requirements for Mission A.

Both of the 5th F.G. squadrons were disheartened, and morale plummeted accordingly. These weren't just any P-40s; they had been carefully prepared, and their crews were justifiably proud of them. Now the special white "haze" camouflage markings would be painted out, the names on the cowlings would be replaced, and their shiny finishes would be allowed to fade and grow dull in the North China elements. The receipt of these replacements by the 3d caused a reshuffling of aircraft among the squadrons to get the proper mix of rocket launcher-equipped fighters in each. In some cases their 700-series tail numbers were retained; on other fighters the 3d's 600 numbers were applied.

With all the preparations made, it remained only to wait for good weather to move the squadrons north. The first break came on April 22, when the first elements of the 2d B.S. were able to fly out of Erh Tong for Liangshan. The bomb is would be commanded by Majors John Foley and Li H.Y., with a mix of flight crews from the 1st and 2d bomb squadrons. Captains John Sanders, William Carson, John Dierkes, and later Charles Miles were flight leaders; Capt. John Sheldon was lead bombardier; and Capt. Wilbur Taxis was lead navigator.

The weather closed back in for another week, but finally on April 28 the combat aircraft were able to begin their deployments. Foley led nine B-25s to Liangshan. In all, the 2d B.S. moved seven U.S. officers and fourteen U.S. enlisted men, plus seventeen Chinese officers and twenty-three enlisted men, in the B-25s. Six more Chinese officers flew in on transports. Also on that day, the 8th and 28th squadrons flew to Liangshan, and the 7th finally made it to Liangshan on May 1, 1944.

The 7th quickly removed the drop tanks and rocket tubes from its P-40s after the 2½-hour flight, then went on alert and scrambled at 1315 to intercept a reported incoming raid. No contact was made with the enemy, however, and the fighters returned to Liangshan. The next day eight fighters of the 7th were sent to Enshih to stage for a mission, but the weather turned nasty again, and the planes went nowhere for three more days. Finally, on May 5 the P-40s of the 7th flew an unopposed mission to Sinyang, then continued on to land at Ankang. Meanwhile, the 28th traded places with the 7th and flew to its new home at Enshih from Ankang on that same day.

The first sorties of Mission A, as well as the first casualty, had been recorded by the 8th F.S. on April 30. Captain Davis and Lt. Lung C.J. took off in the two P-43s at Liangshan on a local alert, but they failed to find any incoming Japanese raiders. On returning to base, Lieutenant Lung, who had considerable P-43 experience before joining the CACW, crashed into a rice paddy and was killed. The cause of the crash was never determined, but the CACW apparently never used the surviving Lancer again.

During May the Japanese pushed south of the Yellow River in several drives. From the infamous bridge at Chungmow they pushed south down the Peking-Hankow rail line to Saiping, with little substantive opposition from the Chinese ground forces. The main drive split off to the west after reaching Hsuchang, then headed back north from Luchow to Loyang. From there the Japanese moved southwest again to Loning and eventually pushed all the way to Lushih, which was only about 100 miles east of the strategic city of Hsian.

Another drive, meanwhile, pushed across the Yellow River north of Mienchih and moved west to Lingpao, also threatening Hsian.

In the face of these drives, the Mission A forces attacked relentlessly from the air throughout the month. The first major blow was struck by the 2d B.S. on May 3, when Major Foley led three B-25s in a withering attack against tanks and trucks south of Hsincheng. On the same day the 32d F.S. flew the first strike against the Yellow River Bridge, dive-bombing the storage area at the single-rail, two-mile-long span. This bridge would remain a major target for the remainder of the war. Heavily defended and simple to repair, the bridge was hit over and over again, but it was never closed for more than a few days.

On May 4 the 3d F.G. lost its Chinese executive officer in a gruesome accident at Hsian. Capt. Wang T.C. was killed on the field when he backed into the spinning propeller of a 32d F.S. P-40.

May 5 and 6 were particularly busy days for the Mission A fliers, and the damage they did to the Japanese on those two days earned them a commendation from General Chennault. On the first day, the B-25s, with the 7th F.S. for escort as mentioned earlier, struck the railroad yards at Sinyang and registered 85 percent hits.

Also on May 5, the 32d registered the first aerial kill claims of Mission A. Eight P-40s were strafing a section of the Luchow-Loyang road, which would become known as "Slaughterhouse Alley" by the end of the month, when Major Turner and Captain Lindell spotted a single-engine Japanese dive-bomber and teamed up to shoot it down. Then Captain Maloney and Lieutenant Colonel Summers, who was assigned to fly with the 32d as fighter control officer, exploded a twin-engine transport.

Several planes were hit during the strafing, and Summers was forced to bail out and walk back to base. Lt. Wang S.C. was wounded when an explosive shell hit his P-40 in the cockpit, and he crash-landed near Loyang. In the strafing, the 32d destroyed forty to fifty trucks, four armored cars, and two pillboxes, and killed about 200 Japanese troops.

The next day the 32d returned to "Slaughterhouse Alley" and shot up fifty more trucks, plus five tanks. This time Lt. Chung H.C. was hit and had to crash-land between Chinese and Japanese lines. He made his way to safety and met up with Lieutenant Colonel Summers at Loning. They hitched a ride into Lushih, where they caught a plane back to Hanchung, arriving May 11.

The 8th F.S. hit "Slaughterhouse Alley" on May 6, too, destroying some 100 trucks in a devastating attack. One of the pilots on that mission was Ray Callaway, who recalls:

"We caught a Jap convoy slowed at a river crossing. I had four P-40s with Capt. [Coyd] Yost on my wing and two Chinese in the second element. The convoy consisted of stake trucks carrying troops, tank trucks, and I suppose regular supply ones.

"As we started in on them, they held up a large Jap flag, apparently thinking we were friendly planes. As they realized we were not friendly, they piled off the trucks and—to my surprise—did not run for cover but started firing at us with rifles. I recall it clearly as it was the first time I had been hit by rifles. It sounds like stones hitting your fender when driving on a gravel road.

"Yost called to me he was hit, and his oil pressure had gone to zero. Expecting him to go down shortly, I went with him and we headed for our staging field. Apparently it was just the line to the oil pressure gauge, and we got to the field okay.

"Didn't know my hydraulic system had been hit until I put the gear handle down and I could smell the fluid. No pressure on the hand pump, so I had to belly it in. The prop snapped off and caught under the wing— thought she was going to go over—but luck or someone was with me, and she settled back. The landing tore the gun camera out of the wing and a Chinese coolie picked up the film, which was uncoiled and lying in the path I made in landing, and started running across the field. Chinese guards took after him in a truck and shot him—no questions asked."[2]

Callaway, an aggressive young Minnesotan, would become the CACW's third ace in August and would be promoted to command the 32d F.S. in September. His squadron-mates knew him to be an adept handyman, being responsible for keeping their record player and other essential gear operational. Nevertheless, the squadron historian noted of Callaway's skill at the card table, "He played a good game of cribbage for low stakes and a poor game of poker for large ones." He finished his China tour in December 1944 with six aerial kills.

On May 6, the bombers also had a field day attacking Hsiangcheng with escort from the 7th F.S. The town was heavily bombed, and then Major Reed's fighters swept the road out of town and caught a concentration of troops traveling in motorized columns. These Japanese also apparently mistook the P-40s for friendly aircraft and began cheering and waving flags at them. They quickly realized their mistake when the fighters returned their greeting with a hail of machine-gun fire. Two swift passes were made, in which twenty-five vehicles were destroyed and about 250 troops killed. Lt. Chang L.M. also damaged a Japanese fighter that ventured near the the P-40s.

Chennault sent his congratulatory message to Colonel Morse on May 10. It read, in part: "I extend my sincerest congratulations to you and your officers and enlisted men, both Chinese and American, who played a part in the success of the operations. These operations are in themselves a vindication of the wing's formation of mixed Chinese and American personnel. The successes are a tribute to their efforts to overcome the handicaps and differences in language and background in achieving the necessary teamwork."[3]

Mission A, for all its ferocity in the opening week, was just picking up steam. In the days to come, all the CACW squadrons would be heavily engaged, inflicting heavy losses on the Japanese and taking a few lumps of their own as well.

As the Japanese drive continued, the 2d B.S. flew all of its missions in mid-May on ground support near Loyang. One mission on May 12, for instance, was flown with Captain Churchill leading five B-25s against artillery emplacements. The next day, Captain Sanders returned from a mission to Loyang with seventy-five holes in his aircraft. Then from the 15th to the 23d bad weather scrubbed all missions. Several were tried, but each time the B-25s were forced to return to Liangshan.

On May 23 Captain Dierkes flew a load of supplies up to Hanchung from Liangshan, and a Chinese crew repeated the process on the following day. Toward the end of the month a detachment of B-25s moved up to Hanchung to be closer to the Japanese advance on Hsian.

Down to the southeast, the 28th F.S. had a particularly tough month of May, for its base at Enshih was located only about 100 miles from the Japanese lines at I-ch'ang. Flying thirty-six missions, the 28th lost nine fighters and several key personnel.

Located as it was, the 28th was responsible for keeping the Japanese Air Force away from the CACW bases to the west. The squadron was successful in denying the Japanese daylight use of their airfields at I-ch'ang, Shasi, Yangyang, and Kingmen. As a result, the Japanese carried out only night attacks against the key base at Liangshan.

Dick Daggett, a pilot who would join the 28th later that month, recalls the base at Enshih:

"The base was good. The fighter strip had mountains on three sides, so we usually took off and landed in one direction. At dusk the P-40s were taxied to the caves. These caves in a nearby mountain were dug out by hand by the Chinese, and these caves helped to keep the few planes we had safe from the Jap bombers, which only came over at night, usually only one bomber at a time. We would usually stay in the sack until we started to hear the bombs going off, and then we would dive for the trenches."[4]

On May 7, Major Strickland's fighter was hit in the windshield by ground fire. He was wounded in the face, requiring treatment at the big hospital in Chengtu. Four days later Capt. Frank Smiley, operations (ops) officer and acting commander in Strickland's absence, was shot down and killed during a rocket attack on a supply boat at Lichiakou.

Capt. Jim Bush then became ops officer and acting commander until Strickland could return to duty. But he was shot down and killed on May 27 when he was jumped by enemy fighters during a strafing attack on riverboats. He, like Smiley, was a West Point graduate, and his death was a great loss to his former roommate, Keith Lindell of the 32d.

Next, Capt. James Sagmiller moved up to operations officer of the 28th, only three weeks after he had been the junior flight leader. His luck was better, however, and he eventually completed his tour and returned home to the United States.

The 28th F.S. scored two aerial victories on May 22, when a pair of Ki-43 Oscars attacked a formation that was strafing boats on the Yangtze River. Strickland turned his flight head-on to the Oscars and hit one of them in the first pass. Then he turned right and came around behind the crippled fighter and shot it down with another burst. The flight concentrated next on the other Oscar and sent it down in flames, too. Captain Bush described the attackers in a precise yet artistic manner: "They were Oscar IIs and painted like speckled trout." Lieutenants Meng C.Y. and Chao Y.H. shared credit for the second Oscar.

A real scrap developed on May 11, when the 7th F.S. provided top cover for a dive-bombing mission by the 32d against rail targets at Mienchih. Seven Ki-43s jumped the P-40s just as Turner's fighters were releasing their bombs. Reed's fighters held off the Oscars while the lower P-40s climbed up into the fight. According to one account, Turner climbed up at the diving Oscars while Reed was chasing them down. As a result, the 32d historian noted, "The two Bills almost shot each other's pants off."

When the smoke cleared, Reed's flight had claimed four victories: Captain Yang and Captain Yieh, one each; Lieutenant Tan Kun, two; Reed, one damaged. Lt. Teng L.C. confirmed one Oscar for the 32d, and Captain Lindell destroyed another with a head-on shot that flamed its engine.

Maj. Bill Reed's most spectacular day of Mission A was May 16, when he racked up three confirmed kills in the course of two missions to become the second ace of the CACW. The task for his 7th F.S. was to find a P-40 of the Chinese 4th F.G. that was down behind Japanese lines and destroy it before it could be captured. Reed and Lt. Armit W. "Bill" Lewis took off that morning to look for the P-40, but they found a lone Japanese dive-bomber instead and promptly took turns shooting at it until the stricken craft went down. Later that day Reed led another flight out to look for the missing P-40. Near Loyang, Reed and Lt. Wilbur Walton spotted a Ki-43 Oscar and shot it down, sharing credit for it. Then another dive-bomber was seen, and Reed shot it down by himself.

Finally the flight ran into three Ki-44 Tojos and attacked. Reed confirmed one destroyed and damaged another. Walton confirmed the third enemy fighter destroyed. Lt. Tan Kun, who had shot down two Oscars only five days earlier, was himself shot down but later returned to the 7th. The CAF P-40 never was found, but Reed was awarded a Distinguished Flying Cross for the day's work.

The 8th F.S. had spent the first half of the month mostly pinned down to air-defense duties at Liangshan, but finally seven P-47s of the 33d F.G. arrived from Chengtu to help out, and the 8th F.S. went north to join the 7th at Ankang.

The two squadrons commenced to wage a furious, four-day campaign of ground attacks against the Japanese Yellow River advance. In one strafing mission near Loning, they wiped out an entire cavalry regiment with their low-level attacks. The hectic pace took its toll on aircraft, however, and by May 22, the two squadrons together only had nine P-40s operational.

An account of the 32d's action during three days in late May provides a good capsulized impression of Mission A, its action, and its frustrations:

During the week prior to May 22 the squadron was grounded at Hanchung by the weather. During that time rocket tubes were installed on the fighters. Then on the 22d the squadron staged through Ankang to make a rocket attack on armored cars, tanks, and cavalry at Loyang.

The squadrons landed from that mission at Hsian, but the next day the Chinese airfield commander there refused to gas up the P-40s because he hadn't been allowed to pick that day's target for the fighters. The planned mission had to be postponed for a day while the feathers were unruffled, and then the next day the 32d dive-bombed and rocketed a target on Yuncheng.

On May 24, Capt. Armit Lewis of the 7th made perhaps the ultimate statement of his feelings about his enemies during an attack on anti-aircraft batteries at Shanhsien. The young officer, according to squadron lore, accomplished a feat worthy of Houdini by somehow lowering his pants, defecating into a brilliant orange scarf, then dropping his stink bomb out of the cockpit onto the surprised Japanese gunners below. Such was the spirit of the CACW.

"Yes, it is true," Lewis confirmed in 1985. "Being an old farm boy at heart, I was used to having my 'morning constitutional' on time, every morning. For some reason on that particular day our takeoff was moved up a couple of hours. When we got over the target area I found I was becoming more interested in a call of nature than I was in looking out for Zeroes. Off with the parachute harness, removal of my fine embroidered silk scarf, and the movement was accomplished—along with frequent interrogations from my Chinese wingman: 'Whassa matter? You all light?' Disposed of the debris, back on with the parachute, and on with the mission. It wasn't easy! And, of course, I never lived it down. Never did get another scarf as fine as that one was, either."⁵

Throughout the month the Japanese struck back at the CACW in night bombing raids against Liangshan. The entire group was saddened to learn that M. Sgt. Clyde "Pop" Casto, the group's well-respected engineering chief, had been killed May 30 by a bomb blast, just days before he was due to return to the United States at the end of his tour in China.

Technical Sergeant McAdams, who had been manning a .50-caliber machine gun mounted near the runway, was knocked out by the bomb blast. In the same raid one CACW P-40 and a P-47 of the 33d were destroyed, and two P-40s, a P-47, and a P-51 of the 51st F.G. were damaged. In addition, two P-40s collided while they were trying to intercept the raiders, and both were damaged.

May ended with a bang for the 32d F.S. when Turner led a rocket attack on Linfen Airfield. Turner and Lindell hit the field first while Maloney and Capt. Herman Byrd, who had transferred from the 8th F.S., covered. When the four had finished, six Oscars and a transport had been destroyed. Then the four flew to Hotsin Airfield, where a P-51 had been captured when its pilot had landed there by mistake, and strafed the U.S. fighter into ashes.

The Japanese got a breather when the weather socked in during the first days of June. By the time it cleared, the enemy had adopted a new tactic of moving at night. The action was about to shift south as the Chinese prepared for a limited offensive against I-ch'ang.

The B-25s at Hanchung and Liangshan were especially stymied by the weather during the month. Captain Dierkes led several strikes in the Yellow River Bridge area, one of which was made in weather so bad that the large bridge was never seen. In another raid, only fourteen of the twenty-four bombs being carried would drop because of faulty release mechanisms in the B-25s.

The 7th F.S. got a shock on June 7. Reed's P-40 was hit in a gas line during a strafing run on the railroad station at Chenghsien, and he was forced to belly it in fifteen miles southeast of the town.

Armit Lewis was flying with Reed on the day he went down and recalls: "He and I had been up around Chenghsien on a recce and target-of-opportunity mission when we both picked up a lot of ground fire. He apparently got hit in the fuel pump area as a visual observation by me showed a lot of liquid streaming back from his ship. Heading for friendly territory, I kept telling him he ought to bail out if his ship conked out completely, which it did about that time, and he decided to belly it in on a sandbar.

"I circled him a few times, saw he was out of the cockpit and apparently OK. I don't believe Bill had ever bailed out, and he seemed to have an inordinate fear of doing so, since bailing out would have been far safer than trying to belly in in that area. He was absolutely fearless in all other aspects, so maybe I am imagining that he had a fear of bailing out. We will never know."[6]

Lewis and a new pilot, 2d Lt. Ed Mulholland, searched for Reed that afternoon but found only the burned-out remains of his fighter. Reed had managed to make good his escape from behind the lines, however, and reached Chinese ground forces. Upon his reaching Laohokow, Chinese generals presented him with a captured samurai sword and put him aboard a B-25 headed for Liangshan on June 24.

The Battle of I-ch'ang opened on June 9, and the 8th and 28th were in the thick of the action. Also, the Chinese 4th F.G. flew in to Enshih to provide top cover for the CACW's ground assault fighters.

On the missions flown the first day, however, the CAF escorts never appeared. The Oscars jumped the CACW formation during one of those missions, but the P-40 pilots fended them off, scoring one confirmed kill by Lt. Chung C.S. of the 28th F.S., two probables, and two damaged.

The escort provided by the CAF improved over the following days, but in the words of the 28th historian, "It never came up to the standard that we had reason to expect."

The American forces' disappointment with their Chinese allies came into focus during the I-ch'ang campaign. Rumors circulated that the Chinese pilots were ordered to avoid combat to conserve their planes, and the information the ground forces provided was often inaccurate concerning the locations of their "advancing" troops.

The Japanese had no trouble holding I-ch'ang and also were able to consolidate their hold on the Peking-Hankow railroad during June. The Chinese 4th F.G. returned to the safety of Chungking. By the end of the month, the Japanese had accomplished all they had set out to do in April, and Mission A was over, but the 3d F.G. and 2d B.S. wouldn't be returning to the south of China. For the rest of the war, their mission would be to strike at the Japanese lines of communication and supply from the bases in North China.

Two P-40s of the 28th flew an interception mission on June 24 that was as unusual as it was symbolic of the differences between the CACW and the other CAF units. Their target was a Chinese P-40 that had taken off from Chungking headed for Japanese territory, its pilot apparently planning to defect.

"Unfortunately," noted the 28th historian, "the traitor was able to escape before we could make our interception."

Despite the disappointing performance of the all-Chinese units and the fact that the CACW had not been able to deny the Japanese their objectives, the squadrons had extracted a tremendous toll from the enemy during Mission A. As a result, the CACW units involved were honored with a unit citation for their action from May 1 to June 30, 1944.

The citation quoted the following totals for Mission A:

"In two months' battle, the wing accounted for 2,317 enemy troops killed or wounded; 1,321 cavalry and packhorses destroyed or damaged; and 110 riverboats—two of them more than 100 feet in length—destroyed or damaged. In addition, extensive destruction and damage was wrought on railroad marshaling yards, dock areas, gasoline dumps, gun positions, and other installations."

This was by no means the sum total of the CACW's toll on the Japanese since May 1, however, because the 5th F.G. and the other B-25 crews of the 1st B.G. had been busy down south fighting a similar battle against the massive new ICHIGO offensive.

In the spring of 1944 Japanese forces were being pushed back all over the Pacific by the Allies. The Solomon, Marshall, and Caroline islands had fallen; the great naval bases at Truk and Rabaul had been neutralized; the carrier strength of the Japanese Navy itself had been greatly weakened. Only in China, where Chiang Kai-shek's massive but ill-trained armies considered starvation their primary enemy, did the Japanese remain the dominant force.

The ground situation had been roughly static, with only an occasional foray by the Japanese toward Changsha, for over two years. That all changed when the Japanese pushed across the Yellow River toward Sinyang in April, but the major thrust of the ICHIGO offensive was yet to come. When it came, the offensive dwarfed anything seen in China since the 1930s, and it would take more than a year for the Chinese and the 14th Air Force to finally stop it.

When the Mission A forces left for North China at the end of April, it meant that action was not far behind for the new 5th F.G. squadrons, the 26th and 29th. They moved from Kweilin up to Lingling on May 1 with their twelve remaining P-40s.

Colonel Branch, meanwhile, had led eight of his 1st B.G. B-25s down to Suichwan on April 28. In addition to the B-25s, Branch's East China Task Force consisted of fourteen U.S. officers, eleven U.S. enlisted men, nineteen Chinese officers and eleven Chinese enlisted men. The U.S.

officers, drawn from the 1st and 4th bomb squadrons, were: Branch, Majors William Dick and Percy Sutley; Captains Chester Jack and John Washington; First Lieutenants Robert Bell, Samuel Brown, Willbraham Hoffson, Donald Keefe, Moncure Lyon, William Waggaman, and Allen Sweeney; and Second Lieutenants Douglas Budden and Theodore Peters.

The first mission flown by the task force was a two-plane sweep along the coast from Foochow to Wenchow led by Captain Washington on April 29. Waggaman led a river sweep near Kuikiang later that day.

The best mission flown by the East China Task Force was a major strike against airfields at Hankow on May 6. Eight of Branch's B-25s plus six more from the 11th B.S. were escorted by forty fighters from the 23d F.G., and good hits were reported while all the B-25s got home without damage despite heavy antiaircraft fire and fighter interception. Three P-38s and a P-51 were lost by the escorts, however. While the bombers were flying from Suichwan, CACW wing headquarters was busy packing. Colonel Morse moved the headquarters down to Liuchow on May 11.

The eager P-40 pilots, who had thus far been only disappointed during their month in China, didn't have long to wait for action. The Japanese attacked Suichwan that night and twice the next day.

The first daylight attack on Suichwan on May 12 came at 0800, and Bob Kruidenier of the 29th F.S. recalled:

"We were up at 4:40 A.M. and on the line by five o'clock, after a breakfast of cold eggs and horrible coffee. We started getting plots on the Jap planes at 5:30, and it was not long before we knew that they were coming for us. The Chinese warning system informed us that there were seventy-two fighters and around twelve to eighteen bombers on their way to wipe us out.

"We had eight P-38s on the field, and they took off with a roar and climbed up to altitudes that a P-40 can never get to. There also were four P-51As, and they took off just ahead of our nine fighters. We were at close to 9,000 feet when the Japs came in. Their bombers came in low, while the sky above them was full of Jap fighters.

"This was the first actual combat with the enemy for us, and it was a real scrap for a while as we were badly outnumbered. We dropped our belly tanks and opened the throttles wide. The next few minutes were busy ones for us.

"I fired at plenty of Jap fighters that day, and while I was squaring away for a sure kill, a Nip let me have it with all he had. Holes appeared in the canopy; oil and smoke filled the cockpit. In a flash I knew I had let myself become a 'sitting duck' for some Jap pilot. I rolled the plane over on its back and headed for Mother Earth, knowing that my would-be killer would not follow down in a high dive as the Jap planes were not capable of withstanding terrifically high diving speeds.

"I found that my wheels and flaps would still function, and I was able to make a safe landing on our own field. Not until I viewed the holes in my plane did I realize what a lucky boy I had been. Except for five small needle-like steel splinters which had entered my right leg I was still all in one piece." [1]

Some of the other pilots had better luck than Kruidenier in the fight, especially a quiet young lieutenant named Ken Elston, also of the 29th F.S. He pulled up behind a flight of twelve Ki-43s as they crossed the field and gave one of them a long burst. The Oscar, badly hit, did a half-roll, went into a spin, and crashed. This was the first confirmed victory for the 5th F.G. Major Hull, plus Lieutenants Wang and Leng P.S., each damaged one fighter in the engagement.

The Japanese weren't finished for the day. A second alert was reported at 1330, this raid consisting of twelve Ki-48 Lily bombers and thirty-five fighter escorts. Capt. Fred Ploetz of the 29th chased one of the bombers across the field, firing from behind during its bomb run, and shot it down for the second kill of the day. His own fighter, however, was damaged by return fire from the bomber and he crash-landed about fifteen miles from the field. He walked into base the next morning. Major Hull damaged his second Japanese aircraft of the day in the afternoon raid.

Also on May 12, the 1st B.G. lost its first crew in several months on a sea sweep along the coast. Lt. L. G. Sheppard, a former Royal Air Force pilot on his first mission in China, was hit by antiaircraft fire during an attack on a gunboat. His B-25 hit the mast of the boat and exploded, killing the entire crew. Lost, besides Sheppard, were Lt. Wu W.W., the navigator, plus S. Sgt. A. R. Kerlin, Sgt. W. A. Grimes, and Cpl. H. G. Sarver.

The fighters flew six more missions, including their first rocket attacks, before being pulled out of Suichwan on May 30. They next went to Hengyang, where they joined the 23d F.G. for twelve missions in the next six days.

The B-25s had been pulled out of Suichwan on May 22, when the gas supply there began to run low, and resumed operations from Kweilin after the B-25s had been serviced at Yang Tong.

From Hengyang, the 5th F.G. fighters flew escort and intercept missions, as well as shipping strikes on Tungting Lake, against the main thrusts of the ICHIGO offensive, which had jumped off May 26. The offensive initially consisted of six lines of attack, which greatly confused the Chinese, then consolidated into three thrusts. One force moved directly south from Yochow toward Changsha while two others ran parallel, one on each side, headed toward points south of Changsha on the Hsiang River. As the offensive pushed south, the fighters were used to attack the advance itself, the final Hengyang mission on June 5 being a strafing attack on Japanese troops west of Yuankiang.

The offensive moved south with such speed that it was soon decided to move the 5th F.G. back to Lingling and then on to Chihkiang, which was about 175 miles northeast of Hengyang. While C-47s were beginning to transport 5th F.G. ground personnel out of Lingling and Capt. Sam Carran was leading a Jeep convoy toward the same destination, the fighters were jumped from above by twelve Ki-43s as they were strafing near Pinkiang, north of Changsha. Maj. George Parker, assistant group ops officer, damaged one, but Lt. Robert Reynolds, flying his first mission with the group, was shot down and killed. The rest of the P-40s were able to drop their wing tanks and climb up into the overcast at 1,000 feet to escape.

June 1944 must be remembered, if at all, as a month of transition by many former members of the CACW. The Mission A squadrons were constantly in flux, staging from one base to another for their next crack at the Japanese; the wing headquarters was settling in at Liuchow, where it was expected the CACW would concentrate soon to support the Chinese forces in South China; the 5th F.G. was moving from Lingling to its new home at Chihkiang, and the 1st B.G. was getting ready for a move from Kweilin up to Peishiyi, near the Chinese capital at Chungking. Then, just as the wing headquarters was getting to know its way around Liuchow, orders were received to move again up to Peishiyi and join the 1st B.G. there. This move couldn't have been mourned much by the headquarters personnel: the rain at Liuchow had been so bad in June that telephone poles had sunk in the soggy ground on either side of a railroad line and began to lean toward each other; when a train came by one night, it snagged the drooping lines around the engine's stack, pulled up the poles by their roots, and dragged them down the track as they banged against the sides of the cars.

In contrast to the war news in Europe, where the Allies had landed at Normandy on June 6 with the most colossal invasion force in history, the Japanese advance in China must have looked even worse than it was. Indeed, the entire operational force of the CACW that day—perhaps forty fighters and fifteen bombers—would hardly have rated a glance in the skies over the D day beachhead.

The 5th F.G. completed its move to Chihkiang on June 9. It wasn't long afterward that Capt. Sam Carran was moved to write this description of his new base in the 26th F.S. history:

"Our field was a picturesque spot. Situated at the western base of the Paima Shan Mountains, it lies in a small, fertile valley formed by the Hung Kieng River as it flows about the feet of the surrounding mountains. Heavy rainfall keeps the valley green . . . colors are vivid and contrasting, sudden strange fogs and brilliant sunsets are frequent. The rugged, off-shaped peaks, with clouds floating through them, form an eerie backdrop for a 'Land of Oz'-like scene.

"These mountains serve for us a useful purpose but represent, too, a difficult problem. They present a reassuring barrier, lying as they do athwart the path the Jap would need to follow should he choose to veer his advancing columns toward our base. However, each mission we run must necessarily cross these towering heights, and they provide a formidable obstacle, with the consequence that many and varied weather as well as navigational difficulties daily confront our airmen."[2]

Bob Kruidenier was another who recorded his impression of Chihkiang:

"At Chihkiang we had 40,000 coolies working on the field repairing runways and building revetments to park our planes in at night. There were coolies everywhere you looked. They carried two baskets hung on the end of a pole, which they carried balanced across their shoulders. The loads they carried were surprisingly heavy, and how they stood up under the hard labor with only a little rice to eat each day will always be a mystery to me.

"There were whole families of Chinese, and everyone worked, including the women and children, with the women carrying loads just as heavy as the men. The picture made by these 40,000 coolies was one of a colony of ants moving in single file, each carrying his load in silence and with one thought in mind, that of completing a task."[3]

Unlike the 26th and 29th fighter squadrons, the last two squadrons of the 5th F.G. did not cross the Hump into China together. The press of operations against ICHIGO, coupled with the loss of half the 5th's P-40s to Mission A back in May, made it imperative that the CACW pilots and fighters in India be sent to China as quickly as possible. The 17th F.S., under Major Wilder, was ready to go first, and its pilots flew into China on May 29. While the P-40 pilots had flown across India, the bulk of the squadron, as well as many of the men assigned to 5th F.G. headquarters, had a long, dusty train ride across India to endure before reaching Chabua and a transport flight over the Hump. Jim Bennie, who was a crew chief with the 17th, remembers the trip well:

"I was one of the people who was designated to go with what they called the 'support force.' The Chinese and Americans and all of our baggage and our tools and all the junk it takes to operate a squadron were put on a train in Karachi. . . . The train trip took about ten days, and we went up to Lahore, over to Delhi, down to Calcutta, and then changed trains and found our way finally up to Chabua.

"We all rode together, Chinese and Americans, in the same kind of a passenger car with wooden seats. It was really crude. We were on that train for ten days with the exception of a layover we had at Lahore. While we were on the train we were given American rations: we had C-rations one day and K-rations the next. That is what we lived on on the way across.

"We did have quite a few things kind of ingenious, I think. We needed water for coffee, and somebody got the bright idea that we had a steam engine up front loaded with it. Every time the train would stop we would all run up front with our canteen cups, and the engineer would fill our canteen cups out of the boiler. When we wanted to take a bath we would run up to the front end and shower. The water the engine takes on at water stops would be pulled for us, and we would have an instant shower. That is how we got across India. It was a wonderful experience for a young person to see India that way.

"Anyway, we got into Chabua, and it was hot and miserable. We flew

C-46s across the Hump into Luliang and eventually got some air transportation on up into Chihkiang with all of our junk and everything.

"The Chinese, when they got into Luliang, had all kinds of black market material they were selling, and they just had a field day counting their money. I have to admit that I managed to sell a couple of cartons of cigarettes at $23 a carton, and I thought that was absolutely beyond belief. Inflation, at the time we arrived in China, was 200 Chinese dollars to one American dollar, and ultimately the inflation figure was 2,000 to 1, but hovered around 1,700 to 1,800 at the very latter part of the war, which in eighteen months was just a fantastic inflation rate.

"When we got to Chihkiang, which was a fighter strip about 3,000 feet long and carved off the top of a hill, they had two squadrons on each end of the runway, and we operated that way. We in the 17th operated from the far end of the runway; we were farthest away from everything. The 27th was the other squadron with us.

"We had our P-40s there, and the other two squadrons had the other end. About a half-mile away was the revetment area, which was down in a kind of rice paddy area away from the main part of the runway. We used to put our airplanes there every night—take them down and park them."[4]

Another 17th crew chief, Glen "Red" Burnham, recalled the difficulty the crew chiefs had moving the P-40s from the alert areas to the revetments. A narrow taxi strip between two rice paddies connected the revetments from the runway, and the crew chiefs had to taxi the nose-high fighters across it every morning and back every night. Burnham said this required even more skill than might be expected because the P-40 seats were designed for pilots wearing seat-pack parachutes, so the crew chiefs had to stand in a half-crouch while they operated the rudder pedals, because if they sat down on the seat they wouldn't be able to see out of the cockpit. Burnham also recalls incurring the wrath of his squadron commander one morning when he gave his P-40 a bit too much throttle and taxied down the runway with the tail wheel off the ground.

Again, Jim Bennie recalls the layout of Chihkiang:

"Approximately a mile from the revetments was the living area. That was divided, the Chinese in one area, the American enlisted in one area, and the officers in one area. They had a couple of buildings there that were designated for the orderly room, the medic's clinic, and the dining hall. The dining hall was set up where the kitchen was in the middle; one side was enlisted and the other side for the officers. The food was predominantly Chinese: rice and water buffalo meat, caribou, bean sprouts, et cetera. We did have eggs in the morning and lived on them quite a bit.

"The quarters initially were just the wooden barracks, but later on the base got kind of crowded as they moved other units in, and they put up some winterized tents. Our barracks were not that bad really. They were not airtight by any stretch of the imagination, and the cold air pretty well blew through. We had a potbelly stove that kept us reasonably warm, and we did have electric light and bunk beds. The beds were two by fours with cords slatted between them and net mattresses, just a cotton pad. You had your two blankets and a mosquito net, which was obviously used to keep out mosquitoes but also to keep out rats. Rats were always a problem. I had one that woke me up in the middle of the night that was eating on my hand. I threw him out of bed, washed my hands with rice wine, and went back to sleep. Nothing ever came of it."[5]

The last fighter squadron to fly to China was the 27th, which left Malir on June 22, 1944. Col. Frank Rouse and his group executive officer, Maj. Clifford Condit, led the formation of twelve fighters. The ground echelon of the 27th left Malir during the first week of July.

Condit had been at Malir since the very beginning of CACW training, spending nearly a year at the base in charge of keeping the war-weary training P-40s and B-25s in the air. He recalls finding out what a small world aviation was in the 1940s:

"The first unusual experience was my introduction to the Chinese training commander who lived in the barracks next to ours: Colonel Li, whom I immediately recognized as a Chinese I had taught to fly in Chicago in 1926. He had served in World War I with the Americans in France. The U.S. government gave him a college education at the University of Pittsburgh, and during his final summer in the U.S. he took a pilot's course with the Heath Airplane Co. in Chicago.

"When I asked him a few questions about his education, et cetera, to prove I was not mistaken, he said, 'You have a remarkable memory.' I saw much of him during the next year as he remained C.O. of the Chinese at Malir."

The maintenance problems he had faced in Malir continued after his move up to Chihkiang, Condit remembers:

"Again lots of maintenance problems as supply lines were so long. The Chinese had an overhaul base headed by a colonel, graduate of MIT, and who proved most helpful to me and our units. They had been dismantling P-40s for quite some time and storing them for use after the war. These planes would be new ones, so when we had to have an engine, prop, or wing I could get them.

"This was a chore as they were stored randomly within fifteen miles of our base in old barns and buildings they had taken over. I always wondered how Lend-Lease was balanced out over there as I had to sign for all parts, yet they went on Chinese-American planes with Chinese insignias. They wouldn't accept the signature of my Chinese counterpart group engineering officer."[6]

The pilots of the 5th F.G. flew twenty-two missions from Chihkiang during June 1944, the first of these on the 9th. On the second mission flown that day, the P-40s caught two steamboats, each pulling a barge loaded with Japanese troops, plus other vessels at a Hsiang River crossing ten miles northwest of Siangyin.

The P-40s blew up one steamboat and one gas-carrying barge, sank three sampans, and killed or wounded about 200 troops. Lt. Bill Johnson of the 26th F.S. was hit, and he bailed out while his wingman, Lt. Phil Colman, watched. Johnson walked into Chihkiang a few days later.

The missions continued until the 13th, when the weather turned sour, but the action resumed on June 17. At 0700 sixteen P-40s flew to Yoloshan Mountain, just west of Changsha, where the Chinese were making a stand against the attacking Japanese. The mission was to dive-bomb, frag-bomb, and strafe the Japanese attackers at the base of the mountain. The attack was intercepted by twelve Ki-44 Tojos, and in the ensuing air battle Lt. Loo Y.P. of the 29th F.S. fired a four- to five-second burst into a Tojo at close range. The enemy fighter began to smoke, then spiraled into the ground, giving the Chinese pilot a confirmed kill. Lieutenant Yoh was shot down, but he parachuted safely from his burning P-40.

The next day brought one of the outstanding feats in aerial combat recorded by the 5th F.G. The morning mission this day was to escort four B-25s to Changsha and over the lower Tungting Lake region. Twelve Ki-43 Oscars intercepted about fifteen miles northwest of Changsha, and Lt. Thomas Brink, assistant group operations officer, was credited with three confirmed kills during the fight. Capt. Lin Y.P. of the 17th F.S.

also was credited with one victory; Lieutenant Tai was shot down and listed as missing.

On another mission that same day, Capt. Glyn Ramsey of the 26th F.S. led twelve P-40s loaded with demolition bombs on a sweep of the lower Tungting Lake channel. They found a big concentration of boats near Siangyin and attacked, causing heavy damage. Lieutenant Colman caused the biggest fireworks when he dropped his bombs on a camouflaged area near the river's edge. Violent explosions sent boats, supplies, and wreckage flying in all directions. He had made a direct hit among some 175 boats that had been tied together under the camouflage.

The 26th's most successful mission of the month was yet to come, however. On June 24 Lieutenant Johnson, just back after being shot down, led eight P-40s to Siansiang. The fighters caught a Japanese support column on the road and shot it up unmercifully. It was estimated that 800 to 1,000 men were killed or wounded and another 200 to 300 pack animals killed. The weather closed in between the formation and Chihkiang, so Johnson led his P-40s into Paoching to spend the night before returning to Chihkiang.

If June had seemed busy to the 5th F.G., July was downright hectic. Finally, all four squadrons were in action, the 27th making its debut as a separate unit (some pilots had been flying while attached to other squadrons) on July 9 when Major Dale led eight of his P-40s on a Hsiang River strafing mission. The next day "dusk patrols" were initiated in hopes of catching the Japanese forces that had been holing up during the day and moving at night to avoid air attacks. The tactic proved successful as Captain DeHaven of the 27th and the three P-40s he led found and blew up a 150-foot steamer, as well as damaging several other vessels.

The Japanese, however, were making steady progress down the Hsiang River Valley in Gen. Shunroka Hata's ICHIGO advance. The Japanese had bypassed Chinese Gen. Hsieh Yueh (nicknamed "The Tiger of Changsha" in honor of his previous defenses of the city) at Changsha and then set out for Hengyang. The base at Hengyang was evacuated and destroyed on June 21 when it became impossible to fly any more missions there because of the Japanese advance. The Chinese army held out at Hengyang until August 8, however, long after the ICHIGO drive had passed them by. Paoching was the next base to go, Gen. Casey Vincent ordering its destruction on July 3.

The drive slowed for a few days then, but a shortage of gas prevented

Vincent's fighters and bombers, including those of the 1st B.G. and 5th
F.G., from capitalizing. In fact, Vincent's bombers were idled for most of
the month. Vincent flew to Chihkiang on July 10 for a quick visit with
Frank Rouse and John Dunning. Despite his frustrations with supply
shortages, he reported cheerfully in his diary: "Frank has a good outfit,
and they're doing good work after us."

The 5th Fighter Group lived up to Vincent's compliment during July,
especially with three devastating raids against the Japanese air base at
Paliuchi near Tungting Lake at Yochow on the 14th, 24th, and 28th.
These are probably the best-remembered missions in the history of the
group, for the combined score was sixty-six Japanese aircraft destroyed,
thirty-one probably destroyed, and twenty-four damaged. In return, the
5th lost but one pilot and plane to enemy action and one other to a flying
accident.

Aggressive low-level flying and superb planning can be credited for the
success of the Paliuchi missions. A measure of the surprise element is
shown in one simple statistic: of the sixty-six enemy aircraft destroyed,
only two were shot down in the air; the rest were caught on the ground
and were helpless before the guns and bombs of the P-40s.

The first mission was led by Colonel Rouse following a coordinated
night raid on the 13th. Of the twenty-one P-40s from headquarters, the
17th and 26th squadrons, and the 75th F.S. of the 23d F.G. deployed at
Chihkiang, two were forced to turn back due to mechanical problems.
Rouse led one element of eight against the south end of the field, Dunning hit the central dispersing area with seven, and the four P-40s of the
75th, led by Lt. Leonard Aylesworth, hit the northern end of the field.

The P-40s approached Paliuchi from the southeast at 0735 and found
most of the Japanese aircraft still in their revetments. Seven or eight
were on the runway, and three Ki-43s were making their takeoff runs as
Rouse's flight peeled off for its dive-bombing run. No antiaircraft fire was
seen until the last plane in the formation made its run.

In the southwest dispersal area Rouse's flight found at least twenty
twin-engined transports in a large revetment, with about ten silver
Ki-43s dispersed among them. Rouse's bombs hit among the transports,
and his wingman, Capt. Tom Reynolds of the 17th, said the colonel
destroyed three of them. Reynolds himself followed his bombs down
toward a group of Ki-43s and set three of them afire with his guns.

The top scorer of the day, however, was Lt. Bill Johnson of the 26th, who burned up four Ki-43s during a strafing run after he dropped his bombs with unobserved results.

Maj. George Parker scored one of the aerial kills when he pulled in behind the three Oscars that had taken off during his bomb run. On that bomb run one of his 250-pounders had hung up on its rack for a moment, and when it released it was flung over the field and out into the Yangtze River, where it almost hit a 250-foot ship moored there. Parker fired a long burst from a range of 600 yards at the nearest Oscar; it caught fire, then exploded. A similar kill was credited to Lt. Chang Y.K., of the 26th, who was in Dunning's flight.

(Major Parker, unfortunately, was killed nine days later in an accident at Chihkiang. He was taking off in his heavily loaded P-40 at 0520 when the plane struck another P-40 that had ground-looped at the south end of the runway the previous day. Cpl. Kenneth Ball of the 26th F.S. tried frantically to pull the major from the burning wreckage, despite the danger that the gas, bombs, and ammunition aboard would explode. He failed to save Parker, but was recommended for the Soldier's Medal for his bravery.)

Dunning's flight found bombers and fighters parked in the center of the field at Paliuchi and gave them the same working over that Rouse's fighters had done at the far end of the field. Major Van Ausdall caught one Oscar that was taxiing and poured a burst of fire into it until the fighter ground-looped, nosed over, and burst into flame. After Dunning's fighters pulled up from their runs, he led them to a small airstrip on an island north of Changsha, where several more aircraft were destroyed.

Lieutenant Aylesworth's flight, armed with fragmentation bombs, found fewer targets at their end of Paliuchi, but they were able to destroy three Japanese planes and damage two others.

In all, twenty-five Japanese aircraft were claimed destroyed, twelve probably destroyed, and ten damaged. That evening, Rouse called a group meeting in the mess hall at Chihkiang to commend all personnel.

The second raid was similar to the first, with pilots from the 26th, 27th, 29th, and 75th squadrons, plus Lieutenant Brink from headquarters. This, too, was a low-level attack, but this time all P-40s were armed with fragmentation bombs. The mission was led by Major Van Ausdall after Major Hull had to return to base with engine trouble.

Glyn Ramsey, who was flying in the 26th F.S., recalls this mission vividly:

"We took off at just about daylight, and we were briefed to stay on the deck. We pulled the gear up and took our course, and the leader simply throttled back until everybody could catch up. We took off as close together as we could and we stayed right on the deck. We got all the buzzing we wanted for a distance of some 250 miles. We were not handicapped by navigation lack too much because once we got within about 100 miles of Paliuchi we could see Tungting Lake, and we flew over it.

"We lost one pilot and an aircraft. That was a Chinese [Lt. Feng P.C. of the 29th F.S.] who got too low over Tungting Lake, and his prop picked up a little water from the vortex. It sucked the prop in, and when he touched the water he just nosed in and made a big splash. I was looking at him, and the airplane dove into the water and then backed out. It looked like it was all together, but then we don't know how deep the water was there, and I am certain the impact must have knocked the pilot out and probably killed him. It didn't tear up the airplane like I anticipated it would.

"We flew our time and distance, and we still didn't know precisely where we were, because flying that close to the ground is almost like trying to read a book with your nose only an inch from the page. You can see the word directly ahead of you, but you don't know what the next word in the sentence happens to be. That was our position: we knew what the ground looked like under us, but we couldn't get any reference points at all. We pulled up and we were not more than three or four miles from the airfield. We could see it clearly.

"We could also see that they were trying to scramble, and some of the engines on some of the airplanes were running. They had upward of twelve to fifteen ready airplanes sitting on the ramp, and people in trucks and pilots were swarming all over those airplanes. We just pulled up to about 1,000 feet and then just peeled off in echelon and started firing as soon as we got in range. The eagerness to shoot at them caused them to misjudge the distance.

"We were carrying parafrags, which is about an eighteen-pound antipersonnel, anti-equipment bomb with a parachute on the tail of it. They had to be dropped at a minimum of 150 feet or they would not arm. The reason they had this delay on the arming was that if a pilot was foolish or careless enough in strafing to drop them below 150 feet the chance of knocking himself down was very good.

"I remember coming in I was trying to slow down to try to get some spacing so that I could shoot those airplanes on the ground without endangering our own airplane that was making a pass ahead of me.

"I finally got to what I thought was the proper spacing and went on in, and I burned my gun barrels up. I shot everything I had. I was too close to the guy in front of me because when I went over I noticed the number of parafrags lying on the ramp by those Japanese planes that hadn't gone off, which means that they had been jettisoned below 150 feet and hit the ground without being armed. That means that some of them were going off under me, and I could have gotten knocked down by our own flak.

"It was most thrilling, yet that's not really the word. It was an exciting situation, but I never took any pleasure in killing people, and we were obviously ripping them apart. I just ripped across the airfield one time, and I think I fired everything I had and dropped every bit of ordnance I had. We were briefed to make one pass and turn for home. When we turned for home that place was literally ablaze. Of course, there were many, many airplanes burning . . . we must have cut it to ribbons. I had been on the receiving end a couple of occasions so I know how those guys must have felt on the ground. I didn't feel very much sympathy for the Japanese. You just can't do that when you're facing the daily situation we were facing." [7]

The attackers had been split up into five flights, each with responsibility for hitting a section of the field. This time thirty Japanese aircraft were destroyed, with seven probables and eight damaged. Top scorers, with three each, were Lieutenants Wei S.K. of the 26th, Chow S.D. of the 27th, and Chou L.S. of the 29th. All were ground kills.

The last of the Paliuchi raids, on July 28, was led by Lieutenant Colonel Dunning. There were eighteen pilots from the 27th and 29th squadrons plus group headquarters. A diversionary raid from Kweilin contributed to the surprise, as it had on the 24th, but the targets were much more scarce after the tremendous destruction of the preceding attacks.

Nevertheless, Dunning's pilots were able to claim eleven destroyed, twelve probables, and six damaged. Top scorers were Major Dale of the 27th and Lt. Chou T.M. of the 29th, who claimed two destroyed and one probable each. On the debit side, Lt. Miles Newell of the 27th reported by radio that his P-40N-15, 42-106336, had been hit in the cooling system and he was bailing out. He went down east of Yochow and was never seen again.

For all their brilliance, the Paliuchi raids weren't the only high spots of July for the 5th F.G. It had started off on a positive and hopeful note on the 5th, when Lt. Chao S.Y. of the 29th F.S. was married in the group recreation hall at Chihkiang by the group chaplain, Maj. Adolph Peterson. American as well as Chinese officers attended, and a big party followed. Everyone there got a lot of practice at "Gombaying," the ancient Chinese bottoms-up toast that flattened more than a few American drinkers of distinction during their stays in China.

The 17th F.S. was shocked twice during the month, both on occasions when its operations officer, Capt. Charles Martin, was shot down. Martin went down the first time on July 3 during a strafing mission over the Hsiang River. He was able to bail out of his P-40 and returned to the squadron on July 7 via Jeep from Paoching. Martin, one of the original pilots of the CACW who had first served in the 28th F.S., was dive-bombing a bridge at Sinshih on July 20 when the wing pulled off his fighter during his bombing run. The P-40 dove straight into the riverbed and exploded, taking with it the smiling Long Islander.

Next it was the 26th's turn to lose a valuable pilot. The Chinese commander, Capt. Yao Jei, was flying a dive-bombing mission against the railroad yards at Hengyang on July 22 when his P-40 was seen to spin out of the clouds and thunderstorms and crash about forty miles northeast of Paoching. He never got out of the falling fighter.

Sinshih, where Martin was killed, was a regular target of the 5th F.G. during July. Major Van Ausdall was leading a fighter-bomber sweep there on the 9th when his fourteen P-40s caught eight Ki-43s below them and attacked. None of the Oscars were claimed destroyed, but Lt. Shu T.S. got good hits on one that trailed white smoke from its wing roots and then disappeared. He claimed a probable, and Lt. Liang T.S. claimed another Oscar damaged.

Two days later twenty-one pilots of the group headquarters and the 27th and 29th squadrons escorted B-24s to hit supply lines at Sinshih. The bombing was good despite interception by about twenty Ki-43s. The 29th pilots did all the scoring as Lieutenant Leng confirmed one kill and damaged another Oscar while Lt. Chou T.M. claimed one probable and a damaged and Captain Ploetz and Lt. Feng P.C. damaged two each.

The 800-foot trestle bridge at Sinshih was the target on the 19th when twelve P-40s returned to the battered city. The formation was bounced by twelve to sixteen Japanese fighters over the target at about 0800, and a wild free-for-all ensued. Again it was the 29th's show, as Lieutenant Leng shot down his second and third victims of the month while single kills were claimed by Capt. Ho H.H., First Lieutenants Feng P.C. and Chiao W.O., plus 2d Lt. Byron McKenzie, who had joined the squadron in June. Major Parker damaged two, and Colonel Rouse and Lt. Chou T.M. damaged one apiece.

Capt. David Green of the 29th was wounded by shrapnel in the left arm and back, but he was able to fly back to Chihkiang. Lieutenant Leng, on the other hand, was shot in the left foot and his P-40 was seriously damaged. He bailed out near Anwha and didn't get back to Chihkiang until July 29.

On July 25, twenty-seven P-40s from the group escorted twenty-one B-24s to Yochow, where they were intercepted by a mixed formation of about twenty-four Oscars and Tojos about five minutes beyond the target. Lt. Phil Colman of the 26th fired a two-second deflection shot at a Ki-44 as it turned in front of him. The Japanese fighter was hit dead center in the cockpit and wing roots, and it crashed into Tungting Lake. Colman then turned his attention to two other Tojos in succession that were attacking P-40s and chased them off, damaging both. Finally, he pulled up behind a formation of six enemy fighters and opened fire on the tail-end charlie, which also was claimed as damaged. Lt. Shu T.S. of the 26th also destroyed one Tojo, as did Lieutenants Kao H.S. and Shen C.T. of the 29th.

July 25 was a big day back at Chihkiang as well as in the skies over Yochow. First, a U.S. nurse flew onto the base for a visit. Normally this would not have been notable, but at Chihkiang she was, as the 26th F.S. historian recorded so succinctly, the first white woman under forty the men had seen in five months. Other visitors on the 25th included Gen. Casey Vincent and the Japanese.

Casey Vincent came to Chihkiang to present awards to three men in the group: Lieutenant Colonel Dunning was to receive the Legion of Merit for the innovations he had introduced in the Foster Field, Texas, gunnery school in 1942; Major Hull was to be given an Oak Leaf Cluster to add to his Air Medal for missions he had flown from Guadalcanal during an earlier tour of duty; and Maj. Edward A. Kelly, group flight surgeon, was to receive the most important award, a Silver Star, for the bravery he had shown in giving medical aid to the wounded during the *Rohna* sinking in the Mediterranean.

At 2100, just before Vincent was to make the presentations, there was an alert as Japanese bombers approached Chihkiang. But evidently they couldn't find the field, because the Japanese jettisoned their bombs nearby at 2115 and flew away. The ceremony proceeded after the all-clear at 2135.

One other CACW outfit that struck hard at the ICHIGO offensive was the 4th B.S., which had remained at Kweilin after the rest of the 1st B.G. moved to Peishiyi in early July. The squadron, with eleven B-25s under Maj. Bill Dick, flew thirty-three of the group's seventy-five missions during the month. Many of these were single-plane night missions that were successful at harassing the Japanese advancing under the cover of darkness, though the actual damage they did was questionable.

The 4th B.S. was pleased on July 13 to welcome Capt. Donald Keefe and his crew back from behind Japanese lines. They had gone down June 11 about fifteen miles southeast of Changsha and had spent a full month getting home. The squadron, despite the heavy action, spent eight days on the ground at Kweilin during July after it ran out of gas on July 16. Finally enough gas was obtained to resume fighting on the 24th.

The 4th B.S. would remain at Kweilin long after the rest of the CACW was gone, not leaving until the bitter end came in September. The squadron didn't have any monopoly on the action, however. Missions came hot and heavy for another 1st B.G. outfit during the summer of 1944—the 3d B.S., which still had not arrived in China.

7

The last CACW unit to reach China was the 3d Bomb Squadron, which didn't bring its B-25s over the Hump to join the rest of the 1st B.G. until mid-September 1944. The 3d was anything but an untested squadron of rookies, however, for it had spent the summer flying missions in support of Gen. Stilwell's advance in Burma.

Maj. Chester "Coondog" Conrad's squadron had finished training at Malir in late May and then moved to the air base at Moran, India. At Moran, the 3d B.S. experienced one of the few incidents involving racial prejudice in the history of the CACW.

Also stationed at Moran was another B-25 squadron, the 83d B.S. of the 12th B.G., 10th Air Force. Before he would let his squadron fly combat with the Chinese-American crews, the 83d commander requested that a practice flight involving both squadrons be flown. Major Conrad agreed, and the flight came off without any problems. The 83d commander, however, demanded a second practice flight.

This time Conrad balked, refusing the flight on the grounds that his squadron already had demonstrated its ability and that a second flight would be a personal affront to his men. As might be imagined, a rift developed between the squadrons. The 83d commanding officer appealed to his wing commander, who wired back to Conrad that his rival was the "supreme commander." Outranked, Conrad had no choice but to fly the second practice mission. This flight was made on June 7, and the Chinese crews did well.

Now both squadrons were considered ready for combat, but on the next day Gen. Howard Davidson, the former CACW training chief who was now 10th A.F. commander, ordered the 83d B.S. back to Calcutta. This left the 3d B.S. and the 90th F.S. (a P-40 outfit of the "Flying Skulls" 80th F.G.) under the command of the 5230th Wing to support Stilwell's advance. The 83d left the base on June 13, and the next day Colonel Branch arrived on his way from China to pick up a new B-25 in India for the 1st B.G. He told his squadron that they could expect to spend the summer in Assam, because the supply situation was so bad in China that another B-25 squadron couldn't be supported there until fall.

On June 16 Conrad flew to Chabua to visit wing headquarters and was given a new assignment for his B-25s. The 3d B.S. was to take over for the B-24s of the 308th B.G. against targets on the Burma Road.

Another week passed without the 3d getting into combat; then Conrad was ordered to China to discuss working with the 69th Composite Wing of the 14th Air Force in support of the Salween offensive by the Chinese Army's Y Force. At that point the offensive was stalled, after a fierce Japanese counterattack had pushed the Chinese back from Lungling.

Finally, on June 25, 1944, the 3d B.S. flew its first combat mission when Capt. Thomas Simpson and Lt. Edwin Ragland, both of whom had previously served in the 1st B.S., flew two B-25s with a P-47 escort in a raid against railroad bridges at Mohnyin, Burma. The next day, the Y Force launched its renewed campaign, this time targeting Tengchung, some thirty miles north of Lungling, as its first objective. The Japanese defending the walled city held out until early August.

During July the 3d B.S. flew 25 missions in support of the Chinese attacks in Burma by the Y Force and the X Force, which was bearing down on the Japanese stronghold at Myitkyina from the north at Ledo. Major targets included the railroad line south of Myitkyina. During one of those missions, on July 8, Captain Simpson's B-25 was shot down during an attack on rail targets south of Hopin. His crew was able to escape, however, and returned to action by the end of the month. Other crews shot down and returning to Moran during July were those of Lieutenants Cunningham and Gene Dorr.

A typical week's action was that beginning on July 19, when four missions were flown. Five B-25s destroyed a railroad bridge at Hzenwi on the first mission, then four B-25s destroyed two road bridges at Mongyu.

Two bombers recorded good hits on a railroad bridge and supply dump at Mawhun, and finally three B-25s damaged a railroad bridge at Mohnyin.

The 3d B.S. continued flying over Burma in August until the 21st, when Conrad's outfit finally began its move to China. The first stop was Kweilin, and then the 3d moved up to Peishiyi in September when Kweilin was evacuated.

July and August of 1944 also had been busy months up in North China, where the 3d F.G. and 2d B.S. were busier than ever, and at Peishiyi, where the CACW headquarters, 1st B.G., and 1st B.S. were settling in at their new base.

The move to Peishiyi didn't prove as fortuitous for the 1st B.G. and wing headquarters as the men had expected. The airfield itself was little more than a cow pasture: a long, flat grass strip among rolling hills. A few sagging buildings stood at the eastern edge of the grass, and the only respectable structure was the operations building, with its glass cupola on top.

The men were housed in the old AVG hostel, which as a mile and a half from the field. The officers lived in a mildly Spanish-styled building with several patios and an inside garden. The enlisted men, on the other hand, lived in a building that was suspected of having been used to house coolies during the AVG days. Water was a problem at the hostel, and the lack of it was exacerbated by the hot weather that set in during the month. The ancient well was completely inadequate, and bathwater was usually tobacco-brown in color, with twigs, scum, and moss floating in it.

During this time the 1st B.S. didn't operate as a separate unit. Its pilots flew with the 2d B.S. from Liangshan and Hanchung until mid-month, when they were transferred back to their own unit. By the end of July they had seven B-25s at Peishiyi and had flown two missions from that base.

Colonel Bennett's 3d F.G. had its busiest month yet in July. With the close of Mission A, the fighter squadrons had adopted a routine of escort and ground attack missions designed to disrupt Japanese lines of communication and supply along the Peking-Hankow railroad line while maintaining control of the airspace over North China.

The weather was good for flying during the month. The 32d F.S., still based at Hanchung, generally staged through Hsian to hit targets along the Yellow River. The other three squadrons flew most of their missions out of Enshih against the Japanese to the east near Hankow. All four squadrons continued to stage through Ankang from time to time. They flew thirty-five missions in July with an average of only twenty-six operational P-40s.

The P-40s flew bombing, strafing, and recon missions up and down the rail line from the Yellow River Bridge to Hankow during the first two weeks of the month, losing two aircraft in the process.

The 28th was the first squadron to score an aerial kill during the month. Strickland's pilots, along with others from the 7th and 8th fighter squadrons, took part in a twenty-aircraft escort of B-25s to Yochow July 9. Just after the B-25s had dropped their bombs the formation was attacked from below by Japanese fighters. Some of the Chinese pilots reported seeing five to seven inline-engined fighters among the attackers, which they took to be Ki-61 "Tonys."

Strickland led the top cover down on the Japanese with his flight; then Maj. Cheng Sung-Ting, who was acting CAF group commander at the time in the absence of Major Yuan, joined the scrap with his flight.

Strickland made five or six passes in ten minutes, with Capt. Art Skidmore, his wingman, covering his tail. On the second pass black smoke streamed out of a Japanese fighter Strickland had hit, and Skidmore and Cheng both saw it crash. By the time the fight was over the 28th had scored four kills. Besides Strickland, Major Cheng and Lieutenants Liu M.Y. and Liu S.Y. confirmed victories. Strickland also claimed a probable and three damaged, and Cheng two damaged.

The next scoring went to the 32d F.S. Major Turner had just returned from Kunming with a new No. 646 P-40 to replace his original one, which had been destroyed in a bombing raid on Hanchung the previous month, and he flew the escort mission July 14 with Captain Byrd and Lt. Chung H.C., along with seventeen other P-40s of the 7th and 8th fighter squadrons. A biplane was spotted over Sinsiang Airfield, and Turner led his flight of three down to attack it. They misjudged their speed, and all three missed the elusive target on the first pass. Captain Byrd then lined up on it again and shot the biplane down with a long burst.

Then Lieutenant Chung spotted two "Lilys" and a "Val" (again, probably a "Sonia") and attacked them. He shot one Lily down, and then Turner noticed another Lily parked on the field below and blew it up on a strafing run. While the three P-40s were down on the deck two Ki-44

Tojos, formidable opponents under the best of circumstances, jumped them. The low and slow P-40s had a few tough moments, but they were all able to escape and get back to base safely.

The group found itself in another good fight on the 18th, when thirteen P-40s from all four squadrons participated in a strafing and bombing mission against a gasoline dump at Kantsun, just north of the Yellow River Bridge. They were jumped by about ten Oscars and Tojos just after their bomb runs.

Major Turner and his wingman, Lt. Yu Wei, were about to line up on a black Tojo when Turner spotted a silver Ki-44 above them. He broke off the attack on the first Tojo and climbed up behind the other one. At 12,000 feet he gave it one long burst of fire; there was a bright flash and the Japanese fighter broke apart, its pieces falling to earth. Yu missed a kill on the black Tojo, which he had stayed behind when Turner broke off, because his guns wouldn't fire.

Lieutenants Wang Kuang Fu and Wang M.T. of the 7th F.S. also were in the thick of the action. Wang K.F. damaged three enemy fighters, while Wang M.T. scored a probable when he hit a Tojo with a good burst from 100 yards behind. The stricken fighter glided into a cloud and wasn't seen again, so the lieutenant couldn't confirm the kill.

The second victory of the fight was recorded by Lt. Cheng T. of the 28th. Flying with Major Cheng, who damaged one fighter in three passes but didn't see it crash, the lieutenant hit one Oscar that went down pouring smoke for his first and only confirmed victory. Lt. Liu M.Y. of the 28th, who had scored his first kill on July 9, was shot down in the fight and listed as missing in action.

The next day, members of the 3d F.G. who had been with the unit since the beginning celebrated the first anniversary of their arrival "overseas." Their timing seems to have been a bit off, but this can be attributed to the fact that all four squadrons were operating out of Ankang at the time, and there was no guarantee that they would all be together on the 22d. The 1st and 2d B.S. originals, being together at Liangshan at the time, were able to hold their celebration on the proper date.

The last big air fight of July came on the 23d, when twenty-two P-40s of all four squadrons escorted six B-25s of the 1st and 2d bomb squadrons to the Yunglowtung railroad yards, which were in the Tungting Lake area, not far from the big Japanese air base at Paliuchi. An estimated fifteen to twenty Ki-43s attacked the CACW formation near Paliuchi from above, but the P-40s quickly got the best of the Japanese. By the time the shooting stopped ten Oscars had been destroyed without a loss to the CACW.

The Oscars dove through the higher escorts, losing a few of their number on the way, only to be met by the 7th F.S. flight on close cover below. Lt. Don Burch was leading for the 7th, and he quickly hopped on the tail of one Oscar that had broken through toward the B-25s. He followed through a loop—no easy task for a P-40 pilot—firing all the way, and the Japanese fighter went down in easy view of the bomber crews, who confirmed the kill. Others in Burch's flight claiming kills were Lieutenants Keh H.S., Ho C.S., and Chang S.C.; Lieutenants Ed Mulholland, Wang K.F., and Wang M.T. each claimed an Oscar damaged.

The effectiveness of the low-level approach tactics used by the 5th F.G. in attacking this same Paliuchi air base is made obvious by the different responses from the defenders. On the 23d, the bombing mission at 9,000 feet drew a whole gang of Oscar interceptors; the next day, coming in on the deck, the 5th's P-40s destroyed thirty aircraft on the field without a single interceptor getting off the ground. In both missions the CACW outfits were clearly superior to their foes, for a total of forty enemy aircraft were destroyed while the CACW lost only two P-40s (one to a flying accident) and no B-25s.

As the summer of 1944 wore on, the weather remained good and action continued for the 1st B.G. and 3d F.G. The bomb group hit a high note on August 11, when it celebrated its first birthday. Colonel Branch hosted a party at Peishiyi, and guests included Brigadier General Morse (with a brand-new star) and his wing staff, Lieutenant Colonel Dunning from the 5th F.G. and Maj. Wang Yu-ken, CAF vice-commander of the 1st B.G.

The 4th B.S. at Kweilin, under Maj. Bill Dick, was the closest of the CACW squadrons to the ICHIGO advance. The B-25s flew seven missions, including a supply drop on the 7th, before Hengyang fell on the 8th. Then on the 9th they went back at it, bombing advancing Japanese forces on the Hengyang-Hengshan road. More missions followed as Siangtan was bombed on the 14th, Kiukiang on the 17th, and artillery emplacements at Changsha on the 18th. Dick submitted commendations for two Chinese crews, those of Lieutenants Wang C.C. and Jen K.C., during the month.

The first aerial victory of the month was scored by Capt. Chang C.M. of the 28th F.S. on August 4 during a strafing mission on the Yangtze River. Chang, who would later be transferred to the 5th F.G. as commander of the 29th F.S., spotted a small single-engine transport and gave chase. A burst from his guns set it afire, and two crewmen were seen jumping out without parachutes before the plane dove into the ground.

The 32d, still flying from its far-off base at Hanchung and often staging through Hsian, was the standout fighter squadron of the month. Its commander, the aggressive Bill Turner, was determined that the 32d's 100th mission would be a doozy, so he set his sights on the Japanese air base at Taiyuan, far north of Hsian and rarely visited by 14th A.F. attackers.

The weather didn't cooperate with Turner's plans, and he flew the 100th mission as a weather recon on August 9. The next day everything was ready, and Turner led all nine P-40s of his squadron out of Hsian at 1105. They climbed up to the bottom of the overcast at 14,000 feet and headed northeast toward the target. En route one P-40 had to turn back. The P-40s, carrying drop tanks but no bombs or rockets, arrived over the target at 1250 and began the first of forty-nine strafing passes they would make in the next twenty minutes.

Some forty to sixty Japanese aircraft, mostly Ki-27 Nate fighters, were caught on the ground. Judging from the obsolescence of these fighters and the fact that they were not very well dispersed, it was thought that Taiyuan was being used as an operational training base.

Only two aircraft were in the air at the time of the attack, and both were shot down. Lt. Tien Y.H. caught one fighter in the landing pattern on his first pass and shot it down. Then Turner and Captain Lindell found another Ki-27 taking off as they pulled up from their first strafing pass, and both American pilots put bursts of fire into it until it crashed.

On the ground twenty-four aircraft were set on fire and another twenty-four were damaged, though some of the aircraft claimed as damaged were destroyed on later passes and so were claimed twice. Lt. Chung H.F. was the top strafer, destroying five and damaging five more in ten passes over the field. The only antiaircraft fire observed was from small arms, but it was fairly accurate. Lieutenant Lu was hit in the chest on his third pass but nevertheless made five more strafing runs and destroyed three aircraft before breaking off and returning to base. Another shot hit the right rudder pedal in Lindell's P-40 and shrapnel wounded him in the leg and chest. In November he would be awarded a Silver Star for the mission.

The formation checked in at the Japanese air base at Linfen on its way home, but by that time ammunition was almost gone and no aircraft were on the field, so Turner's pilots shot up the operations building and then headed for Hsian. The next day General Chennault radioed his congratulations to General Morse at Peishiyi and Major Turner at Hanchung.

Bennett flew up from Liangshan to get a personal report and offer his accolades. Turner later added an Oak Leaf Cluster to his DFC for his planning and execution of the Taiyuan raid.

There was more excitement in the air for the 32d on August 11. A 20th A.F. B-29 returning to Chengtu from a mission over Japan made an emergency landing at the tiny airstrip at Huayin, about eighty miles northeast of Hsian, and the 32d was detailed to patrol over the base with P-47s of the 312th Fighter Wing to protect the big bomber until it could be repaired and flown out.

At about 1430 six Ki-44s appeared over the field, and four of them went down after the B-29, which was stuck in the mud, while two others took on the fighters above. Lt. Chung H.C. of the 32d and Lieutenant Hawthorne of the P-47 outfit each shot down a strafing Tojo, then Lt. Wang S.C. of the 32d attacked another of the strafers. Wang's victim crash-landed near the base and the Japanese pilot jumped out, set his airplane on fire, and then engaged in a shoot-out with approaching Chinese troops. When it became clear that the Japanese pilot was not going to be able to escape, he leaped into the flames of his burning fighter and perished with it.

In all, the 32d flew eight missions and thirty-seven sorties that day before the B-29 was flown out to Chengtu. That night Japanese bombers visited Hanchung and left some explosive calling cards, but little damage was done.

On August 12 it was the turn of the 7th and 28th squadrons to do some damage. They were attacked by Ki-43s during a Yangtze River sweep and knocked down three with no losses. Lt. Li T.T., one of the

7th's top pilots, got one. Major Cheng, the 28th commander, got on the tail of another Oscar and chased it at low altitude until the Japanese pilot misjudged his height and plowed into the ground. Meanwhile, the 28th's Lt. Chao Y.K. got another Ki-43 when he hit it dead center in a head-on pass.

The action returned to Taiyuan on August 17, when Major Turner led eight of his 32d F.S. P-40s back for another shot at the Japanese air base. Again, one P-40 was forced to turn back. This time the weather was clear, and the approach was made at 10,000 feet.

As on the 10th, the Japanese aircraft were caught primarily on the ground, though there were considerably fewer of them than had been seen on the earlier mission. When the pilots came in for their attacks they could see that the remains of aircraft destroyed on the earlier strike had been heaped in a pile near a hangar on the east side of the field. It was also noted that a steel mill in the city of Taiyuan was operating and would make a good target for future attacks.

The 32d attacked in two flights and saw fifteen aircraft on the field. As they pulled up from the first strafing run, Captain Lindell and Lt. Chung H.F. spotted a Ki-27 towing a target near the field. Both fired at it and claimed a kill, but credit was given to Lindell after the gun camera film was reviewed.

Major Turner and Capt. Herman Byrd, who was flying the squadron's camera ship (a P-40N-26CU), strafed two hangars on the north side of the field and saw both of them burst into flames, destroying four aircraft inside. Capt. Hung Chi-Wei, the CAF commander, and Lt. Liao Tan-Ching attacked two aircraft that had just landed and strafed them heavily, but neither caught fire so were claimed as damaged. In all, eight aircraft were destroyed on the ground and another seven were damaged. After the attack Captain Byrd made pictures of the field and the industrial areas of the city before returning to Hsian.

The weather did to the 32d what the Japanese couldn't on August 18, when three P-40s were lost on a dive-bombing mission against the Hsuchang railroad yards. The P-40 of Lt. Liu P.W. was hit in a coolant line, and he made a forced landing at Neisiang for repairs. Lieutenants Lee W., Tien Y.H., and Yu Wei buzzed the field to make sure Liu had landed safely, but then became separated from the formation leader, Capt. Tom Maloney, and his wingman, Lt. Tom Cribbs. All three Chi-

nese became lost in the weather that had closed in, and they each crash-
landed after they ran out of fuel. None of the pilots was hurt, but all
three of the precious P-40s were destroyed, including the photo ship that
Captain Byrd had made so useful on the previous day.

On August 20 one of the rare USO shows to have been seen by
CACW personnel arrived at Liangshan for a performance. The biggest
Hollywood stars were Ann Sheridan and Ben Blue; others were Jackie
Miles, Ruth Dennis, and Mary Landa. After their show, the women
went out onto the field and autographed Maj. Bill Reed's P-40, "Boss's
Hoss."

Another CACW pilot joined the roster of aces on August 22, when
eight P-40s of the 7th and 8th squadrons flew a Yangtze River sweep from
Hankow to Sinti. Four boats were strafed, then twelve to sixteen Oscars
jumped the formation near Kiayu.

In the scrap that followed, Capt. Ray Callaway of the 8th F.S. confirmed one Oscar destroyed for his fifth kill of the war. One CACW pilot,
Lt. Robert Quidley of the 7th F.S., was shot down and killed. He had
been flying Bill Reed's wing and was on his first mission, having just
joined the squadron a week earlier.

The next day Major Reed lost his newly autographed P-40N. The
mission was a B-25 escort, and the target was a railroad bridge west of
Kaifeng. A Chinese pilot from the 8th F.S. was assigned to fly Reed's
fighter, and he crashed on takeoff, writing off the P-40.

The top cover was engaged by seven or eight Oscars and Tojos over the
target, and again the 8th F.S. added an ace to the roster. Capt. Tsang Si-
Lan shot down his fourth and fifth Japanese aircraft of the war and damaged another before he was shot down himself. He crash-landed near
Tungkwan and later returned to the squadron. Captain Tsang was the
first Chinese ace of the CACW and perhaps of the Chinese Air Force,
though several Chinese pilots claimed some pretty impressive scores in
the early days of the Sino-Japanese conflict.

Maj. Bill Turner of the 32d scored his last aerial kill of the war, and his
fifth in the CACW, on August 25 during a recon and sweep mission of
railroad targets near Loyang.

Just as his four P-40s were about to drop down and strafe along the rail
line, Turner spotted four Tojos above them. He led his flight up above
the Ki-44s, which went into a mock dogfight in an attempt to draw the

P-40s down to them. Turner smelled a trap, however, and kept climbing. Soon four more Tojos came into view above and behind the first four, so Turner climbed up to their level before he pulled his P-40s down into a dive toward the lower formation.

Turner attacked three fighters of the lower flight from the rear. He hit one with a ten- to twenty-degree deflection shot an saw it roll away smoking. He didn't follow the fighter down, because there were too many other Japanese fighters close by. About this time Lt. Liao T.C. pulled in behind another Tojo and opened fire. This Tojo immediately burst into flame and plummeted to the ground. Then Lieutenant Liao saw another Tojo on the tail of a P-40 and dove down to help out. The Tojo burst into flames and dove into the ground for Lieutenant Liao's second kill of the engagement (and his third of the war).

Meanwhile, Turner had noticed the leader of the lower flight of Tojos and his wingman begin to climb up above the P-40s. Turner gave chase, and the wingman made the mistake of pulling up in front of him about 1,000 yards ahead. Turner fired bursts as he closed in to a mere thirty yards, observing strikes along the cowl, cockpit, and wings. This plane caught fire and plunged down in heavy smoke and flame. The pilot jettisoned his canopy, but never was able to bail out.

By now Turner was up to 18,000 feet, and another Tojo, probably from the top cover flight, pulled in behind him and opened fire. The shots missed, and Turner pushed over into a screaming dive that pushed the airspeed needle to 415 mph before he pulled out of range. Turner flew through a cloud, then pulled a tight 180-degree turn and climbed back, looking for his pursuer. The Tojo had broken off, however, so Turner turned around and returned to Hsian. Lieutenant Liao had fired on another Tojo in the meantime and saw it spin away, but he could only claim it as a probable kill. Lt. Tung P.C. also got in a burst that hit one Tojo in the early going and claimed one aircraft damaged.

When the four P-40s (Lieutenant Cribbs was the fourth) returned to Hsian at about 1300, not one bullet hole was found in any of them.

On August 26 Major Turner flew up to Lushih, where Lt. Yu Wei of his squadron had been waiting since his crash landing on the 18th. Turner originally had intended merely to drop supplies (quinine, a first-aid kit, and emergency rations) to Lieutenant Yu, who was reported to be suffering from malaria and injuries sustained in his crash. Turner found that about 1,800 feet of the airstrip at Lushih was usable, though soft, so he decided to land. He found that Lieutenant Yu was indeed sick with fever and chills, so they decided to try to fly him out. The Chinese pilot curled up into the baggage compartment of Turner's No. 646, and the Major gunned the P-40 down the runway with 15 degrees of flaps. Turner had to make a sharp turn almost immediately after lifting off to avoid hitting a low hill, but the out-of-balance P-40 was equal to the task, and they made it. Turner flew to Hsian, where Lieutenant Yu was placed in the hospital until he could be evacuated by the CACW's borrowed Beechcraft on the 29th.

Down at Enshih, fourteen P-40s led by the newly promoted Lt. Col. Bill Reed flew a Yangtze shipping sweep on August 29 that saw the 3d F.G. score its 100th aerial kill. In all, eight victories were scored on the mission, so credit for Number 100 couldn't be singled out.

The mission was briefed to fly the river from Hankow to Sinti, attacking river traffic and shore installations. After dive-bombing a storage area and sinking a river steamer, the P-40s were attacked from above by Ki-43s near Yuanti. Medium cover was hit first, then the top cover, which had been trailing by several miles.

Down low Lieutenant Colonel Reed got a good burst into an Oscar during a quartering turn head-on attack. The Ki-43 went into a steep turning dive and continued straight down into the river. Lt. Ed Mulholland spotted an Oscar lining up on Reed's P-40, so he fired a ninety-degree deflection shot that hit the Japanese fighter in the fuselage. The Oscar broke off his attack, but Mulholland didn't follow him.

Also in Reed's flight was Lt. Tan Kun. He put a long burst into an Oscar that was lining up on a P-40, and the Japanese pilot flipped his plane over and went into a dive. Lieutenant Tan followed him down until he saw the Ki-43 crash into the ground.

Three Chinese pilots from the 28th scored kills while flying top cover for the mission. Lt. Tien C.C.—flying P-40 No. 732, which Major Cheng often used—saw four Oscars attack from above. The first one looped up and away, for some reason, and the second did one and a half rolls to the right, then went into a dive. Lieutenant Tien followed him down, firing, and then climbed back up into the fight after he saw the Oscar crash. He was jumped on the way up and his P-40 was damaged, but then climbed up again and made passes on several more Oscars before breaking off for home.

Lt. Wei H., in No. 638, spotted four Oscars behind his flight leader,

Lieutenant Meng, shooting at him. Lieutenant Wei fired at them from behind, and one started smoking before it rolled toward the ground. The lieutenant followed, then pulled up when he saw an explosion on the ground below him where the Oscar had been going down.

Lt. Chao Y.K. was flying No. 639 and gave this account:

"I was leader of the second element in the top-cover flight. When the Zeroes came I followed Meng and Wei down after them. I made seven passes. The whole thing was a hell of a mess: Zeroes and P-40s whirling around everywhere. I knocked one Zero off a P-40's tail and followed him down to the ground; I saw him hit. The Japs that attacked the top cover came from high out of the sun. I knocked a Jap off Wei's tail. I gave this Jap several good bursts, but I do not know what happened to him." [1]

This fight was a fitting end to an outstanding month for the 3d Fighter Group and for Bill Reed, who would be awarded the group's first Silver Star for a mission on August 8 in which he, Lieutenant Mulholland, and Lt. Tang C.C. all scored confirmed victories. Reed also was the group's newest lieutenant colonel.

The first week of September brought rain to North China, and that meant that the 3d F.G. would get a breather. Personnel changes were in the works, however, that would affect group headquarters and all the squadrons.

Weather was a tremendous factor for the men of the CACW throughout the wing's history. The weather had decided when they could fly the Hump, often making them wait long, empty days in Chabua before they could even get to China. Upon arriving in the combat area, the weather determined when the planes would fly missions, and thus when the fliers' lives would be on the line.

China is a land of extremes: when the weather is bad, it can be really awful, so when it's good, an air force has to make the best of it. That was the case at Chihkiang in August 1944, when all four squadrons of the 5th F.G. found themselves in constant action against the ICHIGO offensive.

The P-40s struck at the Japanese anywhere they could find them, attacking sampans, trucks, buildings, cavalry, and troops mercilessly. In seventy-nine missions, 566 sorties were flown and ten Japanese planes shot down. The P-40 pilots also destroyed 577 sampans, seventy-two motor launches, and 246 trucks, all vital to the supply effort for the advancing Japanese.

On August 11 the 17th and 27th squadrons moved into a new alert shack at the south end of the field, leaving the two senior squadrons at the far end. The following week the last of the support personnel for the newer squadrons arrived, consolidating the 5th F.G. once and for all. Colonel Rouse announced that henceforth aircraft maintenance would be performed exclusively by CAF personnel, with the U.S. technicians doing only supervisory work. Despite this order, the American crew chiefs continued in much the same role as they had before, doing much of the highly technical work that was beyond the means of many Chinese mechanics.

Glyn Ramsey, then operations officer of the 26th F.S. and recently promoted to major, filed a report on the capabilities of the Chinese at about this time and noted that they seemed to make better armorers, and especially sheet-metal workers, than mechanics. He considered engine-trouble diagnosis and engine repairs to be particularly bad areas for them.

The first good aerial scrap of the month came on August 4 and involved Colonel Rouse and Lt. Bill King, and American citizen of Chinese descent who had joined the CAF in 1938.

King, who eventually returned to his native California some years after the war ended, recalls this mission as his most exciting:

"Four of us, flying P-40s with a 1,000-pound bomb under the belly, were supposed to dive-bomb a steamer unloading next to a Jap airfield [at Siansiang]. Takeoff was at dawn; however, only two of us, Colonel Rouse and myself, got off—the other two planes aborted. Anyway, the two of us reached our target and dive-bombed at about 5,000 feet with Col. Rouse going in first and me following.

"The first bomb missed, and as I pulled up from my dive I noticed a bunch of Jap Zeroes diving toward the colonel. I hollered, 'Zero! Zero! Dive! Dive!' Never determined where my bomb landed.

"When the colonel dived with about eight Jap Zeroes after him, I proceeded [on] my upward climb and flew between the colonel and the Japs shooting all the way until I just about stalled. I heard a loud explosion and the plane rocked all of a sudden. I thought, 'Damn, I've been hit and not by those eight Zeroes that were after the colonel!'

"Just as I prepared to bail out I looked down, and damned if I wasn't exactly over the Jap airfield. My P-40's motor seemed to be still working so I decided to stay with it and hit the deck. I got away with a couple of Japs in hot pursuit. But this time I had lost contact with the colonel and he with me.

"I headed for friendly ground and force-landed—wheels up, low on gas—not hurt. I returned to base after about three days; received the DFC."[1]

King's is a fascinating story. After studying aeronautics at a junior college in California, he joined the CAF in 1938 in San Francisco. He recalls:

"The whole deal was supported by contributions from all over the U.S. If my recollection is anywhere near correct, there must have been around fifty volunteers. Perhaps about half were in ground-crew training and half in flight training. Most instructors were hired U.S. [Air Corps] reserves. After a year's training we were sent to China.

"Arriving in the interior of China [Kunming] we found that the CAF [Chinese Air Force] school was more or less run by U.S. personnel under the leadership of then-Colonel Chennault. We were given flight tests by American pilots, and some were washed out right there and then.

"Others who passed the test were assigned to primary training or basic training. Fortunately, I was assigned to basic and then advanced, too, and graduated from advanced with a fighter-pilot classification. So I actually learned how to fly in the U.S. but graduated from CAF officers flight school in China.

"Planes used in training were all American-made. Primary trainers were Fleets; basic trainers were BT-9s and a few Douglas biplanes. Advanced trainers were Curtiss Hawk IIs and IIIs.

"I did not join the CACW immediately. After graduation from the CAF school a few of us (four, to be exact) were assigned to regular combat squadrons. However, about that time there was a great shake-up among the only three fighter groups of the CAF. So after some time in the 3d F.G. I found myself transferred to the 5th Fighter Group and headed for India. After three or four months of training we flew our planes over the Hump back to China."

How well did the Chinese and American personnel get along in the CACW? According to King:

"As far as I can remember, I can truthfully say that we got along swell. Being an American Chinese and speaking the Chinese language, I was called to interpret a lot."

King also denied the contentions made by some that the Chinese pilots were instructed to avoid dangerous combat situations with the Japanese because the high command wanted to save its air strength to use later against the Chinese Communists. He says:

"As a matter of fact, the Americans always told the Chinese pilots to save themselves when in real danger: pilots are hard to come by; we can always get planes. When I wanted out after the war, the CAF wanted me to stay because of the Communists."

He had a few thoughts on the value of the CACW:

"The CACW gave a give lift to the CAF. They finally had some planes to fight with. They knew that the CACW had been fighting hard. The CAF wanted in, too!"[2]

On August 25, Lt. Bill Johnson of the 26th F.S. was shot down for the second time that summer. Again, his wingman was Lt. Phil Colman. Johnson's P-40 took a hit in the cooling system while the pair were strafing Japanese cavalry near Siansiang. The 26th F.S. historian recorded the radio conversation between the two pilots this way:

> Colman: Johnson, your coolant is hit and trailing white smoke! Head northwest. [Johnson was positioning himself to make another pass.]
>
> Johnson: Yeah, I guess I am.
>
> Colman: Better get some altitude, Johnny, and head for those hills northwest.
>
> Johnson: Okay. [He prepared to bail out.]
>
> Colman: Well, you know how to do it.
>
> Johnson: Reckon ah do. See you in about two weeks.
>
> Exit Lt. Johnson.

Colman circled Johnson's parachute as the future commander of the 26th F.S. floated down, then flew off after he was sure that Johnson had landed safely. As luck would have it, the Ann Sheridan USO troupe arrived at Chihkiang the next day. Johnson, being otherwise engaged, missed the show, which was described as "slightly risqué" in the best 1940s style. Miss Sheridan left an autographed photo for Johnson, however, on which she wrote:

"To Bill Johnson—many happy landings, kid."

The high point of the summer at Chihkiang, if anything could top a USO tour featuring pretty girls from back home, came the following night during an air raid on the base. Again Glyn Ramsey and Mac McCullough were in the thick of the action. Ramsey recalls:

"The Japanese came in often enough at night that Dunning decided that we could put fighters up at night, one at a time. We would just fly around and listen to the tower, and he would tell us where the airplanes were coming from and at what height. We would fly parallel that course looking for their exhaust. Of course it was a fool's game, but it was a way of possibly getting them, and everybody wanted to do it.

"It came my night to be the night fighter pilot, and I had an airplane on the end of the runway. It was all ready to go, and the engineering officer, Bill Stiles, was going to go down with me and help me get started. He and I were pretty good friends, and he was a good engineering officer. Of course, we got a report that they were coming in, and we went into a *jing bao* [air raid] and everyone went to their gun pits. We had used guns from aircraft, and the Chinese blacksmiths had made a device similar to bicycle handlebars. They mounted the gun on the handlebars and then they had a rod that went down in the ground, a pipe, and a rod in the bottom of the handlebars that sat inside the pipe. In other words, we had a 360-degree, dual-firing, .50-caliber machine gun. They were air-cooled aircraft guns, not designed for firing in a stable position like that because they were cooled by the air from the airstream. You would fire one burst on that thing and both barrels would be red-hot, but that's all we had.

"Well, Dunning was just off the end of the runway, and Stiles and I ran down the runway. I jumped in the airplane and started it, and then I wheeled around to take off in the dark. I was just heading the airplane in the direction I knew the runway ran, and I figured I could get off at full power before I ran off the end.

"I opened the throttle, and the airplane coughed and caught again, then coughed and died before I picked up any speed at all. Fortunately for me. If it had run for fifteen seconds until I got up to 80 to 100 mph and then coughed it would have been duck soup. But it coughed and died. It had water in the fuel, which often happened, and it killed the engine.

"When the airplane finally quit turning over so I could hear, Stiles was standing at the edge of the runway and he was screaming at me as loud as he could yell, saying, 'They're coming now! Get the hell out of that airplane!' I bailed out of that airplane, and he and I ran about 100 yards to an old gun pit on the end of the runway.

"We hardly made it to the gun pit before I could hear the first Lily bomber coming in, and he was coming from right to left. We had about 2,000 feet overcast, which was very thin, and behind that overcast was a bright moon. You couldn't imagine a more translucent screen arrangement. Of course the Japanese on top of that thin overcast couldn't see the ground, so they were ducking through and coming right under it over the base.

"They just looked like a fly on flypaper. It was just clear as a bell even though it was night. As Stiles and I jumped in that pit I started tracking that airplane, just manually, for speed. I'd shot a lot of skeet and birds and had a gun in my hands long before I was in the military. I was tracking those planes, and I said to Stiles, 'When I shoot I won't be able to see a thing. I'm just going to keep on tracking the speed I think he is moving.'

"I started shooting at the airplane, and Stiles starts jumping up and down; I couldn't see anything, I was blinded. He said, 'You're hitting! You're hitting him.' I stopped firing after I swung through the complete arc, and sure enough the airplane was going straight in. It just maintained a shallow dive that it was doing when we hit, and one of the engines caught on fire. Flames strung out behind that airplane 100 feet, and it flew right into the hill beside the field about a mile from where we were. It was one of those improbable kills because shooting with machine guns that didn't have any sights on them is just more psychological than anything else. But in this case it worked."[3]

Unknown to Ramsey and Stiles, a second gunner hit that Lily on its run across the field. In another pit was Mac McCullough of the 29th, freshly promoted from warrant officer to second lieutenant. Fire from both pits was seen to hit the Lily, so credit for its destruction was split between Ramsey and McCullough. The all clear was sounded at 2100, and afterward the gun crews were treated to a taste of whiskey, rum, and brandy by Colonel Rouse. The Lily wouldn't be the last to fall over Chihkiang.

On August 29, the Japanese offensive began a new push after taking three weeks to rest and rebuild its supplies following the fall of Hengyang on the 8th. The Japanese forces first swept south down the rail line toward Canton, then turned west toward Lingling and Kweilin.

That same day saw the 5th F.G. claim its last scores of the month when pilots of the 27th and 29th led by Major Hull took part with squadrons of the 51st and 23d fighter groups in an escort of B-24s to Yochow. The force, which included thirty-four P-40s and ten P-51s, met Japanese interceptors over Lukiroshi. The Oscars and Tojos made single attacks, apparently trying to avoid the escorts and get in close to the B-24s.

In all, six kills were claimed, and Major Hull got the only one for the 5th F.G. when he pulled in behind an Oscar and fired at slight deflection from about 150 yards. Heavily hit, the enemy plane went down as its pilot bailed out. Lt. William "Buck" Joyner, who had just joined the 27th, claimed one fighter damaged. The 27th's Lt. Chow S.D., who destroyed three aircraft on the second Paliuchi raid the previous month, was shot down and listed as missing in action.

On returning after the mission there was one last bit of excitement. A B-24 crash-landed at Chihkiang (not surprising, given the length of the landing strip) and caught fire. Once again Lieutenants Stiles and Mc-Cullough were in the thick of the action, braving the danger to extinguish the fire and save the crew. Both received medals for the bravery they displayed that day.

As busy as the 5th had been in July and August, the group got no respite in September, which would turn out to be the busiest month yet as the Japanese offensive pushed past Hengyang and ever closer to Chihkiang. No less than 109 missions were flown in September.

A new technique for using the P-40s as fighter-bombers against the advancing enemy was pioneered as a ground liaison officer, Captain West, experimented with pinpointing strikes for the fighters by radio from his position on the front lines with the Chinese troops.

Despite these efforts, the Japanese were able to take Paoching on September 15, and this immediately threatened both Chihkiang and Kweilin. The last CACW bombers flew out of the Erh Tong air base at Kweilin on the 14th, and demolition of the base began that night. The B-25s of the 3d and 4th bomb squadrons flew in to Peishiyi at about the same time, and many men who hadn't seen each other for many months were reunited, with much festivity. One other unfortunate note that day came when the 3d B.S. commander, Major Conrad, tried to put his wheels down to land at Peishiyi and found his nosewheel stuck. He crash-landed the bomber at Chungking with no injuries to his crew, but major damage to the B-25.

At Chihkiang, the threat of being overrun by the Japanese was so great that about 150 personnel who were not considered essential to the day-to-day operation of the 5th F.G. were flown out to Enshih for safekeeping until either the threat eased or the base fell. As it turned out, the former came to pass, and the men returned to Chihkiang seventy-five days later. The closest the Japanese were able to get to Chihkiang was 100 miles away on September 16, but the Chinese forces held them there. Another drive from Sinning later in the month got to within seventy miles at Wukangshien, but it, too, was halted. Flying with the 5th F.G. from Chihkiang during September was the famous 75th F.S. of the 23d F.G.

A good example of the ground-support missions flown during the month was a weather recon attack on Paoching flown September 29 by Lieutenant Colonel Dunning and Capt. Tom Reynolds of the 17th F.S. Reynolds's fighter carried two pairs of fragmentation bomb clusters, while Dunning's P-40 was loaded with six rockets.

The two planes ranged east of the river at Paoching and together made some thirty strafing passes. One rocket hit a large, stablelike building and destroyed it. Another flew off on an erratic course, and the rest missed their targets. Reynolds dropped his frags over a building compound two miles east of the city, and it was estimated that fifteen Japanese were killed.

Aerial kills were made on only six missions during September, but the totals were impressive: thirteen destroyed, five probables, and twenty-nine damaged. Another sixty-two ground kills were claimed.

Captains Ramsey and Reynolds each damaged an Oscar in a scrap September 12, but Lt. Tom Brink, considered one of the hottest pilots in the group, was shot down and killed when the P-40s were caught low and slow by the Japanese fighters.

Later that day Lt. Phil Colman of the 26th F.S. shot down an Oscar over Siangtan, in addition to scoring a probable and two damaged.

Lt. "Buck" Joyner of the 27th was next to score when eight Oscars jumped an equal number of P-40s near Changsha on the 16th. Also registering kills that day were Lieutenants Wang W.W. and Yueh K.C. Lt. Loo Y.P. destroyed a Hamp on the 19th, but the biggest fight of the month was to come two days later.

Mission 279 of September 21 called for eleven P-40s to bomb and strafe Japanese warehouses at Chuliangkao and sweep north of Sinshih in the Tungting Lake area looking for targets of opportunity. After one aircraft was forced to turn back, the formation split into an assault flight of six with a four-plane top cover consisting of Colonel Rouse, Major Van Ausdall, and Lieutenants Colman and Yang S.H.

Near Sinshih, a formation of eight Japanese fighters attacked the lower flight, apparently not spotting the top cover. At the same time, another flight of eight enemy fighters was seen in the distance.

Colman called out the first flight of Japanese to Van Ausdall, who was leading the top cover, and they peeled off to dive down behind the enemy fighters. The Japanese finally spotted the P-40s behind them and dropped their belly tanks just as the "sharks" came into range.

Colman closed in on one Hamp from behind and fired three bursts, hitting it in the fuselage and left wing. The wounded fighter rolled and went down in a diving turn, with Colman right behind, taking occasional shots. Finally the Hamp caught on fire and then crashed.

Colman then climbed back and formed up with P-40s of the 75th F.S. that had joined the fight. Spotting four Oscars below him, Colman dropped down and took some shots at the leader. Looking back, Colman saw another Japanese fighter pulling in behind him, so he broke off the attack and went into a dive and gradually pulled away.

Just as he pulled out of range, Colman did a violent 180-degree turn to the right and up. The Oscar pulled up and to the left but was attacked by two other P-40s, so the Japanese pilot rolled and came back toward Colman in a dive.

Colman half-rolled and got a forty-degree deflection shot from above. The Oscar belched black smoke, and then Colman saw fire in its left wing root. It continued its rolling dive straight into the ground about twenty miles northeast of Sinshih.

Climbing back into the fight again, Colman scored heavily on an Oscar with blue wings. The fighter trailed black smoke from under its fuselage, but Colman lost sight of it and could claim only a probable.

Colman, whose two kills made him the 5th's first and only ace, didn't have a monopoly on excitement; in all, eight pilots of the 5th registered claims in the scrap. Colonel Rouse himself was able to tack up a confirmed kill next to his name on the big scoreboard behind his desk back at Chihkiang.

Rouse had attacked with the top cover, but he blacked out when he pulled up on the first pass. Recovering, he did a 360-degree turn and found that his only company were two Oscars coming in from the left. He fired at them as they passed, then attacked another Oscar to his left.

The first burst of fire was high, the second behind. The third burst, however, caught the enemy fighter flush from five degrees deflection astern at very close range. The Oscar was suddenly blanketed with hits and exploded in midair. It fell from the sky, trailing a long, red flame, as Rouse dove out to evade two other Oscars on his tail.

Total claims for the fight were as follows: Rouse, one Oscar destroyed; Van Ausdall, one Oscar destroyed, one probable, and three damaged; Colman, one Oscar and one Hamp destroyed, one Oscar probable, two Oscars damaged; Sub Lt. Lin Y.S., one Hamp destroyed, one damaged; 1st Lt. "Bobby" Yang S.H., one Oscar probable, three damaged; 1st Lt. Liang, half an Oscar destroyed; Lt. Chang Y.K., half an Oscar destroyed; Lt. Chang Y.S., one Oscar probable.

One other mission in September was worthy of special note. On the night of the 24th, Capt. Bill "Bonnie" Bonneaux of the 17th F.S. was scrambled from Chihkiang in an attempt to intercept Japanese bombers that were raiding the field. Climbing out in the darkness, Bonneaux made radio contact with one of the ground antiaircraft crews, who told him a bomber was making a run over the field from south to north.

At that time, Bonneaux was northwest of the field over the town of Chihkiang at 4,000 feet. As the bomber came across the blacked-out field it turned head-on to Bonneaux's course at 1,000 feet below. He considered attacking from the front, but decided instead to do a 180-degree turn and circle in behind the bomber.

The turn brought him dead astern and slightly above the Ki-48 Lily, which turned on its running lights just as Bonneaux came into firing range. He cut loose with a short burst that raked the bomber nose to tail. The first burst didn't do the job, so Bonneaux fired again, this time hitting the cockpit area. The second burst was enough, and the bomber exploded, fell into a spin, and crashed just north of Chihkiang.

Bonneaux saw another bomber then, silhouetted by the burst of its bombs, but he was unable to close on it before the intruder disappeared into the dark night.

In October the skies filled with rain, and flying practically stopped at Chihkiang. The mud was incredible, at one point becoming so bad in the 27th F.S. dispersal area that P-40s were sinking in the mud to their belly tanks. The overcast reached from the ground all the way to 20,000 feet, and only toward the end of the month did the skies begin to clear.

With the rain, the pace of life slowed down, and there was time for such diversions as card games, reading, and a spate of "Battleship" tournaments. Four members of the 26th F.S. found time for something else, thanks to their flight surgeon, Dr. John Forgrave.

Forgrave had discovered that the men had never been circumcised, so when the weather turned bad and there was time to burn, he convinced them to go under the knife. Glyn Ramsey recalls:

"We didn't have any dispensary—I mean hospital. We had a little room, and they had the field kits of medicine. Forgrave and Kelly [Dr. Edward Kelly, who had received the Silver Star for his bravery on the *Rohna*] did circumcisions on those guys. It was common knowledge that he was going to do it, and then he did it.

"The next morning early I walked into those guys' room to hooray them a little bit, and I saw [some] sick guys. Their faces were pale, and they were lying out flat on their beds, and they were not moving around. I made a couple of what I thought were light remarks about the situation, and I had to duck to get the hell out of there. I could hardly get out the door fast enough to keep them from hitting me, but I was so tickled I could hardly find the door.

"I've told people since then it's maybe a case similar to having a tonsillectomy: when you're little it may be okay, but when you're a grown man it's something else. I wouldn't recommend it to anyone, because those guys were tough . . . that is, they thought they were tough. But they sure were pussycats that next morning."[4]

About the only 5th F.G. pilot who saw much action during October was the 27th's Lt. Buck Joyner. He was forced to bail out of his plane in the dark on September 21 after a strafing mission.

Encountering heavy haze as his radio and lights failed and night was falling on the terrain below him, Joyner decided to try to follow a course that would take him to Liuchow, southwest of Kweilin. The P-40 he was flying ran out of gas before he could reach his destination, so he left the aircraft at 1,600 feet over a town. A strong wind blew his parachute fifteen to twenty miles from the town, and he landed in trees on the side of a mountain.

After getting out of his chute harness and cutting loose his jungle pack, Joyner started down the mountain. He made slow progress, all the while hacking at dense undergrowth, then dropped his flashlight and fell down an incline while trying to retrieve it. Battered and cut, he decided to curl up and call it a night. He walked all the next day and finally found a path late in the afternoon.

Joyner walked several miles before he found some Chinese sleeping along the path. He woke them up and was recognized as an American pilot, so the Chinese took him to where his plane had crashed. He was finally taken to a nearby village, where he made his wants known, and the Chinese agreed to take him out to Liuchow. Traveling by houseboat, in which he was hidden in the cabin, Joyner was taken downriver until he reached a tiny U.S. radio outpost. He stayed with the three radio men in the shack for five or six days, then was taken to Liuchow.

"You know," Joyner said over thirty-five years later, "I never saw those three guys in that radio shack again."

At Liuchow the weather was considerably better than at Chihkiang. During October Joyner flew thirteen missions with the 76th F.S. of the 23d F.G., then returned to Chihkiang when the 76th was evacuated from Liuchow in the face of the advancing Japanese.

The most significant event of November for the 5th F.G. was a change of commanders. Col. Frank E. Rouse, who had led the group from its beginning in Malir, was sent back to the United States, and Lt. Col. John Dunning, another original member of the group, took his place as commander.

The two men had been a study in opposites during their time together. Rouse was older, smaller, and less personable than Dunning. He was a by-the-book officer who nevertheless had created a top-notch outfit in the face of some enormous obstacles.

Dunning, already extremely popular with the men in the group, would prove equal to the challenge of command—and then some.

Dunning's elevation to group commander left the group operations officer job open, and Maj. Charlie Wilder of the 17th was chosen to fill the job. This in turn left command of the 17th open, and Maj. Glyn Ramsey moved in to take that job.

The weather improved during November, and a number of effective ground-attack missions were flown. By far the most noteworthy was flown on the 11th, when Capt. Tom Reynolds, now flying with the 26th F.S., led ten P-40s on a surprise attack against the Hengyang air base. The former 14th A.F. stronghold had been rebuilt by the invading Japanese, and Reynolds's P-40s caught about twenty-five aircraft parked on the field. The pilots dropped eighteen fragmentation clusters and made thirty-seven strafing runs before departing for home.

In six passes, Reynolds destroyed four Oscars and damaged three more before climbing up to 8,000 feet for top cover while the flight of three led by Lt. Wang W.W. made its runs. Reynolds soon was jumped from behind by an Oscar that hit his P-40, an N-30 model, serial number 44-7402, several times in the horizontal stabilizer.

Reynolds dove for safety while Lt. John Miller of the 26th, who had just finished making five strafing passes himself, pulled in behind the Ki-43. Miller fired from 300 yards range and hit the Oscar, causing it to cough up a stream of white smoke. Miller hit the plane with another burst, and the Japanese fighter fell off in a steep dive, pouring black smoke behind it. No one saw it crash, however, so Miller was credited with a probable victory.

In all, seventeen Japanese planes were destroyed and eighteen damaged, in addition to the Oscar that Miller clobbered. Reynolds was awarded a Silver Star for planning and leading the mission. Reynolds, an Arkansas native, had graduated flying school in December 1941, and was then sent to a fighter training outfit in Baton Rouge, Louisiana. Finishing training, he was made a fighter-pilot instructor with the 338th F.G. in Florida. There, he said, "I led student pilots to the gunnery range day after day for at least two years. In fact, I participated in the training of a number of Chinese pilots." He had been one of the pilots who sailed to China aboard the aircraft carrier U.S.S. *Mission Bay* in early 1944 and had then been one of the original flight leaders in the 17th F.S. A lot more action was ahead for this aggressive pilot.

In these waning weeks of 1944, the press of operations and the paucity of replacement planes began to show on the performance of the 5th F.G. Engine failures in the P-40s became more common as the hours mounted, and some of the Chinese pilots began having accidents with their fighters. Attacks continued to be made on airfields, bridges, and traffic; major targets were Changsha, Hengyang, Lingling, and Paoching.

On November 18, insult was added to injury for the men of the 5th F.G. when Barracks C and the BOQ at Chihkiang burned down. Japanese fifth columnists were suspected of causing the fires, from which little was salvaged by the men who had been living in those quarters.

Also during the month of November, radar was installed at Chihkiang. By this time, however, the threat of Japanese bombers was diminishing, and only three air raids took place from December 1 through the end of the war.

The 1st Bomb Group was not to be left out of the action entirely at Chihkiang during late 1944. Though the group was concentrated at Peishiyi, Liangshan, and Hanchung, a small detachment flew missions out of Chihkiang. The detachment, made up of two planes each from the 3d and 4th squadrons, was called Task Force 34. During December, Task Force 34 flew missions against the Japanese advance in the Kweichow-Kwangsi area, where the heaviest fighting of the month took place. Of the eighteen missions flown, eleven took place at night, and one of them, against the searchlights of Hankow, was considered especially effective.

Weather and wear and tear took their tolls on the 5th F.G. during December, though the squadrons were able to average about thirty missions each for the month. Several planes were lost when aircraft malfunctioned or the pilots became trapped in the weather. The Japanese antiaircraft gunners accounted for several lost planes as well. The squadrons averaged about nine operational P-40s apiece, and Lieutenant Colonel Dunning's personal P-40, nicknamed "Sam," was finally retired. It was the last of the 5th's original "hot-rod" P-40Ns.

If equipment was hard to come by, at least the squadrons at Chihkiang began to get replacement pilots during December. Some of them, such as Capt. Frank K. "Pete" Everest of the 17th, Capt. Winton "Slick" Matthews of the 26th, and Capt. Charles Souch and 1st Lt. Bob Glessner of the 27th, had combat experience from previous tours. Others were veteran instructors, and hardly any were recent flight school graduates.

Glessner had hardly even learned his way around base at Chihkiang when his luck ran out. On Christmas Eve day the veteran of a tour in Europe was strafing Japanese vehicles on a road when he crashed into a hillside while pulling up from the run in his P-40. The fighter exploded on impact, and Glessner died instantly. It was only his ninth mission in the CACW.

December 18 marked the high point of the month for combat operations. On that day the combined aerial might of the 14th Air Force was thrown against Hankow in an effort to smash this vital link in the Japanese supply lines. Missions were flown night and day against airfields, railroad targets, supply dumps, and other targets in the Hankow area.

Pilots from all the squadrons except the 17th registered claims that day while escorting B-24s over the city. Scoring kills were Lts. Chiao W.O. ("Fred") of the 29th and Chang E.F. of the 26th. Chiao was leading left close escort when he spotted an Oscar below him and dove after it. He pulled in behind the Japanese fighter at 5,000 feet and fired a twenty-degree deflection shot from 100 yards. Hits covered the cockpit and canopy, the Ki-43 belched black smoke, and then it plunged into the ground. Fred Chiao remained in the Chinese Air Force and retired as a general before moving to the United States and making his home in Tennessee.

The treacherous weather of December, with its impenetrable cloud formations and vicious icing conditions, would get worse in the opening months of 1945. Dramatic and exciting events were nevertheless ahead for the 5th Fighter Group as the war made its last change of calendars.

9

September 1944 was a month of transition for the CACW forces in North China. As the weather began to turn wet and hint at the soggy winter ahead, changes in the leadership of the 3d F.G. and 1st B.G. headquarters and squadrons were made.

First to go was Lt. Col. Tom Summers of 3d F.G. headquarters, who was transferred to the 10th A.F. in India. Maj. Harvey Davis of the 8th F.S. took his place as group engineering and technical officer, and Maj. J. T. Bull, group operations officer, took Davis's place as 8th F.S. commander. This, in turn, left the group operations officer job open, and Maj. Bill Turner of the 32d F.S. came down to Liangshan from Han-chung to fill the slot. With that, Capt. Ray Callaway transferred from the 8th F.S. to become the new 32d F.S. commander. With his new job, Callaway got a promotion to major.

Also in September, some of the U.S. pilots began to complete their tours and receive orders home. First in the 3d F.G. to leave were Captains Tom Maloney of the 32d F.S. and Wilbur Walton of the 7th. Over in the 1st B.G., Majors Tom Foley, Bill Carson, and Winston Churchill—all original members of the 2d B.S.—got orders home at about the same time.

With the departures came replacements to the squadrons, most notice-ably in the fighter outfits. To the 7th F.S. came 1st Lt. Heyward Paxton, who had considerable instructor duty behind him, and 2d Lt. Ralph

Marx, fresh from training. The 8th F.S. was most changed: First Lieutenants Frank Klump and Walt Michaels (Michaels had been an instructor at Malir since the early days of the CACW) plus 2d Lt. Van Moad
joined 2d Lt. Charles Wagener, who had arrived in mid-August.

The only new face in the 28th was Capt. Keith Lindell, not really new
since he was a transfer with much combat behind him in the 32d. He
replaced Capt. Jim Sagmiller as ops officer when Sagmiller was sent to
group headquarters. Lt. William Storms, a veteran of ninety-plus missions
in the Mediterranean theater, replaced Lindell in the 32d. He was joined
at Hanchung by Second Lieutenants Tom Cribbs and Jim Silver, who later
were referred to by the squadron historian as the "Gold Dust Twins"
because of their friendly rivalry. With all the changes in the 32d, the only
remaining original officer was Maj. Mike Hitchko, the flight surgeon.

Down at Peishiyi, Colonel Branch became the first CACW combat
group commander to be replaced when he was relieved on September 6
by Lt. Col. David J. Munson, former wing operations officer. Lt. Col.
Austin Russell replaced Major Foley as group operations officer and exec,
and Maj. Lawson Horner replaced Major Carson as 2d B.S. commander.
The 1st B.S. was moved up to Hanchung on September 15.

The Chinese also made some changes at the top in the 1st B.G., as
Maj. Wang Yu-ken replaced Major Lee as commander and Maj. Chen
Yu-Feng became vice-commander.

The bad weather that limited operations during early September was
something of a blessing, for the squadrons were beginning to run out of
airplanes. The 28th F.S., for instance, flew only nineteen missions during the month and averaged four P-40s in service. The 32d wasn't much
better, with seven fighters assigned, an average of five of them service-
able, and just sixteen missions flown. The 8th F.S. flew only eleven
missions.

Only three confirmed victories were scored during the month. The
first two were shared kills by Captains Callaway and Yost of the 8th F.S.
on September 15 and 16. Their first victim was a Ki-46 Dinah reconnaissance aircraft, which they caught on the way to Hankow. The pair
chased the Dinah at low level until the Japanese plane dug in a wingtip
during a low turn and crashed into the ground. The next day Callaway
and Yost took turns shooting at an Oscar and brought it down with a
succession of deflection shots.

The last kill of the month was scored by Capt. Herman Byrd of the 32d F.S. While flying top cover September 17 on a strafing mission over the Siang River, he shot down one Oscar and damaged another. Lieutenant Cribbs, flying one of his first missions, damaged another Ki-43.

The biggest mission of the month was flown on the 21st, when nine B-25s of the 3d and 4th bomb squadrons dropped 1,000-pound demolition bombs on the Yellow River Bridge with escort from the 7th and 32d F.S. plus P-47s of the 312th Fighter Wing, normally an air-defense unit for the B-29 bases at Chengtu. The formation was jumped by six to ten Oscars that got through the P-47 top cover unscathed. The P-40 escorts turned into them, and Lieutenants Chung H.F. and Chung H.C. of the 32d each damaged one. Unfortunately, Capt. Don Burch, 7th F.S. operations officer, was shot down in P-40N No. 674 of the 8th F.S., which carried the fuselage code M2. Burch survived the encounter, but later was sold into captivity by a corrupt Chinese official.

The 28th F.S. completed a successful project during a rainy September that culminated on the 13th, when Major Strickland test flew the "C-40," a two-seat P-40 converted under the direction of T. Sgt. Morris Satlikoff. Satlikoff got the first ride in the C-40, and after that a number of uses were found for it. On one occasion, a mechanic was flown up to the advance base at Laohokow to repair a grounded P-40 that had been waiting there for a month to be fixed. The C-40 was damaged October 1 when its pilot (history does not reveal his name) tried to land it in the dispersal area at Hanchung. The two-seater bashed into P-40 No. 652 of the 32d F.S., wrecking both fighters. Luckily, Cpl. James Webb, who was painting No. 652 at the time, saw the C-40 coming and jumped clear quickly enough to avoid being injured.

October brought three weeks of rain to North China, and with the precipitation, action pretty well stopped for the CACW forces there. Missions were flown by the 3d F.G. on only five of the first twenty-two days of the month.

Two of them proved notable in retrospect, for on October 4 the 8th F.S. flew two missions from Laohokow. This base, east of Hsian and formerly used as an emergency field, would become the 3d F.G.'s major base during the first three months of 1945, but for now the action was limited: both of the October 4 missions were local alerts in which no enemy aircraft were encountered.

On October 7, newly arrived Lt. Jim Silver of the 32d F.S. got a real introduction to the China air war. He was on a four-plane strafing mission to Houmachen when his P-40, No. 657, developed engine trouble. Silver bellied it in near Tsishan and was cut over an eye in the crash landing. He thought he heard firing, so he ran from the fighter while Captain Byrd circled overhead. Silver walked all night before reaching a village, where the Chinese warned him that there were Japanese in the area. From there he traveled by foot, sedan chair, mule, and finally truck for two weeks before returning to his squadron at Hanchung.

Silver recalls the incident:

"I had a love affair with the P-40. I felt so confident while flying it. I opted to belly-land rather than bail out of a P-40 that was badly shot up. . . . I wouldn't even have considered that option had I been in a P-51."

By far the brightest spot in the dreary month of October was the mission by the 3d F.G. on the 27th, four days after the weather finally broke. The formation for the mission, an afternoon sweep of the railroad from Hankow to Puchi, with alternate targets of I-ch'ang, Kingmen, and Tangyang airfields, consisted of six P-40s from the 7th F.S., four from the 8th and three each from the 28th and 32d. Lt. Col. Bill Reed was the leader.

Reed led four planes in the strafing flight, while Lieutenant Michaels of the 8th led the four-plane intermediate cover and Captain Lewis of the 7th and Major Callaway of the 32d led four-plane top cover flights. Their first victim was a southbound train of twelve to fifteen cars on the railroad, some twenty miles south of Hankow. The engine, which had been pulling the train at about twenty miles per hour, was hit first and spouted steam in all directions before it rolled to a stop. The strafers made eleven passes over the train, from ninety degrees and lengthwise, setting three or four tank cars at the back of the train on fire and killing a considerable number of troops who were riding in coal cars farther forward. The gasoline spilled fire back down the tracks for about a half-mile, where the burning gas set a single-span wooden bridge on fire.

Leaving the train, the formation proceeded down the railroad for a distance, and then Reed turned the P-40s northwest toward Kingmen. There is no way to know if Reed's long experience in air combat over China or just blind luck led him to Kingmen, but when the P-40 pilots got there they found a sight that must have made their hearts leap. Nine

Lily bombers and eight to ten Oscars were in the landing pattern, circling over the advance Japanese air base. Several bombers were already on the ground as well.

Reed wasted no time wading into the middle of the Japanese, and shot down a Lily in flames for his ninth and last victory. Lieutenant Paxton was credited with two and a half Oscar kills in the air; one crashed and tore itself apart when it hit the ground, and the other two exploded. The other 7th F.S. pilot scoring was Lt. Wang Kuang-Fu, a veteran flight leader, who was credited with two and a quarter Oscars plus a Lily, all of which he saw crash. Capt. Bill Lewis of the 7th developed engine trouble in his P-40N, "House Mouse," No. 664 (serial 43-23610), and bailed out in guerrilla territory. He arrived safely at Laohokow on November 21.

Two Chinese pilots in Callaway's top cover flight did all the scoring for the 32d F.S. Lt. Wang S.C. spotted a Lily below and dove down to attack. His burst set it on fire, and the bomber went down in flames. Lt. Lee W. followed Wang down and attacked an Oscar, which crashed and exploded. Then Lee pulled up and shot at another Ki-43, which also went down in flames.

The only 28th F.S. pilots to get in on the scrap (Lt. Tom Hallman was Lewis's wingman and accompanied him toward home early) were Lieutenants Chang C.M. and Tien C.C., both of whom had scored previous victories in August. Chang was credited with two air kills and one ground kill at Kingmen, and Tien got one aerial victory.

The four 8th F.S. pilots on intermediate cover also did well in the scrap. Upon spotting the enemy aircraft, the flight dove to attack. Lieutenants Frank Klump and Ku Po went on down to the deck and destroyed one Lily apiece on the ground, then zoomed for altitude. Meanwhile, Lieutenant Michaels got one Lily in the air while Lt. Mao C.P. covered him. At that point the Oscars accompanying the bombers intervened, and Lieutenant Klump knocked one down while Lieutenant Mao got another. The other pilots filed claims for Oscars damaged, but they couldn't confirm their victims because of the general mix-up in the massive dogfight.

In all, sixteen Japanese aircraft were confirmed destroyed in the air and four on the ground. It was believed that the Japanese aircraft were staging at Kingmen for a night mission against the CACW bases when they were so rudely interrupted. The pilots noted that the Oscar fliers

Trains carrying supplies for the Japanese advance on the Peking-Hankow line were frequent targets for pilots of the 3d Fighter Group. Here, a locomotive spouts steam after being hit in the boiler by gunfire from a strafing fighter. (Charles Lovett)

Maj. Bill Reed (left) and Col. Al Bennett shake hands in the summer of 1944 at Liangshan, probably during a party celebrating the 7th Fighter Squadron's 110th mission. Surrounding them, from left, are N. P. Nardelli, Homer Nunley, Moose Rumen, Edward "Blackie" Lydon, Carl McAdams, Harvey Davis (commanding officer of the 8th Fighter Squadron), Wilbur Walton, and Clarence Davis. The samurai sword was Reed's, given to him by a Chinese officer in June while he was returning to the squadron after being shot down in Japanese-held territory. Bennett has a 3d Fighter Group patch on his flight jacket. (Charles Lovett)

Maj. Bill Reed's P-40N serves as a backdrop for a USO troupe that visited Liangshan on August 20, 1944. From left are Major Reed (partially visible), Col. Al Bennett, next two unknown, Ruth Dennis, Ann Sheridan, Mary Landa, comedian Ben Blue, Maj. Joe Gayle, Capt. Armit Lewis, Maj. Harvey Davis, and unknown. All three women autographed the cowling of "Boss's Hoss," but the plane was destroyed in a takeoff accident the following day. (John C. Hamre)

Capt. Armit W. Lewis clowns with an aerial camera atop the fuselage of "Pal Jim" at Liangshan during the summer of 1944. (Note the upturned smile on the shark mouth, a trademark of 7th Fighter Squadron P-40Ns.) (Wilbur Walton)

Capt. Chuck Lovett, 7th Fighter Squadron intelligence officer, plays catch in front of the squadron's operations shack at Liangshan, 1944. Above the door is a sign that says: "REED & HSU Inc., EXTERMINATORS, Open Day or Night." (Wilbur Walton)

P-40Ns of the 17th (foreground) and 27th fighter squadrons are loaded with belly tanks and fragmentation bomb clusters at Chihkiang, summer 1944. The nearest aircraft carries tail number 765 and a white propeller spinner, which was a standard marking on 5th Fighter Group P-40s. Note the chalked-in shark mouth on the next P-40 in line. (Bill Mustill)

A tired Col. John Dunning poses in his full 5th Fighter Group gear at Chihkiang. Note that both his scarf and his flying jacket display the group badge. In time, the men of the 5th would come to call themselves "Dunning's Demons." (Jane Dahlberg)

Chinese and American officers of the 5th Fighter Group enjoy a banquet following a decorations ceremony at Chihkiang during the winter of 1944–45. (Jane Dahlberg)

The co-commanders of the 17th Fighter Squadron, Majors Hsiang Shih-Tuan (left) and Charles Wilder, discuss plans for a mission at Chihkiang, 1944. Note the wooden structure built on the Jeep behind them. (Jane Dahlberg)

B-25H No. 625 of the 1st Bomb Squadron had picked up some replacement parts by the time this photo was taken in late 1944. Note the camouflaged cowling and nose-pieces, obviously scavenged from another aircraft. At this time, the 1st Squadron was attacking targets in North China from its base at Hanchung. (Jim Kinder)

A B-25 of the 1st Bomb Group is refueled at Liangshan in early 1945. Even at this late date in the war, facilities were ex-tremely crude on forward bases in China. Here, the ground crew transfers gas from fifty-five-gallon drums into smaller tins that can be carried up the ladder and dumped into the bomber's wing tank. (Wayne Senecal)

Three B-25Js of the 1st Bomb Squadron fly in formation, summer 1945. Note that all three are equipped with underwing rocket racks and .50-caliber cheek guns. They are, from foreground, No. 622, 44-31132; No. 620, 44-31117; No. 614, 44-30837. Capt. G. A. Smith flew No. 620 regularly during May and June 1945. (Jim Kinder)

Capt. Ed Mulholland (left) and Lt. Heyward Paxton (right) of the 7th Fighter Squadron both were shot down in P-51s near Hankow on January 14, 1945. Here, they pose with Lt. Col. Bill Turner in the Chinese clothes they wore while escaping from Japanese-held territory. (Lonnie Neal)

Snow halted operations of the 3d Fighter Group at Laohokow for several days in early 1945. Here, Sgt. Homer Nunley and two Chinese mechanics have a snowball fight while a P-40 of the 7th Fighter Squadron and a P-61 of the 426th Night Fighter Squadron stand idle behind them. (Lonnie Neal)

Red-haired Maj. Keith Lindell (right) was one of the CACW's original fighter pilots. He was first assigned to the 32d Fighter Squadron, then commanded the 28th F.S. from December 1944 through May 1945, scoring three confirmed victories and one probable. "Albakirk Jerk," P-51K serial number 44-11414, was named for Lindell's hometown in New Mexico. He flew it with the 28th in the spring of 1945 at Ankang. (Jeff Lindell)

Lt. Bob Gardner prepares for a mission in "The Stud," P-51K serial number 44-11422, of the 8th Fighter Squadron. Gardner was shot down by small-arms fire in this aircraft on April 13, 1945, and spent the rest of the war as a prisoner of the Japanese. (Bob Gardner)

Col. Eugene Strickland (right) turns over command of the 3d Fighter Group to Lt. Col. Bill Yancey in late July 1945 at Ankang. Strickland, one of the longest-serving and most respected officers of the CACW, scored two confirmed victories and one probable while he was commander of the 28th Fighter Squadron. (Charles Lovett)

Maj. Glyn Ramsey flew "Dippy Did," a P-51, in early 1945 while commanding the 17th Fighter Squadron at Chihkiang. Originally assigned to the 26th Fighter Squadron, Ramsey assumed command of the 17th in November 1944. (Jane Dahlberg)

Lt. Yoh Kung Chen poses in front of a 27th Fighter Squadron P-40N in 1945. Note the squadron insignia on the P-40's upper cowling. The 27th was the last squadron in the CACW to trade in its P-40s for P-51s, not doing so until June 1945. (Santo Savoca)

The last pilot of the CACW to die in combat was Lt. Max Dixon of the 26th Fighter Squadron, shown here reclining on the cowl of his P-51K at Chihkiang shortly before he was shot down over Yochow on August 9, 1945. Note the fancy headgear. (David Bowers)

The Japanese sent a team to sign surrender papers at Chihkiang on August 22, 1945. When the Japanese transport plane carrying the team landed at the base, it was surrounded by armed troops immediately to maintain order while the surrender team proceeded to the base hospital to sign surrender documents. (Glenn Burnham)

were probably quite inexperienced, given that they attempted to evade the P-40s by diving away. This tactic had never been effective against the heavier and faster American fighters and had been exploited by P-40 pilots since the days of the AVG. It was noted with satisfaction after the jubilant fighter pilots returned to base that but a single Japanese raider was reported by the warning net that night.

October was most miserable for the 1st B.G. and wing headquarters personnel at Peishiyi. In addition to the hangovers experienced on the 9th, the morning after the CACW's wingding first birthday party, the men had to contend with mud, mud, and more mud. There was no personnel or equipment on the base available to maintain the roads, and as the rain fell the mud grew ever worse. Finally, on the 23d and 24th everyone was called out for road-repair duty, because the mud threatened to shut down the base.

The first of November brought at least one bright spot for the men at Peishiyi a USO troupe featuring the noted model Jinn Falkenburg and actor Pat O'Brien arrived for a show.

Nevertheless, the rain continued and gas supplies dwindled. On top of that, there were no stoves in the quarters at Peishiyi, and it was starting to get cold. Some of the men made their own stoves. Predictably, when they started buying significant quantities of charcoal to burn in the stoves, the Chinese raised the price considerably.

It was a very slow month operationally for the 1st B.G., with only the B-25 crews down south at Chihkiang getting much flying time. When the weather cleared late in the month, the 3d B.S. Mitchells were moved back to Chengtu because they were safer there from night attack, and there wasn't enough gas at Peishiyi to fly them on missions anyway.

Gas wasn't the only thing in short supply. When Thanksgiving came on the 23d, there wasn't any turkey to feed the men. They got duck for dinner and a promise of turkey later. The delayed turkey dinner finally was served on the 30th.

The shortages continued into December for the 3d Fighter Group and 1st Bomb Group, but the month was far from uneventful. On December 6, the command of the wing changed hands as Brigadier General Morse was sent off to Europe to check out ways and means of redeploying air forces there to China. Col. T. Alan Bennett moved up from command of the 3d F.G. to become acting wing commander. Bennett brought Lt.

Col. Gene Strickland with him to become operations officer for the wing. These two changes brought a major reshuffling of commands within the 3d F.G.

Lt. Col. Bill Reed moved into the command of the 3d F.G., with Lt. Col. Bill Turner as operations officer. Capt. Keith Lindell took Strickland's place as 28th F.S. commander, and Capt. Bill Lewis replaced Reed as commander of the 7th F.S. Maj. Ray Callaway completed his combat tour that same week and was replaced as 32d F.S. commander by Capt. Herman Byrd. When he went home, Callaway's victory total stood at six.

Changes also were made in the 1st B.G. command during the month. On December 17, Lieutenant Colonel Munson got his orders home, and Lt. Col. Austin Russell assumed command. A quickly organized party, attended by Morse and Bennett, marked the occasion.

The shortage of supplies limited missions by the B-25s of the 1st and 2d bomb squadrons to just ten. The 2d B.S. got in nine of them, primarily skip-bombing bridges and medium-altitude drops against railroad yards. Over in the 1st B.S. only one mission was flown, a four-plane strike on the 16th led by the squadron commander, Maj. Ray Hodges. The Mitchells were escorted by sixteen P-40s of the 3d F.G. and encountered no enemy fighters. Nevertheless, Sgt. C. E. Lewis was killed when Lt. "Tex" Waggaman's bomber was damaged by antiaircraft fire.

During the month, the 3d F.G. established Laohokow as its principal staging base in order to reach farther behind Japanese lines with its P-40s, but gas shortages and bad weather hampered operations. The 28th F.S. made a permanent move from Enshih to Ankang to be nearer the action.

The last big mission of 1944 was the aforementioned 14th Air Force destruction of Hankow on December 18. The 3d F.G. put up thirty-two P-40s, split into two groups; Lieutenant Colonel Reed led one, Lieutenant Colonel Turner the other. Their assignment was to sweep the airfields around Hankow and destroy any enemy aircraft that might try to oppose the 14th and 20th A.F. bombers over the city.

After staging at Laohokow at 1125, the formation led by Turner headed for the Japanese airfield at Siaokan. A few enemy aircraft were spotted on the field, and Captain Lindell and Lt. Fang C.C. each destroyed one. From Siaokan the formation headed for Hankow, and Jim Silver of the 32d F.S. takes over the narrative:

"Colonel Turner timed our arrival over Hankow so as to avoid any contact with the [20th A.F.] B-29s. I was Turner's wingman, and Bill Storms was flying No. 3 position.

"We sighted a Lily bomber heading eastward and gave chase. Turner fired and nothing seemed to happen; I fired and the Lily exploded. (We should have shared the victory, but when I suggested it later that evening, he refused to even consider it.) Shortly after shooting down the bomber, we chased a Tojo and fired a few rounds at extremely long range, but the Japanese pilot used his superior speed to escape.

"The real excitement came toward the end of the mission, when several of the pilots reported that their fuel tanks were almost empty. Colonel Turner calmly instructed them to land first while the rest of us circled the field. It was kind of nervous up there because we all expected our engines to quit."[1]

The next day a combined mission, with twenty-four P-40s at Laohokow escorting fourteen B-25s of the 2d, 3d, and 4th bomb squadrons, was flown to Pengpu in Anhwei Province. The bombers hit railroad yards and an oil-tank farm with no opposition from the Japanese, but the mission resulted in one of the most heartfelt losses in the history of the CACW, when Lt. Col. Bill Reed was killed that evening returning to Liangshan.

Again, Jim Silver of the 32d F.S. recalls that day:

"The day after the big Hankow raid, we flew cover for B-25s of the 1st Bomb Group, which bombed railroad yards at Pengpu. Over the target, Tom Cribbs's fuel tanks began to siphon out gas after he had jettisoned his belly tank. Tom tried an attempt to stem the flow, but to no avail.

"Colonel Reed, who was leading the mission, gave Tom a compass heading toward what was thought to be a relatively safe area. I accompanied Cribbs and watched as he bailed out and landed safely. Then I turned for home. Much to my surprise, I was joined by Reed and several others. The colonel didn't like to have his kids flying around alone.

"We landed at Laohokow to refuel. As dusk approached, we took off. [Capt. Keith] Lindell and I headed west. Colonels Reed and Turner and Lieutenant Van Moad [of the 8th F.S.] flew toward Liangshan. Lindy and I landed well after dusk at Ankang. We were aided in landing by two oil-burning smudge pots that were placed at the east end and on both sides of the airstrip. The lights were immediately doused while we taxied in. And shortly afterward, we had a full three-ball alert. The Japanese bombers were out in force to avenge the previous day's smashing raid against Hankow."[2]

Reed, Turner, and Moad were not so fortunate as Lindell and Silver. When the three P-40s arrived over Liangshan they found the field already under a three-ball alert and completely blacked out. Unable to land, they continued southwest toward Peishiyi but found the weather there socked in, so they headed back toward Liangshan.

The field was still blacked out when they returned, but now another problem faced them: their fuel supply was getting low. There was nothing for them to do now but circle until the lights came on or their gas tanks ran dry. Unfortunately, the latter happened first.

One by one, the pilots bailed out of their P-40s as the Allison engines drank the last ounces of fuel. Moad was luckiest, getting down uninjured and walking into Liangshan the next day. Turner broke his leg when he landed but was found by villagers and carried into Liangshan the following morning.

Luck had run out for Reed, however. His body was found the next day a mile west of Lao-Yen-Chang village, about twenty miles from Liangshan. Capt. Charles Lovett, his good friend and intelligence officer in the 7th F.S., was detailed to go pick up Reed's body. Lovett recalls:

"He bailed out, and we don't know what he did, but we speculate he turned the P-40 upside down and dropped out. The pilots used to talk about what they were going to do if they had to bail out. What they were supposed to do was to throttle it way back and put the nose in an up position a little bit and roll the canopy back, then step out on the wing and dive off. That was the approved procedure, but we don't know what Bill Reed did.

"Whatever he did, he must have hit the tail plane with the back of his head because his body wasn't damaged at all other than there was a flap of hair loose on the back of his head that was scalped there. The chute did not open. His hand was on the rip cord."[3]

When Chuck Lovett gave this account of Reed's death nearly thirty-seven years later, he was sitting in his law office in Portland, Oregon. On a credenza at his left elbow was a small photograph of a handsome young man in a military uniform. The face was that of Bill Reed.

Reed, by all accounts, was the kind of man who inspired that level of respect and affection. He was born January 8, 1917, and grew up in

Marion, Iowa, not far from Cedar Rapids. He graduated from Marion High School in 1935 and Loras College in Dubuque in 1939. Athletically inclined, he played on his high school and college football teams and also was an excellent golfer.

Reed joined the Army Air Corps in February 1940. He completed advanced flight training and was commissioned a second lieutenant in October of that year, then was assigned as a flight instructor at Barksdale Field, Louisiana. When recruiters for Claire Chennault's American Volunteer Group approached Reed in the spring of 1941, they found an eager prospect. He resigned his commission and sailed for China from San Francisco on July 21, 1941.

Reed was assigned as a flight leader in the AVG's 3d Pursuit Squadron, the "Hell's Angels." He got his first crack at the Japanese on December 23, 1941, when a formation of twenty-one bombers attacked Rangoon. He gave this account of the fight to reporter Loyal Meek of the Cedar Rapids Gazette after he returned home in August 1942:

"I made three ineffectual passes at the formation before I got around to following Chennault's instructions. The bombers were flying in a V of Vs formation, and I picked the end man on the right flank as my prey.

"I caught him with a hit as my fire raked past him. Evidently I crippled him, for he dropped down about 500 to 600 feet and turned away from the formation. He was easy picking then. I made two passes at him and got the biggest thrill of my life when I saw him burst into flames and drop.

"During the foray, a Jap gunner had nicked my tail assembly but didn't do any damage. The bomber I had downed was found in the jungle, thirty miles from Rangoon. That was my first verified kill."[4]

Two days later Reed was back in action, knocking down two Japanese fighters in the Hell's Angels' famous Christmas Day massacre, during which twenty-three confirmed kills were scored. These rounded out his confirmed aerial kills with the AVG, but Reed was far from finished. On March 18, 1942, he and fellow Hell's Angel Ken Jernstedt flew an armed reconnaissance from Magwe down to Moulmein and found an auxiliary field full of Japanese aircraft. They immediately swept down in strafing runs and raked the enemy aircraft, which were lined up neatly in rows. By the time they finished, Reed had destroyed eight and Jernstedt had seven more.

The AVG's emphasis switched to ground attack after that as the Japanese continued their push up through Burma, and Reed didn't register any more air kills. The strafing attacks on trains and other ground targets would prove valuable training for his later missions with the CACW, however.

Reed returned home after his contract with the AVG ran out on July 4, 1942. He reentered the U.S. Army Air Force in January 1943 after a rest and some war bond tours. Now a major, he spent six months in training posts, then left for his new assignment with the CACW in China in July 1943.

At the time of his death, Reed had flown seventy-five AVG missions and sixty-six more with the CACW. He had nine confirmed aerial kills, nine more on the ground, plus many probables and damaged. He was the highest-ranking member of the CACW to be killed during the war. His awards included the Silver Star, the Distinguished Flying Cross with Oak Leaf Cluster, the Air Medal, the British Distinguished Flying Cross, and the Fifth and Sixth Order of the Chinese Cloud Banner.

A postscript to the Bill Reed story and an example of the respect with which he was held in the 14th Air Force:

Reed wrote to his mother back in Iowa shortly before his death to tell her of the Japanese sword that he had been given by a Chinese officer at Laohokow in June 1944 while he was returning to base after having been shot down near Japanese lines. He told his mother that it was too valuable to entrust to the mail and that he would carry it home himself or send it with a friend. After he was killed the sword was quickly forgotten, but that following summer Mrs. Mayme Reed received the sword, and it had indeed been brought home by one of Reed's friends: none other than Maj. Gen. Claire Lee Chennault.

Reed's death resulted in yet another change in the command of the 3d Fighter Group. Turner replaced him as group commander, though his fractured leg precluded him from flying any more missions. Replacing Turner in the number two spot at group was Lt. Col. J. T. Bull. When Bull left the 8th F.S., 1st Lt. Frank Klump was chosen to replace him. Klump had only been assigned to the squadron for three months and was short on rank for the commander's slot, but when the members of the squadron were asked their opinion they gave Klump their vote of confidence, and he got the job. Unfortunately, his tenure would be short-lived. In the 7th F.S., Capt. Armit Lewis completed his combat tour and was transferred to nonflying duties with group headquarters prior to getting orders home. His place as commander was taken by Maj. Tom Reynolds, who was transferred up from the 5th F.G. at Chihkiang to take the reins.

Reynolds arrived at Liangshan to take command on the 29th, and the following day the squadron, along with a detachment from the 16th F.S. of the 51st F.G., flew twenty P-51C Mustangs to Laohokow to begin Mustang operations. The plan was to base the 7th F.S. at Laohokow with the detachment and to rotate pilots from the other 3d F.G. squadrons into Laohokow to ease the transition from their aging P-40s to the new, longer-ranged P-51s.

On the last day of the year eight P-51s, four flown by CACW pilots, flew the first all-Mustang mission from Laohokow. The target was Wuchang Airfield at Hankow, and the 16th F.S. pilots scored one air kill plus two more on the ground in the surprise attack. It was the beginning of a hot string of operations at Laohokow that would only be halted when the Japanese mounted a ground offensive and took the base three months later.

As 1944 ended, it was a logical time to be taking stock of the progress that the CACW had made since its formation nearly a year and a half earlier. Unofficial totals listed at the time for the wing included 190 enemy aircraft destroyed in the air and 301 on the ground. In addition, 1,467 vehicles had been destroyed, 131 probably destroyed, and 1,074 damaged by the fighters and bombers of the wing. Also, several hundred thousand tons of shipping had been sunk, plus a heavy toll taken on enemy troops, facilities, railroads, and bridges. From the miniature force of three B-25s that flew the first combat mission in November 1943, the wing had grown to eight squadrons of fighters and four more flying B-25s.

Since that first mission, the wing had lost thirty-five fighters and eight bombers to enemy ground fire, and twenty fighters had been shot down by Japanese aircraft. Not a single CACW bomber had been lost to enemy interceptors, a tribute not only to the abilities of the B-25 pilots, but also to the quality of the escort protection they had been given by the fighters of the wing.

The end of the year was also a good time to take stock of what the Americans had learned about their Chinese squadron mates. Maj. Mike

Hitchko, 32d F.S. flight surgeon at Hanchung, turned in a report on December 20 that served the purpose. It was titled "Notes and Observations on the Chinese Fighter Pilot." The nine-page report went into great detail and gives valuable insight into the spirit and abilities of the Chinese airmen. Excerpts from Major Hitchko's report follow:

"During the past eighteen months I have had the opportunity of working with a large number of the members of the Chinese Air Force assigned to the Chinese-American Composite Wing and have had numerous occasions to witness the Chinese fliers at work and play. During this period the occasion presented itself of being with from two to four separate squadrons, so I believe a fair cross-sectional view was obtained. Regarding the Chinese flier in combat, information has been derived from mission reports, individual combat reports, and from American fliers who have flown daily with the Chinese.

"In order to gain a more clear conception of the Chinese flier, his actions and reactions, and general ability as a fighting man of the skies, it is necessary to mention a few facts. . . . During the first two years of the war, the Chinese were fighting an enemy equipped with modern implements of war and led by well-trained and efficient leaders, while they in turn had outmoded weapons and matériel, and too few capable officers. Yet in spite of these great handicaps, the Chinese as a people fought back. Though defeated almost at every turn during this phase, the morale and spirit of the Chinese people was high, and there was a decided effort to stem the tide. But constant and repeated defeats, both on the ground and in the air, promoted a feeling that the Japanese fighter was well-nigh invincible. This feeling has been evident and is still a part of the Chinese flier, for he possesses a fear of the Japanese Zero and the capabilities of the Japanese pilot. During the past five years, apart from small-scale sporadic fighting, no concerted effort has been made to fight back. This fact has much to do with the attitude and behavior of the Chinese pilot in action.

"The average Chinese pilot is a highly selected individual, and there is no doubt that these men represent 'the best manhood in China.' These fliers are, as a rule, much more capable and intelligent than their 'brother officers of the line.' The average Chinese flier spends from six months to one year at a military academy before entering flying school. [The] curriculum is intended to acquaint the future flier with problems of ground units and also serves to 'weed out' physically unfit individuals. . . . After this course, if the individual passes his written and physical examinations, he is ready to enter primary flying school. It is of interest to note that little or no emphasis is placed on eliminating candidates because of factors that we consider disqualifying from an 'adaptability rating for military aeronautics' standpoint. We have Chinese pilots with history of severe skull fractures with prolonged periods of unconsciousness; men with known attacks of fainting spells; men with past medical histories that are not compatible with flying combat.

"The course of flying instruction appears to be patterned after our own. At primary school an individual usually solos after twelve to sixteen hours of instruction and remains until he has completed sixty hours of flying time, before he goes on to basic. Here he receives another sixty hours of flying time before he goes on to advanced training. During the past few years the Chinese flying cadet has been completing his basic and advanced training in the United States. . . . After advanced training the cadet receives his wings and undergoes a slight period of O.T.U. [Operational Training Unit] before being assigned to a combat unit. During the past seven years, because of existing conditions, it has required some classes as long as five years to complete their training from primary through advanced. As a result, the average Chinese fighter pilot in our organization is twenty-five years of age.

"In the notes that follow, reference is being made at all times to the average Chinese fighter pilot with whom I have had contact. The average Chinese fighter pilot in our organization has between 200 and 300 hours of flying time, and he does not compare in fighting efficiency to an average American airman with equal or less flying hours to his credit. There are several reasons for this:

"1. Generally speaking, the Chinese flier does not possess the mechanical aptitude and coordination that the American pilot possesses; he does not take part in a particular coordinated effort (teamwork) with the coordination of the American flier, and he definitely acts more independently. There have been numerous instances when Chinese pilots have broken away and left their formations, in spite of orders not to do so, in order to strafe a likely-looking target or to 'take off' after an enemy aircraft. He is a better flier as an individual than as part of a team.

"2. He definitely experiences difficulty in thinking out proper solutions for new situations. For example, if a Chinese pilot runs into an unexpected emergency in the air during routine flight or combat, his actions are difficult to explain. To the flier, 'new situations' do not appear to bear any relation whatsoever to past experience. In normal and tried situations, the Chinese pilot has proven himself quite a capable airman, yet when that situation changes to an unfavorable one that does not run 'according to the book,' or in the manner in which he has been taught, his actions and response generally reveal poor judgment. On one occasion (and such examples have been numerous) a better than average Chinese pilot who was a flight leader had his electrical system shot out during aerial combat. He came to his home field and made a crash landing, totally demolishing his plane because he was unable to lower his landing gear. Examination of the plane showed that his hand hydraulic pump was intact.

"The Chinese pilot, unless led by American leaders, is fearful of the Japanese and of his aircraft. The Chinese flier is in need of good leadership, for his individual initiative is not of high caliber. This may be attributed to the fact that the leaders of the country have been doing the 'mass thinking' for a good many years. Any American flier who has flown with Chinese airmen generally remarks to this fact, namely that the Chinese flier does not do 'too much thinking on his own.' The Chinese pilot has to be told repeatedly how a certain job should be performed and yet in most instances he will proceed to do the particular task as he so desires. This is a common characteristic that continually tries the patience of those men working with the Chinese.

"During the battle of Honan [Mission A] in May, June, and July of 1944, I had the opportunity to observe the Chinese fliers of the 4th and 11th groups of the Chinese Air Force, who were led by Chinese. These units flew few missions, evaded heavily defended areas and rarely engaged in aerial combat, yet the Chinese members of the Chinese-American Composite Wing led by Americans came through with some fine results and records. It must be emphasized that with proper leadership the capabilities and potentialities of the Chinese airmen are high. . . .

"Generally speaking, the older Chinese pilots trained under the old system are jealous of the younger and better-trained Chinese fliers. This seems particularly true when the younger men have been trained in America. These older men will not pay attention to good advice or modern tactics and continue to do things in the old manner. This is a definite carryover of the provincial warlord days and has hampered and continues to hamper the efforts of the Chinese Air Force.

"Flight fatigue seems more prevalent among the Chinese, in our units at least, than among Americans. At the present time the Chinese Air Force does not recognize flight fatigue. The Chinese flight surgeon with a tactical unit has little or no say regarding a flier's condition, and has no authority for grounding, for recommending consideration pertinent to a flier's status, or any of the recommendations that the American flight surgeon may make. The following example actually occurred in a unit stationed at our field. A Chinese navigator had been having repeated attacks of a pernicious type of airsickness after being in combat for several months. He had no difficulty before flying combat. His commanding officer spoke to the American flight surgeon and asked what was wrong with this man. The flight surgeon explained that the man was suffering from extreme anxiety neurosis and recommended temporary grounding. The commanding officer replied, 'No, I will shoot him if he does not care to fly.' As a result of not recognizing flight fatigue, most cases when seen are overt and far advanced."[5]

It is important to keep in mind that Major Hitchko was reporting on the elusive "average" Chinese pilot, for the CAF certainly produced its share of outstanding aviators and leaders in the CACW. Capt. Wang Kuang-Fu of the 7th F.S. provides a good example.

Wang was one of the "old school" pilots, having won his wings in 1939. He was one of the original flight commanders in the 7th and survived a number of scrapes early in the squadron's history, including a major collision while landing at Liangshan in May 1944. In his first combat against Japanese aircraft, on July 18, 1944, he was credited with three aircraft damaged, and then he damaged another fighter, a Tojo, five days later. He scored his first confirmed kill on July 28, then was credited with three and a half victories in the famous Kingmen massacre of October 27, 1944. Wang scored once more, on March 7, 1945, to reach the rarefied status of "ace" with five and a half confirmed kills, and on March 22 he was named Chinese commander of the 7th.

Wang, who is remembered as a friendly man who liked his American comrades and spoke English reasonably well, was sent to Peishiyi in May 1945 to take the examination for attending CAF Staff School. Despite the fact that the school would have been very beneficial to his future career in the CAF, Wang decided that he preferred to stay with his squadron. He knew that the school lasted a year and suspected that the war would end before he could get back into combat, so he feigned illness on the day that the examination was given and returned to his squadron a few days later. Wang continued flying missions until the end of the war.

10

As new 1945 calendars went up on the walls of offices and barracks at 14th Air Force bases all over China, the men of the CACW were as hopeful as any that this would be the final year of the war. For many of the Chinese, it would be their ninth year of war against the Japanese.

The 3d Fighter Group, especially its 7th Fighter Squadron, found itself in a particularly good location to strike at the enemy as the new year opened. The 7th, under new American commander Maj. Tommy Reynolds and long-timer Capt. Yieh Wan-Fie, was still getting settled in a Norwegian mission house near the airfield at Laohokow as the pilots began flying missions in their long-range P-51 Mustangs.

The arrival of Mustangs had been long awaited by the CACW fighter squadrons, and the 7th got the first twenty, which they shared with the 16th F.S. detachment, also flying from Laohokow. These were P-51Cs, identical to the Mustangs that had been flying over Europe for more than a year. They were fully 50 mph faster than the CACW's P-40Ns and capable of operations at much higher altitudes. Perhaps the P-51's greatest attribute, however, was its range. While the P-40N boasted a respectable 750-mile range that had made it a favorite of General Chennault earlier in the war, the new Mustang's range was 900 miles, and later models would extend that figure to 1,000.

The Mustangs were not without their drawbacks, however, as the CACW pilots would discover. The streamlined design of the aircraft dictated moving the cooling system back along the fuselage under the trailing edge of the wing. This made the P-51 much more vulnerable to ground fire than the P-40, which had its engine and cooling system grouped in the nose. Often, the slightest damage to the cooling system could overheat the engine and cause it to fail. By having its cooling system and engine grouped together, the P-40 therefore presented a smaller target. Another disadvantage of the radiator scoop under the Mustang's belly was that it made the aircraft more dangerous to land with its wheels up in the case of a hydraulic failure. The P-51C model also was equipped with two fewer machine guns (four) than the P-40N, though later P-51D and -K models would carry six.

Regardless of the design trade-offs, the CACW pilots were glad to get Mustangs and wasted no time putting them through their paces against the Japanese. During the months at Laohokow, the P-51s were often used on strikes in conjunction with P-40s. Generally, the P-40s would be loaded down with ordnance to dump on ground targets, and the P-51s would fly escort. When the P-40s were finished working over a target, the P-51s would swoop down to strafe whatever was left . . . unless, of course, the mission was intercepted by Japanese fighters.

Later, the P-51s would be used on long-range sweeps of targets out of range for the P-40s, and some of the 3d F.G.'s greatest triumphs came on these missions. P-40s and P-51s both were used to escort B-25s of the 1st B.G., but these missions were not numerous during the opening weeks of 1945.

It was clearly seen that the use of Laohokow as a major staging base for operations would require beefing up the 3d F.G. considerably. Replacement American pilots were assigned to all squadrons, and about eight transports were assigned to the group for hauling supplies and gas out to Laohokow. In fact, group historian Ken Kay noted at the time that January 1945 was the first month the 3d "ever had enough of anything."

Soon after the first of the year, the 3d F.G. had yet another change in American commanders. Lieutenant Colonel Turner, still unable to fly because of his broken leg, was replaced by Lt. Col. Gil Bright. Turner became executive officer, then was sent back to the United States in March for gunnery training (read: a much-deserved rest).

Lieutenant Colonel Bright was one of the most widely traveled fighter pilots in the USAAF. He had won his wings as a U.S. Navy pilot before the war, then was recruited to fly in China with the AVG. Bright scored three kills as a flight leader in the Second "Panda Bears" Squadron of the AVG, then chose to join the USAAF and stayed on in China after the AVG was disbanded. As a major, he scored his fifth victory while flying with the 75th F.S. on July 31, 1942.

Bright returned to the United States late in 1942 after having spent some eighteen months in the Far East. He was not long in getting back into action, however, and scored his sixth kill while flying P-38s in the 12th Air Force over the Mediterranean. There was plenty more action in front of him when he took command of the 3d.

The man on the hot seat in the 3d F.G., nevertheless, was Major Reynolds. For Reynolds, that hot seat was located in the cockpit of a P-51. As commander of the 7th F.S., it fell to him to plan and lead the bulk of the missions flown from Laohokow, and he jumped into the job with both feet.

Reynolds recalls those days at Laohokow:

"It was a grass strip with holes here and there. You had to be real careful to keep from clipping your prop in the ground. . . . I realize now that I was extremely fortunate to have had experienced officers in charge of each nonflying department and some experienced enlisted personnel. They kept the squadron operating. My total time was spent planning missions and leading most of the flights. I had a ball.

"I reported to Colonel Bennett, who was at [Liangshan] a few hundred miles away. He would send a letter now and then saying, 'Sweep the railroads,' 'Sweep the Yangtze River,' 'Hit the Yellow River Bridge,' et cetera. We would run missions every day unless the weather closed in, and that was not often. The weather was similar to north and east Texas. . . .

"Most of the time only four airplanes were used, to conserve fuel and ammunition. We hit the airfields time after time at Hankow, Nanking, and Shanghai. After a few missions we knew that the Japs had no advance warning, so we would go direct to the target, make a few passes, and get out. After a while the Japs would get the antiaircraft going after the second or third pass. We lost a few pilots that way.

"We wondered at the time why the Japs didn't raid us in the daytime. Once in a while they would send a bomber at night and drop fragmentation bombs. Never much damage.

"While at Laohokow every week or so we would get a wire through channels from General Chennault or General [Albert] Wedemeyer [Stilwell's replacement] saying congratulations on the results from numerous missions. That would set us on fire, and we would put together missions that would produce recognition."

The first missions from Laohokow during the new year were sweeps of the railroad from Hankow north to the Yellow River Bridge. Again, Reynolds recalls:

"There were so many trains that we only strafed the locomotives. We went back out every day, and the trains did not move for at least a week. The latter strafing was done at everything—rail cars, trucks, anything that looked like a target. Once in a while the car or truck would blow up, and we would know that it would be gasoline, ammunition, or something of that nature."[1]

The last of three missions flown New Year's Day was a sweep by eight Mustangs, half flown by 16th F.S. pilots, over Suchow Airfield. The pilots found the field packed with aircraft, and a total of twenty-three were claimed destroyed. This was the first day of many during early 1945 that the Japanese would feel the sting of the 3d F.G.

The first aerial kill of the year by a CACW pilot was scored by Lt. Heyward Paxton, 7th F.S. operations officer, on January 3 during a Yangtze River sweep. Flying over Siaokan Airfield, Paxton spotted an Oscar in a revetment and swooped down to destroy it in a strafing run. He led the formation on to Hankow, where the Mustangs found a formation of Oscars and Tojos. In the scrap that followed Paxton and Lt. William Harbour of the 16th each destroyed a Japanese fighter before they broke off the fight and went home to Laohokow.

The next day, Paxton scored again, this time while flying a P-40 with Lt. Jose Muniz, one of the new 7th F.S. pilots. The two, plus four P-51s, were sent up at 6:45 A.M. to intercept an incoming Japanese attack and found six bombers with two Oscars for escort about five miles northeast of Laohokow. Paxton and Muniz each knocked down an Oscar on his first diving pass at 3,000 feet, and then the bombers salvoed their loads and ran for home before any more attacks could be made.

The first of three devastating January attacks on the airfields at Hankow was flown January 5. In those raids (the other two were on the following day and the 14th) no less than seventy-one Japanese aircraft were claimed destroyed and another fifty-seven damaged, for the price of eight P-40s and P-51s plus four pilots. Reynolds alone scored twelve ground kills and four damaged.

The raids were flown with two or three assault flights and one to three top cover flights. Reynolds led the attackers and Paxton the top cover on all three missions. The formation would fly out at eight to ten thousand feet, then start to let down about nineteen miles from the target.

Obviously, the first assault pass was made at high speed. The parafrags would be dropped on the first run, then pilots would pick out individual targets to strafe. Twenty-nine aircraft were used in the first mission, twenty-four in the second, and fourteen on the third. Pilots of all four 3d F.G. squadrons plus the 16th F.S. took part.

On the January 5 mission, the top cover flights led by Paxton, Capt. Tan Kun of the 32d, and Lt. William Zimpleman of the 16th were jumped by thirty to forty Oscars and Tojos out of the overcast at about 10,000 feet over Hankow. As the Japanese fighters dropped down out of the clouds, the top cover Mustangs broke up their formations.

On his second pass, Paxton caught a Tojo with a burst of fire into its cockpit and engine from thirty degrees deflection, and it went down, streaming fire. Paxton then turned head-on to another Tojo, but his bullets missed their mark. By now there were three or four Japanese fighters on Paxton's tail, so he dove out of the fight, lost them, and then climbed back up to look for more targets.

Next Paxton registered good hits on the fuselage and wings of an Oscar, but it dropped out of sight, and Paxton lost him. With more fighters on his tail, Paxton dove out again, and he repeated the maneuver three more times before the strafers radioed that they had finished their attack on the airfield below. With that, the Mustangs and P-40s reformed and headed back to Laohokow.

Besides Paxton's kill, Captain Tan confirmed two, and Lt. Walter Ferris of the 16th got two more. Reynolds was the top strafer, with five of the thirty-nine ground kills confirmed. Another pilot who confirmed a strafing kill was Lt. Kuo Ju-Lin of the 28th F.S., who eventually became the commander in chief of the Chinese Air Force (before retiring in Taipei).

On January 6 Reynolds led a formation of nineteen P-40s and five P-51s back to the same targets, but the Japanese response was considerably weaker. Only four Oscars rose to challenge the attackers, and one of these was shot down quickly by Lt. George Patrick of the 16th. Anti-aircraft fire was heavy, as it had been the day before, but only one P-40 was lost. Again, Reynolds was the top scorer, with four more destroyed on the ground and five damaged.

A stretch of bad weather closed down flying for the next week at Laohokow, but on January 14 eleven P-40s carrying parafrag bombs and eleven P-51s with 100-pound demolition bombs went back for another crack at Hankow. The plan was that the top cover Mustangs would drop down and dive-bomb the airfield after Reynolds's P-40s had finished their parafrag attacks, but Paxton's P-51s ran into between twenty-five and thirty Japanese fighters and had to jettison the bombs before they could make their attacks.

The pickings were slim for the P-40s, Reynolds destroying three and Lt. J. T. Moore, a newcomer to the 7th F.S., two more. The Mustangs upstairs had their hands full, however.

Flying with Paxton was Capt. Ed Mulholland, by now the longest-serving U.S. pilot in the 7th F.S. He followed Paxton in on the first pass and hit an Oscar in the fuselage and wing root with a thirty- to forty-degree deflection shot. The Oscar dove straight in to give Mulholland his second confirmed kill of the war. Next he got in ninety-degree deflection shots on two more Oscars, but then his own aircraft was hit badly from behind and he broke off, heading for home. Soon the P-51 became uncontrollable, however, and Mulholland elected to bail out.

Meanwhile, Paxton had watched Mulholland's Oscar crash, then climbed back up into the fight. He spotted Lt. Elwood Smith of the 28th F.S., his wingman, with an Oscar on his tail, so Paxton gave the Japanese fighter a good burst to chase him off. Smith, who got one Oscar of his own and shared another with Lt. George Walston of the 16th in the fight, later confirmed seeing Paxton's Oscar crash. This gave Paxton six and a half aerial kills, the most scored by a pilot while serving in the CACW.

Paxton, however, had other things on his mind as his last victim fell, for he was in trouble himself. A Japanese fighter had clobbered his Mustang, and he dove out of the fight.

Unable to keep his Mustang in the air, Paxton elected to belly it in. Paxton suffered a leg injury in the crash, but he eventually linked up with Mulholland, and the two pilots returned to Laohokow about two weeks later. Because they both had escaped from behind enemy lines, they were taken out of combat. Paxton, because of his injuries, was sent home soon thereafter. Mulholland was assigned to air-defense duties at Liangshan, then finally sent home in June.

Operations continued at a frantic pace, and by January 17, the 3d F.G. had destroyed 100 Japanese aircraft since the first of the year. On the 21st, Reynolds caught a Tojo in the landing pattern over Nanking Airfield with its wheels down and sent it crashing to the ground, then destroyed two more aircraft strafing, while Moore added two others.

The 8th F.S. suffered a grievous loss on January 23, when its popular young commander, Frank Klump, was killed. He led four P-51s that day on a sweep of the railroad from Suchow to Yenchow. The Mustang pilots had destroyed seven locomotives by the time they reached Yenchow, and then they spotted a formation of Japanese troops and dove to strafe them.

Ground fire hit Klump's P-51C (serial number 44-11104), and it began to stream gasoline and coolant. He pulled off the target and headed toward home, but ten miles later he radioed to the others that he was going to bail out. As he popped the canopy at 1,000 feet, the Mustang suddenly nosed over and went straight in. One of the pilots in the formation reported seeing Klump struggle out of the cockpit and onto the wing just before the Mustang hit and exploded.

It was the third loss in nine days for the 8th. Lt. Van Moad, who had survived the night jump with Reed and Turner, was killed on the Hankow mission of the 14th, and Lt. Freeland Matthews was shot down in a P-40 near Hankow on the 17th. Capt. Eugene Mueller arrived from the 51st F.G. in early February to take permanent command of the squadron.

As the month closed, the men at Laohokow could be proud of the score they had tallied: twenty-three aircraft destroyed, one probable, and four damaged in the air; ninety-four destroyed, five probables, and sixty-six damaged on the ground; 155 locomotives destroyed. And the action was by no means over.

Operations continued at the same pace in February, though aerial opposition by the Japanese was lacking after the drubbing they had received during the previous month at Hankow. More Mustangs arrived to supplant the CACW's weary P-40s, and many of the Chinese pilots were rotated to India for transition training on the new craft at a school that Lieutenant Colonel Bull had been sent to establish at Ondal. In their place, pilots from the 25th and 26th squadrons of the 51st F.G. arrived to join the action.

The job at Laohokow remained to disrupt Japanese supply lines north of the Yangtze River, and that the pilots did. In the process they lost eight aircraft in action, and another thirteen were destroyed in "operational failures." In all, fifty-eight missions were flown from Laohokow during February, the majority of them against ground targets such as railroad and river traffic.

In addition, a detachment from the 3d B.S. was sent to Laohokow. These B-25s, along with two from the 22d B.S. of the 341st B.G., flew day river sweeps on the Yangtze from Hankow east to Nanking, railroad strikes, and sea sweeps near Shanghai. The 2d B.S. and the rest of the 3d B.S. continued to fly from Liangshan, with night intruder missions against convoys and trains along the Peking-Hankow line and day strikes against tracks and bridges. The 1st B.S. sent a detachment to Hsian to use the 75mm cannons of their B-25Hs against rail targets in the Tsing-Pu area north of the Yellow River. These missions proved fairly successful. The remainder of the 1st B.S. aircrews flew missions against the Yellow River Bridge and the Peking-Hankow rail line from their base at Hanchung.

By far the most successful mission of February for the Laohokow flyers was an attack by the far-ranging Mustangs on the airfields at Tsingtao. On February 8 two P-51s flew a six-hour recon mission to scout the area, about 400 miles north of Shanghai on the Shantung Peninsula. Two days later Reynolds and Lieutenant Colonel Bright were ready to take thirteen Mustangs back to the lucrative-appearing target airfields.

Bright, unfortunately, never got much past the end of the runway at Laohokow, because the engine of his P-51D (44-11281) failed on takeoff and he washed out the fighter. He missed a field day.

Lieutenant Walston assumed lead of Bright's flight after the crash, and he turned over the formation lead to Reynolds, who was leading the second flight. Maj. Ed Witzenburger of the 51st Fighter Group led a third flight, and each one was assigned a different airfield to attack.

The assault was a complete surprise, and Reynolds noted that even the ground fire at his target, the main Tsingtao airfield, was "extremely meager and inaccurate." His first pass was made east to west over five "Kates" (probably Ki-51 Sonias), and he saw the first and third planes catch on fire. When he came across the field again he spotted six more of the light bombers parked between two hangars on the west side of the field. Three of these caught fire, and the other three were damaged. On the next pass he strafed a row of ten bombers and saw two catch fire. Reynolds burned three more and damaged perhaps ten others in six more runs across the airfield. He noted that the enemy aircraft appeared to have a fresh coat of brown paint and that they were concentrated on the north and west sides of the field.

Lieutenant Moore was in Reynolds's flight and he made ten strafing runs over the field, destroying ten more bombers and a gasoline truck. He estimated that he also damaged ten Japanese aircraft.

Major Witzenburger's flight attacked the southernmost Tsingtao airfield and also found plenty of targets on the ground. The major destroyed four, plus claiming five probables and four damaged. Two pilots from the 26th F.S., Capt. Stanley Hedstrom and Lt. Gerald Ravenscroft, destroyed four and two aircraft, respectively. A further fifteen aircraft were claimed destroyed by Lt. George Walston's flight, which attacked the northernmost airfield, at Liuting. Flying with Walston were Lieutenants Bill Zimpleman, Walter Wyatt, and George Koran.

On February 20, nineteen Mustangs went back to Tsingtao for another shot at the airfields, and this time Lieutenant Colonel Bright was able to lead the attack. He destroyed two Ki-46 Dinahs, Major Reynolds was credited with three more ground kills, and Capt. Don Minnick of the 7th F.S. got three others. Lieutenants Walston and Koran each claimed single ground kills to bring the total to ten. Lieutenant Zimpleman of the 16th F.S. and Capt. Donald Rauch of the 26th F.S. were both shot down; Zimpleman survived, but Rauch was listed missing in action.

The action continued nonstop, and some thought was even given to flying a shuttle mission to Siberia in the P-51s, but it was never done. River and rail targets felt the sting of the Laohokow-based P-40s and P-51s through the first two weeks in March.

The next encounter with Japanese aircraft came on March 7 during a dive-bombing mission to Nanking by ten Mustangs. The inexhaustible Reynolds led the mission and shot down two Ki-44 Tojos, both of which exploded, when the Mustangs were jumped over the target. Capt. Wang Kuang-Fu of the 7th F.S. added another to bring his total aerial kills to five and a half, making him the second Chinese ace of the CACW after Major Tsang of the 8th F.S.

Weather shut down operations at Laohokow from March 12 to 21.

During those nine days the Japanese began an advance against the base that would quickly bring to a close the fruitful operations from Laohokow. Also, the 16th F.S. detachment was pulled out of Laohokow on March 16 to rejoin the 51st F.G. in southeastern China.

The Japanese offensive began at Lushan, about 120 miles northwest of Laohokow, where a force of about 4,000 troops had been concentrated for the assault. Three similar columns left almost simultaneously from Paoanchen, Shengtin, and Shahotin, which are between Lushan and the Peking-Hankow railroad line. By March 21 the Lushan force was only sixty miles from Laohokow, and the first contact with Chinese defenders was made. The Chinese decided to defend the strong points at Nanyang and Tengshein, which both lay in the path of the advance from Lushan, but in fact no effective resistance was mounted.

Beginning on March 22, the aircraft at Laohokow pounded relentlessly at the advancing Japanese. As the Japanese shifted gears and began moving only at night, the P-40s and P-51s searched out and attacked their day hiding places while the P-61 night-fighter detachment from the 426th Night Fighter Squadron at Laohokow flew night sweeps. B-25s from the 1st B.G. added their firepower in both day and night missions from Laohokow, Ankang, and Hsian. Fighter missions flown against the advance increased from five on the 22d to fourteen on the 25th, and seven aircraft were lost during that time.

If the Chinese ground troops weren't putting up much of a fight, the CAF pilots at Laohokow certainly were. Sad proof of this is found in the fact that several Chinese pilots in the 3d F.G. were killed during those four days. Most notable was Capt. Yieh W.F. of the 7th F.S., an original squadron member who had recently assumed command from Captain Hsu. He tried to make a belly landing in his damaged P-40 on March 22 but was killed when the aircraft flipped over after it touched down. American losses were Captain Minnick of the 7th F.S. on March 22, and Capt. Phil Parker of the 28th the next day.

A report by Capt. Herbert Martin, base commander at Laohokow, provides a detailed account of the last days at the base. It was filed on April 4, 1945, after Martin had reached safety at Ankang.

"Laohokow was situated in Hupeh Province on the Han River. This base was east of the mountain ranges of Central China, being on the coastal plain north of the Yangtze River, elevation approximately 300 feet. Because of its accessibility to the coastal region and the Peiping-Hankow Railroad, this most easterly of U.S. air bases was always considered vulnerable to enemy action should they decide to move. Lying in a pocket with Jap forces north, east, and south, many times it was thought evacuation would have to take place sooner than it did.

"The seriousness of the situation developed toward the middle and end of the week of March 19–25. General Morse visited the base on Saturday and Sunday, March 18 and 19. Sunday morning a conference was held with General Liu, commanding general of the 5th War Area, at which General [Winslow] Morse requested from General Liu that his cooperation would be appreciated in pushing to a speedy conclusion improvements to the airstrip then taking place. This assurance was given. However, the following day General Liu moved his headquarters back over the river, and as the week developed more and more Chinese evacuation was noted. On Friday, March 23, Captain Martin withdrew remaining funds from the Central Bank of China, which were to be used on deposit, and the remainder of the balance for construction was resubmitted to Chungking. That evening pilots of the 426th Night Fighter Squadron reported seeing twelve miles of enemy vehicles lined up bumper-to-bumper in a large concentration to the east. Saturday morning orders were received by radio from CACW headquarters to evacuate all nonessential personnel.

"A unit of the 559th Aircraft Warning, which had operated a radar set approximately thirty-five miles to the southeast, had been forced to retreat and arrived at Laohokow Saturday morning. Lieutenant Bronillard was commanding that unit. The next day at a conference held with Major Reynolds, commanding officer of the 7th Fighter Squadron, it was decided that the radar unit would be evacuated by plane with 7th Squadron equipment. A weapons-carrying trailer and Jeep and trailers were taken from them.

"By noon Sunday, March 25, intelligence reports indicated the urgency of evacuating the field that day. All personnel, baggage, and equipment with the exceptions noted below were evacuated by air that afternoon.

"The base engineer, Capt. James G. Bohlken, was requested to start destruction that afternoon. Ten planes, including three B-25s, one transport, three P-51s, and three P-40s, were destroyed by fire. Gasoline in revetments was fired except for a quantity on the west side of the field where transports were taking on loads after all other equipment had been evacuated. This gas was later fired by the stationmaster after the last plane had departed. Several drums had been moved onto the field, waiting to be taken out by transport, but were fired by a strafing run the next day. Belly tanks unable to be removed were shot full of holes.

"In that late afternoon, all personnel and equipment not air-evacuated were transported from the hostel area to the field, and all but three vehicles were loaded with supplies for the evacuation by convoy and told to cross the river and wait on the opposite side. The bridge across the river was a difficult problem as it was crowded with refugees, ox carts, broken-down Chinese trucks, wheelbarrows, and Chinese troops, all streaming to the west. There was no order or military control at the bridge. It took considerable work for the convoy personnel to get a lane opened in the mob for four vehicles to get through. The bridge was a pontoon bridge approximately a half-mile long with wooden platforms supported by river sampans connected by wooden planks. Planks were constantly having to be readjusted to suit each vehicle's wheel width that went over the bridge. . . .

"By 7:30 that evening the last intelligence report came through. Japanese cavalry were eighteen miles down the road in a northeast direction, having bypassed Nanyang. Other cavalry forces were reported coming from the southeast, and more were reported to have crossed the river at Fancheng. The Laohokow radio station went off the air at 8 P.M., and they began packing up. A convoy was organized immediately and started out. The convoy consisted of nine vehicles: one 6 × 6, three weapons carriers, and five Jeeps. This included the weapons carrier with trailer and Jeeps with trailers taken over from Lieutenant Bronillard and the 559th Radar Unit.

"The following day they suffered considerable mechanical difficulty with some of the vehicles and did not have more than four hours' running time all day. That day Captain Boardman, who had been out east of Laohokow, joined the convoy with his Jeep and one 6 × 6 and a weapons carrier. The 7th Fighter Squadron, who had waited farther down the road for us, joined the convoy, making a total now of ten vehicles. The following day they drove from 7 A.M. to 7 P.M., covering approximately 120 miles. Much of this terrain was over high mountain ranges with many hairpin, twisting turns. On Wednesday, March 28, the convoy arrived at Ankang Air Base in the late afternoon, having also picked up by this time three Chinese nuns and an Italian priest from Piling."[2]

By taking Laohokow, the Japanese had severely damaged the Allies' projective strategy of coordinating the 14th Air Force coastal attacks from the inland and seaborne coastal attacks by Pacific Fleet forces on Japanese lines of supply. Nevertheless, Laohokow was the last 14th A.F. base lost to the Japanese during the war, and the offensive that had swallowed it soon petered out as the ever-increasing demands for defense of its home islands sapped Japan's strength.

In the midst of the drama at Laohokow, Brig. Gen. Winslow Morse bid his final farewell to the CACW. The general had returned temporarily from his liaison trip to Europe, but he had now received orders to return to the United States. Farewell banquets were given in his honor at Peishiyi on March 24 by officers of his staff. In addition, all wing personnel at the base marched in reviews on the airfield that day. Morse, recorded the wing historian, "gave a typically brief, rumbling, bumbling farewell to the men he was leaving behind." Col. T. Alan Bennett resumed command of the CACW.

Ankang was now the most important base for the CACW forces in North China. It was described as "a gravel strip between denuded mountains in the valley of the Han River" by Maj. Ken Kay, of the 3d F.G. headquarters. "Ankang proper is a village in a shallow valley hard by the turgid waters of the cooling Han. At the head of the valley, across the river and in the gravel of the tributary, lies the airfield, a bare streak between wheat fields. Craggy mountains overpower it on every side," Kay recorded.

Thirty missions were flown by the 3d F.G. fighters from Ankang between March 25 and the end of the month. In addition, the 1st B.G. was quite busy during the period, flying nearly all of its 158 March missions during the final week of the month. Most of these, as most of those flown by the fighters, were against the advancing Japanese forces.

On March 31, Lieutenant Colonel Bright decided to lead the P-51s on a long-range mission to Shanghai to strafe the airfields at nearby Wingpo. The hunting was not as good as had been hoped, and only three Japanese aircraft were destroyed. The long distance involved in striking the target from Ankang proved disastrous: six P-51s ran out of gas and had to be abandoned on the way home. One of these was flown by Bright himself, who bailed out near the secret base that had been established at Valley Field in the Chinese-held pocket of territory east of the Peking-Hankow rail line. Bright eventually returned to Ankang, but he was taken out of combat and turned over command of the 3d F.G. to one of its old favorites, Col. Eugene Strickland. At about the same time that Strickland returned to the 3d from his job as wing operations officer, in mid-April, the CACW was further cheered by the news that the word "provisional" had been dropped from the names of its units. Strickland had become one of the youngest full colonels in the USAAF when he was promoted in February at age 27.

With April also came the reunion of the 3d F.G. at Ankang. Group headquarters and the 8th F.S. were moved up from Liangshan to make room for the 1st B.G. to move onto that base, and the 32d F.S. relinquished its pleasant accommodations at Hanchung as well to join the 7th and 28th fighter squadrons, which were already at Ankang. In effect, it was the first time the group had ever lived together, save for a week in mid-February 1944 at Erh Tong when no missions were flown.

The 92d F.S. of the 81st F.G. was also stationed at Ankang, and living conditions were crowded. One fighter from each 3d F.G. squadron was based at Liangshan for air defense under Capt. Ed Mulholland.

The Mustangs returned to Shanghai on April 1 in force, but the hunting was considerably better than it had been the previous day. Major Reynolds scored his final two ground kills, bringing his total to thirty-eight and a half plus four aerial kills and making him the top-scoring fighter pilot in the 14th Air Force. A total of eight ground kills were reported, but the big score was Lt. Chung H.F. of the 32d F.S.

Lieutenant Chung and his squadron commander, Capt. Hung Chi-Wei, were pulling up from their first strafing run when they spotted a formation of nine twin-engine enemy aircraft over the field at about 150 feet altitude. Chung shot up the last aircraft in the formation, which crash-landed near the field, then turned to attack the rest of the formation from the side. He hit a second aircraft, which trailed black smoke, then crashed and burned. At this point one of the enemy aircraft tried to turn back and land on the airfield, but Lieutenant Chung followed its turn and shot it down before it could reach safety. Captain Hung, meanwhile, had shot down another of the Japanese aircraft and saw it crash-land near the base.

The heavy action in North China continued through April, with the 3d F.G. flying 313 sorties, as compared to 337 the previous month during the fight to save Laohokow. Missions were mixed between close air support of the Chinese forces opposing the waning Japanese advance past Laohokow and the continued pounding of Japanese lines of river, road, and rail supply from the Peking-Hankow railroad east to the coast. Attacks by the B-25s of the 1st, 2d, and 3d bomb squadrons were considered effective at holding rail traffic to a minimum.

All this action didn't come without cost. The 3d F.G. lost ten fighters in the first two weeks of the month to enemy fire, weather, and accidents. Two examples are provided by pilots Joe Page of the 8th F.S. and Robert Gardner of the 28th.

Joe Page was a veteran of twenty-five missions over Italy with the 81st F.G. before he came to China and transferred to the CACW. He already had experienced a three-week walk out from the mountains after a bailout when he took off April 10 in a flight of four P-51s for a strike on Shanghai airfields. He recalls:

"It took two drop tanks and seven and a half hours to make that run in good weather, and if you had dysentery—which I seemed to have all the time in China—it was a rough trip. On April 10, when we got back to the foothills on the return flight, the weather had turned bad and we had a solid deck of clouds over the mountains. Our field was closed, so we turned to go to Chungking. As my tanks ran dry, one by one, I knew the only option was to bail out when the engine quit.

"I watched two bail out, and then my turn came. The only one left was Capt. James Spurgin. I jumped, and Spurgin waved his wings. I came down in the yard of a Chinese family who thought I was some kind of devil after them. After I convinced them I was friendly, they escorted me to a village where a riverboat was going down the Yangtze to Chungking the next day. The next morning about 10 A.M., as we went down the river, I heard a lot of shouting, and when I looked over the side, there was Captain Spurgin grinning at me from a sampan.

"The boat carried us to Chungking, where we stayed in Ambassador [Patrick] Hurley's quarters. He was in Russia at the time. We had fine treatment from the Chinese and embassy personnel. We caught a ride out on a military transport plane back to base. I hurt my leg when I bailed out, but it was only bruised and was soon as good as new."[3]

Gardner was far less lucky than Page. He had arrived in China in

January 1945 after a stint as a flight instructor. He had been fortunate enough to get back to base, following the ill-fated March 31 mission, with just seven gallons of gas left in the tanks of his P-51, which was nicknamed "The Stud." But on April 13 Gardner's luck ran out. His recollection:

"My last mission was a milk run against locomotives on the Kaifeng-Soochow railroad. While leading a flight of four 51s, all carrying drop tanks, I destroyed a locomotive, but the low and slow pass resulted in taking a hit in the oil line from small-arms fire. I was forced to bail out. . . .

"This was a virgin bailout, and I pulled the rip cord too soon, thus enabling the enemy to track the descent of the chute for a bonus of two minutes or so. The Mustang went straight in and exploded. The ammo kept popping off, and I feared, irrationally, that the Japs were using me for target practice. Upon touchdown, I was unable to collapse the chute and was dragged about seventy-five yards across a rice paddy. Lt. William A. Elmore made a low pass while I waved.

"The above action took place about 11 A.M. in or near an area known as 'the pocket,' which was an enclave inside enemy territory presumably controlled by Allied forces. Be that as it may, Chinese puppet troops located me within twenty minutes, and under the guise of escorting me back to friendly territory moved from village to village until about four o'clock the next morning, when Jap infantry placed me in handcuffs.

"The next time I saw a white man was two weeks before the surrender in an internment camp located on the outskirts of Peking. Interned there were several dozen British, French, and Dutch civilians—businessmen and consular people from Shanghai. Also, five or six of the Doolittle boys, one of whom died of malnutrition three days after the war. There was a Marine color guard at our embassy in Peking who had been interned December 8, 1941. In addition, three other fighter pilots from other units who had been shot down since I had and were in reasonably fair physical shape.

"As for myself, I had been incarcerated in a half-dozen civilian jail cells in towns on the Hankow-Peking railroad. I ended up with beri-beri [malnutrition] and dropped from 147 to 104 pounds. On the journey to Peking via train and ox cart, I was paraded through a number of Chinese villages where the populace turned out to see a rare 'blue-eyed devil.' On one occasion, a drunken Japanese cavalry colonel rapped me rather forcibly on the base of the skull with the blunt edge of his samurai sword. Neither the Chinese populace nor the Japanese enlisted men were amused, and the colonel moved on.

"While awaiting return to free China (after the truce), several of us were quartered in the Grand Hotel de Peking. The Marine guard and I were roommates. He was visited by two absolutely gorgeous White Russian girls he had known before the war and who had sweated out the war in Harbin, Manchuria. These girls wore silk stockings, high-heeled shoes, cosmetics, Max Factor hairdos, and spoke impeccable English. What they really wanted was to marry us so that they could get into the U.S.A. However, our debilitated condition was so apparent that they were forced to look elsewhere."[4]

May 1945 brought hot weather to Ankang, but gas supplies ran low late in the month as the 14th Air Force devoted most of its strength to the job of reversing the Japanese ICHIGO offensive in southern and eastern China. Bridge cutting and supply burning were the 3d F.G.'s main job, as they were for the 1st B.G. The bomber squadrons were beginning to receive B-25Js, some of which mounted eight .50-caliber machine guns in their noses for strafing, to replace their aging B-25Ds and -Hs.

At Ankang, thousands of coolies descended on the air base in May to begin work on extending the runway. This led to three gruesome accidents. On May 7 a P-47 of the 92d F.S. loaded with napalm bombs crashed on takeoff and hit three fighters of the 7th F.S. The napalm exploded, destroying all four aircraft and killing scores of coolies. Later in the month landing crashes by a P-61 and a P-40 repeated the tragedy. Burr Shafer, operations and intelligence NCO in the 32d F.S., recalled the P-61 crash vividly:

"There was also a night fighter and recon outfit operating out of Ankang during those last months. I can recall a night fighter coming in with a load of napalm still undelivered—the prop blades cut the arms off several coolies, and I can still see them running down the runway holding their arms high as the ambulance crews tried to chase them down to help them. Meanwhile, the P-61 itself crashed into a work gang of about fifty coolies, and the napalm exploded upon impact. I helped gather the bodies afterward, and it was a scene right out of Dante's *Inferno*!"[5]

The last confirmed aerial kills scored by the 3d F.G. came on May 2, when a flight of P-51s from the 32d F.S. (the same squadron that had scored the CACW's first victory back in December 1943) caught four "Vals"—again probably Ki-51 Sonias—over Suchow Airfield at 1,000 feet. Lt. Leo Bugner opened fire first, hitting the No. 4 aircraft and seeing it begin to smoke but then overshooting his target. Capt. Bob Ferguson hit the lead enemy aircraft in the cockpit and tail, and it crashed into a field. Lt. Richard Tonks damaged the No. 2 aircraft, then No. 3. He then put a good twenty- to thirty-degree deflection shot into No. 3, killing the rear gunner and sending the airplane into a glide. Unfortunately, no one saw this airplane crash, so it was claimed as a probable.

Then Bugner picked up the No. 2 aircraft and began firing from 700 feet dead astern, pulling right up behind it as he continued to fire. The mortally wounded aircraft finally crashed near the airfield. During the engagement, Tonks flew so low at one point that he scraped the wingtip of his Mustang (serial number 44-11439) on the ground, but he was able to maintain control and return safely to Ankang.

May also saw the beginning of staging missions from Valley Field in "the pocket" and the end of combat tours of three squadron commanders. Major Reynolds was replaced in the 7th F.S. by Capt. Bert Welch; Maj. Herman Byrd's replacement in the 32d was Maj. Jesse Harris; and Captain Ferguson took over for Maj. Keith Lindell in the 28th. Captain Mueller remained in command of the 8th F.S. until the end of the war. Welch would soon turn over command of the 7th to Maj. Ross Bachley, and Maj. Don Campbell replaced Ferguson in the 28th during the summer.

May had seen the operations level of the 3d F.G. drop, with seventy-one missions—250 sorties—flown and only four Japanese aircraft destroyed, two of them on the ground. The 1st B.G. flew 234 sorties, dropped 326.9 tons of bombs, and fired sixty-two rounds of 75mm shells. Quite a bit of the bomb group's total was piled up, however, by the 4th B.S., which had its hands full down in Chihkiang with the 5th F.G. After a slow winter, April and May had been action-packed for the men at Chihkiang.

11

Operations of the Chinese-American Composite Wing were subject to a variety of influences throughout its history, and enemy action was just one of them. The chronic shortage of aircraft finally began to ease in early 1945, but fuel supplies remained a problem, and there wasn't always enough ammunition to go around. Having balanced these factors, combat commanders next had to take a look up at the sky and see what the weather looked like, for the days of all-weather combat operations were still years away, especially on the primitive airfields of central China.

Nowhere was the weather more of a factor in January 1945 for the CACW than at Chihkiang, where John Dunning's 5th Fighter Group and Maj. Bill Dick's 4th Bomb Squadron were trying their best to maintain pressure against the Japanese advance along the Hsiang River. They began the year with thirty-eight P-40s in various states of repair and about ten B-25s, and these numbers fell as the month progressed, despite the fact that bad weather limited flying to only sixteen days during January.

During the month, the Japanese chose to take the railroad lines between Hankow and Canton, thus completing another rail link in China and eliminating the 14th A.F. bases at Suichwan, Namyung, Kanchow, and Sincheng. These eastern bases had put much of the Japanese coastal shipping route within range of 14th A.F. aircraft, which had sunk millions of tons of valuable cargo bound for Japan. The Japanese advances were hardly opposed, and when these bases fell, Chihkiang was left as the most advanced 14th A.F. base in China.

Some important changes in personnel were made in the 5th F.G. during January, and the new American pilots who had arrived the previous month began to settle in with their squadrons. Two command changes of note were made. The Chinese changed group vice-commanders, as Maj. Cheng Sung-Ting transferred from the 28th F.S. of the 3d F.G. to go to work for Col. Chang Tang-Tien. Major Cheng, who had commanded the 28th throughout its combat history up to that time, was a seasoned fighter pilot with an aggressive nature and three confirmed kills.

In the 27th F.S., Maj. Jim Dale completed his tour and was replaced as commander by Maj. I. A. "Buck" Erickson. Dale had been one of the original CACW fighter pilots, first serving as operations officer of the 32d F.S. in 1943 and early '44 before getting command of the 27th.

Dale had scored one aerial kill over the Aleutian Islands during 1942 before joining the CACW, and the Floridian had also scored two ground kills on the third Paliuchi mission while leading the 27th. Another long-time pilot to leave during January was Maj. John Wilcox of the 17th F.S., who had spent a year in India training Chinese pilots before getting into combat. He earned an Air Medal and Distinguished Flying Cross during his eleven months with the 17th.

Most of the missions flown from Chihkiang during January were against ground targets. As a result of these attacks, the Japanese were unable to use the rail lines between Hengyang and Kweilin, as well as the airfields at those cities.

One mission of a different nature was flown on January 14, when twenty-nine fighters, including sixteen P-51s of the 75th F.S., which was then stationed at Chihkiang under 5th F.G. control, escorted B-24s to Hankow. The Japanese attempted to intercept the bombers as they hit their target from 16,000 feet, but the enemy pilots were unable to break through the escorts and attack the Liberators.

About twenty-five miles southwest of Hankow, Capt. Phil Colman of the 26th F.S. spotted two Tojos below the bombers and dove to attack them. He caught up with them at 1,000 feet, and the first Ki-44 turned to the right and came at him head-on. The action took place so fast that neither pilot had a chance to fire at the other.

Colman then switched his attention to the other enemy fighter and put a two-second burst into it as the pilot attempted to turn away from him. The Tojo caught fire in its fuselage and wings, then did a half-roll and dove into the Yangtze River below with a splash. This was Colman's sixth victory in China, though he is officially credited with only five. He scored four more times as an F-86 pilot during the Korean War.

Also scoring a kill in the scrap was Lt. Yueh K.C. of the 27th F.S. He got on the tail of a Ki-43 at 9,000 feet and proceeded to chase it until the Oscar finally crashed into the ground and exploded. These were the only aircraft destroyed by the 5th F.G. during the month.

Four days later, on January 18, what was probably the most dramatic event in the history of the CACW took place. Ironically, the action took place on the ground at Chihkiang rather than in aerial combat.

On that day, a B-25 Mitchell bomber from a USAAF squadron was landing when it overshot about two-thirds of the 4,400-foot runway. The bomber touched down, then took a forty- to fifty-foot drop off the end of the runway and crashed into the rice paddy below.

One man who remembers the crash vividly is Glyn Ramsey, who at that time was a major in command of the 17th F.S. He was talking to Lt. Don Lopez, a pilot in the 75th F.S., in the 17th alert shack when the B-25 came in to land. His story:

"This guy swung around to land from north to south. The alert shack was right at the edge of the runway, and I always stood out there with a flare pistol. Any pilot who came in there and wasn't low enough and slow enough to stay on the runway—we were pretty good judges since we flew it every day—I would fire a red flare at him to warn him. I found the flare pistol when I could see this B-25 was high and fast. I never believed he would land, but he kept coming right on down, and he didn't hit the ground until he had about 1,500 feet left—not more and probably less.

"I stood there and watched him and figured he would just go around. We had no control tower in those days. We had one up there, but it wasn't manned with any controllers. I never did fire a flare, and I later wished a thousand times that I had. He touched down and immediately they saw how short they were, so instead of going around they just chopped the power and locked the brakes. Rocks were flying in all directions and mud and clay, and it was jerking those rocks out of the runway and throwing them in all directions. When he went off the end of the runway he was doing about 70 miles per hour.

"He went off the runway not more than 300 feet from where I was standing. He went off with those brakes locked, and of course that nose went straight down. Though the slope was only about forty-five degrees, the forward speed of that airplane was such that as it went down the nose hit the ground and sheared the nose gear and drove that greenhouse on the nose right back up to the engines, just drove the whole thing back. The airplane came to a crunching halt with the tail sticking up in the air.

"Lopez and I ran down there with a bunch of people, but we had absolutely no fire fighting equipment—not even a five-gallon can. There were guys hurt in the back, and someone was in there trying to get them out. The airplane's spars were broken at the engines, and the pilots' compartment and the bombardier's greenhouse compartment were just shoved back so that they extended hardly at all beyond the engines, which means they were shoved back about six to eight feet. There was a big hole in the front opening, and I looked in there and saw a guy with blood all over him. He was dazed, but he could hear me, and I kept telling him, 'Come out this way.' Finally he began to comprehend; I said, 'Here, here'; I could almost reach that guy. I got that guy to come out of that hole. It turned out to be the pilot. The copilot was killed.

"The right engine was dripping a little fuel, and it had caught on fire. It was not even burning behind the nacelle, which was off the ground about three feet. The fuel was dripping out onto the rice paddy and burning on the ground. We could see that it was going to burn enough there that eventually the plane was going to catch on fire.

"As we were facing the plane from the front, there was a small hole in the left wing, and we could see a guy in [the fuselage] through it; he was a young kid and he had blond hair. He had on a field jacket and a parachute harness. It was a chest-type harness, but he didn't have the parachute on; just the harness. He was perfectly rational and we kept telling him to come on out, but he said his leg was hung up. He couldn't get out. It was like looking in a can, and there were control cables and junk all jammed together. We could see him clearly from about his hipbones up, and we could see part of one of his legs, but I could not get him to come out. He was the flight engineer.

"The top turret had fallen down, so you didn't have the normal space you would have had. This boy was not crushed. He had plenty of space to breathe and move around. He just had a leg caught. Lopez and I had taken time out and gotten down on our knees in the rice paddy along with the night soil and everything, just scooping that mud and stuff up and putting it on that fire. Droplets would come down and catch on fire, and we would get this mud and slap down on it. You can't trap gasoline fumes. The tragedy of this whole thing was that we couldn't do it, so we turned our attention to trying to release that man.

"Finally Lopez and I were out on the wing, and we finally figured out that he wasn't going to get out of there, and somebody said, 'Well, what are we going to do?' By this time the 75th flight surgeon walked up. He was a real mature man, a real fine-type guy. We said, 'Doc, can you cut his leg off?' He said, 'I can if I can get to it.' Finally that flame leaped up that drip and caught on fire behind the engine nacelle at the source of the gas leak. We knew then it was just a short matter of time.

"It began to burn and get hot, then suddenly the top turret's oxygen supply bottle's fitting melted off, and that fitting blew out of there. If that bottle hadn't been pointed toward the tail of the airplane, Lopez and I would have been cremated. That thing blew out, and then for about three or four seconds—long enough to burn us up—it blew flame down that fuselage parallel to us. The heat was terrible. When that went off it blew that flame onto the ammunition canister, and the ammunition started going off.

"After talking to the flight surgeon about cutting the kid's leg off, we decided to try to pull him out because the doc said he couldn't get to him. About three of us grabbed that parachute harness, and we put all the force on it we could. You could hear that guy scream a country mile. It was terrible. By this time he was not rational; he knew he was about to burn. We could not budge him. It got hot enough that his field jacket caught on fire, and he was still talking to us, and he said, 'Please get me out of here.' Lopez and I were in mud and blood from head to toe, and we would grab up this mud with our hands and rub it on his arm to put the fire out. By the time we would get another one up there it would be burning again.

"The reason Lopez and I left was a .50-caliber going off. That shell casing came flying out and one of those hit Lopez right above the eye and cut a gash about three-quarters of an inch long. It was deep enough that it addled him. I grabbed him by the arm and said, 'Hey, Lope, you've got to get out of here.' He was just like a fighter who had been given a knockout punch: he was on his feet, but he was incapacitated there for about thirty seconds.

"When I turned around to take Lopez out of there, Lt. Mac Mc-

Cullough had just arrived or I had just become aware of his presence. McCullough is the type of individual who would have been right there on that wing where we were. The group's Chinese engineering officer was there and jerked out his .45 pistol and said, 'There, shoot him.' I said I didn't want to shoot the trapped man. That is an odd feeling. All the Chinese were in a chorus saying, 'Shoot him. Don't let him die like that.' I took the gun in my hand, but I wasn't about to shoot him, and I knew I wasn't about to shoot him. There never was any doubt in my mind, but I thought, 'This is insane, but still he is on fire.' McCullough said, 'Let me have the gun,' so I gave it to him and took Lopez out of there.

"When I went out, McCullough charged the gun and shot it into the ground once, and of course we were all at fever pitch at this time. Not over the accident, not the fact that a couple of guys had been killed, but what was so horrible to us was that a guy was about to burn to death and we couldn't do anything about it. He fired that gun into the ground and that is the last I remember. I just didn't pay any attention to it after that. Lopez had to be gotten out of there. I figure Dunning was arriving about that time."[1]

Indeed, the thirty-one-year-old group commander had arrived, and true to form, he took charge of the situation. He was not a man to pass off a tough job, and it was reported that he already had been burned trying to rescue the trapped man.

The following account of the next few minutes was written based on official documents by Robert E. Hays, Jr., in 1964, after Dunning's death.

"On hearing the suggestion that the man should be shot, and seeing the drawn weapon, Dunning took the pistol away from McCullough with the comment that, '. . . If there is any shooting to be done I will do it. I am the senior officer here.'

"With gun in hand Dunning walked toward the front of the plane and looked at the trapped airman. Later there was conjecture as to whether any words passed between the two, but no one denied that the man in the plane was conscious at the time. Turning, as though to walk away, Dunning seemed to be engaged in some inner struggle. A decision had to be made, a decision that was foreign to everything John Dunning had ever been taught, a decision which called for a courage of the type few men had ever been called upon to exercise with calm deliberation. Turning to look at the plane, he saw that the flames were then licking around the legs of the trapped man. His flying clothing was burning, and there was no one to put out the flames. Seeing that, Dunning raised the pistol, took deliberate aim, and fired two shots into the head of the doomed man. Turning, he threw the gun into the mud and walked away from the burning plane."[2]

Lopez and Ramsey differ from this account on only one point: they say that Dunning fired but one shot. Regardless, the deed had been done, and the man had been put out of his misery. Back to Ramsey's account:

"I went straight to the alert shack . . . and by that time Lopez was completely rational. It wasn't more than two or three minutes until I came out, and Dunning drove up in a Jeep from the direction of the plane. By this time the airplane was just one big ball of fire. Obviously, anything that could be done was long past. I remember that Dunning drove up there looking straight ahead, and he was in shock. Now I won't say it was clinical shock, but I mean when a guy is sort of a zombie. He was not alert to what was going on around him, but he drove up there and stopped.

". . . I walked out there and said something. I didn't know he had done it; I didn't know what had happened. He said, 'It's terrible,' and I said, 'Yeah, it is, but Colonel, there is nothing we can do about it.' I didn't know for an hour until somebody else told me. I knew he was in a terrible mental state. I knew something terrible had happened, but I didn't even guess that he had shot the guy. . . .

"None of the guys in the group drew any judgments. We didn't look down on him because he did it. We felt pity for him because that's the kind of man he was. . . . I was sitting in a bar someplace years later—it could have been in Canada; it could have been in Southeast Asia—and I heard somebody start telling this story. My first inclination was to lower the boom on him . . . because the story I was hearing was obviously an inaccurate repeat. That's the only time I ever heard anybody mention it after that."[3]

A month later Dunning was charged in a general court-martial with voluntary manslaughter. His trial took place on the afternoon of March 2, 1945, in the recreation hall of a 14th Air Force hostel in Kunming. Seven colonels heard the case.

Dunning's defense, mounted by Lt. Col. John H. Hendren, was based on the contention that the defendant had acted irrationally under a great deal of emotional strain, rather than stressing the mercy-killing aspect. A main point of the defense, however, was that the condition of the man's charred body, when it was finally recovered, left a reasonable doubt that he had died from the gunshot rather than from burning.

The principle factor in the colonels' decision was not recorded, but a considerable weight of testimony on behalf of Dunning's qualities as an officer and airman probably worked in his favor. Whatever the case, Dunning was acquitted when the prosecution failed to gain the two-thirds majority needed for conviction.

It was a fortunate ruling not only for Dunning, but for the 5th Fighter Group and, as his future career would show, for the entire U.S. Air Force. For John Afleck Dunning was perhaps the finest leader to serve in the Chinese-American Composite Wing.

Born in 1914 in San Antonio, Texas, Dunning showed his qualities of leadership and a bent for the military early when he participated in his high school's ROTC. At the time he graduated in 1931 his ambition was to become a physician, but the Depression was in full swing, and his family had no money to send him to college. He worked as a laboratory technician in two San Antonio hospitals, and by 1933 was able to move to St. Louis and attend Washington University while continuing to work part-time. He balanced jobs and school for the next five years before joining the Missouri National Guard in January 1938.

The course of Dunning's life changed almost immediately, for he was sent to flight school at Randolph Field, Texas, in March, and by the time he won his wings in February 1939 he wanted to do nothing but fly. Returning to civilian life didn't appeal to Dunning, so he resigned his commission in the National Guard in the summer of 1939 and joined the Air Corps as a private. Soon, however, he passed the officers' examination, and he was commissioned as a regular second lieutenant in August 1939. He topped off the year of 1939 by getting married in November to Jane "Sam" Craighead, whose nickname he would carry into war four and a half years later on the nose of his P-40.

Dunning was sent back to Randolph Field after he was commissioned, but this time he was an instructor, not a pupil. In October 1941 he was assigned assistant commander of the 1st Training Group (though he was still just a first lieutenant) at Foster Field, Texas. In that position, he became one of the pioneers in Air Corps gunnery training. He was promoted to captain in April 1942, by which time the war had begun and gunnery training had taken on an even greater importance. He was named director of gunnery training for Gulf Coast Training Command. In that capacity he played a key role in the development of the BB Link Trainer. With this device it was possible to give future fighter pilots gunnery training on the ground and greatly speed their development to full-fledged combat status.

Finally, Dunning got his combat assignment in September 1943. He had served with the 5th Fighter Group ever since he arrived in India that same fall. At six feet two inches and 200 pounds, Dunning was almost too big to be a fighter pilot, but he already had eighty combat missions behind him, and he held numerous decorations. A Silver Star earned during a mission the previous summer would be awarded in the near future.

It was not long after Dunning assumed command of the 5th F.G. in November 1944 that the group adopted the nickname "Dunning's Demons" in honor of the boss. By the time he finished his overseas tour and returned to the United States in June 1945 he had flown 103 missions and chalked up 258 combat hours. He was credited with five enemy aircraft destroyed on the ground, but it is also likely that he shot down several Japanese planes. These scores can't be confirmed because, characteristically, Dunning refused to make personal claims, preferring to chalk up his successes to the group as a whole.

Dunning returned to Training Command after the war, then was sent back to China in November 1948 as air attaché to the embassy in Nanking. Soon after his arrival, the Communists took over control of the nation, and the embassy staff was incarcerated in their compound. The ambassador and his staff finally were allowed to leave the country on August 5, 1949, and they flew out of China in a C-47, with Dunning at the controls.

By that time the USAF was well into the jet age, and Dunning's next assignment was command of the 20th Fighter-Bomber group and wing, which flew F-84s. He led the first ferry flight of Thunderjets to Europe, then flew several combat missions during a two-week tour of F-84 outfits in Korea during August 1951. The 20th was assigned the task of becoming the first tactical unit equipped with atomic weapons, and in the summer of 1952 Dunning led the outfit to its new assignment in England.

After a year in the National War College during 1955–56, Dunning was assigned to the Pentagon's War Plans Division. Ironically, during this time he worked on plans for combating the crisis between the Nationalist and Communist Chinese over Quemoy and Matsu islands. In June 1960, after having gained his first star, Dunning was reassigned to a combat unit as commander of the 831st Air Division (TAC), which contained the 479th and 31st fighter-bomber wings. During this time he flew the wings' F-104s and F-100s as much as his schedule allowed.

In March 1962 Brigadier General Dunning received his last assignment. He was sent to Saigon to coordinate aerial activity for the military assistance effort under way for the government of South Vietnam. Then recurrence of back pain that resulted from a slipped disk in 1959 sent him to Clark Field in the Philippines for an operation on a ruptured disc in his spine on August 13, 1962. Unfortunately, his heart failed during the operation, and he never regained consciousness. "Big John" Dunning, who had been equal to every situation that confronted him during his military career, was dead at the age of 48.

It would be difficult to capture the esteem with which he was held by the men of the 5th Fighter Group. Nevertheless, here are two examples.

First, Glyn Ramsey, writing some thirty-six years after he and Dunning served together in China:

"Big John was a magnetic personality who could do what was needed to be done. He was not a renegade, but neither did he allow protocol and convention to stand in the way of getting a job done. He was a handsome, big man—a man's man—and a very active pilot. I don't believe I ever saw him drunk, and when he entered a room people naturally took notice. He had confidence and he could validate it by action. I flew with him, planned with him, and knew him, I believe, as well as anyone and better than any other pilot in the group.

"He was my boss all the way, but we were very good friends. Nearly everything he ever got involved in that he wanted to consult anybody about he eventually got around to talking to me. We kept up after the war, but I never worked for him again." (Ramsey made a career of the USAF and retired as a colonel in February 1970.)[4]

A second impression of John Dunning was written by Capt. Sam Carran, 26th F.S. intelligence officer, in June 1945 at the end of Dunning's combat tour:

"Colonel Dunning has been responsible for all the outfit has been able to achieve. It is difficult to restrain oneself sufficient to describe in a sober fashion the many capabilities of this brilliant officer. His talent in handling tactical operations, the patience, tact, and understanding shown in achieving the coalescence necessary to weld both Chinese and Americans into a unit such as the 5th F.G., his thorough understanding of the strategic situation, his unlimited energy activated by a deep sense of responsibility and his insistence on participating as a fighter pilot during our most dangerous and successful operations all contributed most vitally to the ability of the organization to wage successful aerial warfare and gained for him the esteem and fervent devotion of all those who served under him. His leadership was responsible for carrying the outfit through its early and most rugged days in China. . . . Colonel Dunning leaves us a developed organization, experienced, war-wise, and confident of its ability."5

Bad weather prevailed at Chihkiang through February and March 1945, limiting operations, but changes were in the wind. On February 25 Major Van Ausdall of the 26th flew in to the base with the 5th's first P-51, and Capt. Jim McCutchan followed the next day with another. The reequipment with Mustangs would take place gradually over the coming months, but in fact it never was completed. The P-40s were lumped primarily in the 27th F.S. and flown through the end of the war.

More command changes were made during this period, as many of the experienced U.S. pilots completed their tours. During February Maj. Bill Hull got orders sending him to Foster Field, Texas, for gunnery training, and he was replaced by Maj. Fred Ploetz. Capt. Frank Everest moved over from the 17th F.S. to become operations officer in the 29th. Hull wasn't finished in China, however, for he returned to the 5th F.G. during the summer of 1945. Over in the 26th, Major Van Ausdall was relieved on March 3 and sent to command and general staff school at Fort Leavenworth, Kansas. His replacement was Capt. Bill Johnson, who had been with the squadron since the previous May. His operations officer was Captain McCutchan, one of the originals in the 26th.

During this period, the primary job of the 5th F.G. remained to harass the Japanese lines of supply in the Hsiang River valley. Eventually the squadrons were assigned specific sectors to patrol. The 17th covered Yochow; 26th, Hsiangtan to Hengyang; 27th, Hengyang to Kweilin; 29th, Kweiyi to Hsiangtan; 75th (still under 5th F.G. control), Hankow to Changyeh. The 26th found hunting particularly good on the roads of its sector, destroying 115 trucks during the month of February. Capt. Winton "Slick" Matthews, the new operations officer, was tops, with thirty-eight trucks destroyed and forty-three damaged; Major Erickson was second with twenty-one destroyed; and Lt. Jack Fetzer was third with sixteen destroyed. Most of the flying during this time was done by the American pilots, because many of the Chinese had been sent to India for transition training to P-51s. This was especially true in the 29th, and as a result the 26th F.S. used the 29th's P-40s on many missions during February and March.

Only two enemy aircraft were destroyed by the 5th F.G. during February, as Japanese air power over central China dwindled. On February 8 Lt. Wei S.K. of the 26th F.S. spotted a Topsy transport near Changsha while on an escort mission and swooped down for the kill. The Topsy dove as Wei approached on his first pass, but when Wei lined up again and opened fire he was able to set the enemy aircraft afire in the fuselage and wings. The Topsy crashed into the ground, and no parachutes were seen before it hit.

The other victory of the month was scored by Capt. James Russell of the 17th F.S., and it was actually a ground kill—but just barely. On February 25 Russell spotted a Sally twin-engined bomber flying near Hengyang and gave chase. The bomber quickly made for the airfield at Hengyang and landed, but Russell followed it down in a strafing pass and blew it up as it rolled to a stop at the end of the runway.

New American pilots began to arrive in numbers during March, and with them came enough P-51s for them to begin thinking about some long-range penetration missions. Bad weather scrubbed flying from March 9 to 24, but then the 5th was ready to get back in action.

On March 29, the first long-range Mustang mission by the 5th F.G. was flown by the 17th and 29th squadrons. Led by Major Ploetz, the formation consisted of nine aircraft from the 17th and eight from the 29th, and the target was Ming Ku Kung Airfield at Nanking. The 1,500-mile mission took six hours and forty-five minutes to complete. The pilots were disappointed that there was no interception attempted by the Japanese and that targets on the airfield were sparse. Nevertheless, a number of Oscars and Tojos were destroyed. Top scorer for the 29th was Captain Everest, a recent transfer from the 17th. He approached from the north and spotted four Tojos parked in a revetment on the east side of the field. He circled down to 150 feet altitude, then swept in on a strafing run that set two of them on fire and exploded a third. He circled the field once to confirm his targets, but then the engine in his Mustang began to miss, so he headed home. Single Oscar fighters were destroyed by Lieutenants Shen C.Y. and Chen K.C., while 2d Lt. Roy Marker and Sub Lt. Liang T.K. each damaged one aircraft. Major Ploetz shot up four hangars and blew up a pile of bombs. None of the 17th F.S. pilots were able to confirm any aircraft destroyed, though several were damaged.

Throughout the first months of 1945 rumors had persisted that the Japanese were building up for an offensive to take Chihkiang, and on April 10, the rumors became reality. Time was of the essence for the Japanese, for the Chinese 4th Area Army, which was stationed in the Chihkiang area, was in the process of reorganizing and rearming. With a successful offensive, the Japanese could eliminate the threat posed by an effective 4th Area Army and at the same time drive the 14th Air Force out of its most forward base. Even if the drive didn't take Chihkiang, if the Japanese could advance close enough their threat would be too great to continue using the base. At the same time, the Japanese would be in better defensive position to fend off a counterattack by the Chinese.

On the face of it, the Japanese appeared to be pitifully outnumbered. They pushed off with six divisions totaling perhaps 25,000 men against twelve divisions of Chinese and ten more in reserve, numbering nearly 125,000. The Japanese, however, were banking on past experiences that had shown the Chinese forces to be far less effective than their own well-trained, well-fed, and well-equipped troops. It would soon become evident that times had changed.

The Japanese advanced in one of their classic three-pronged attacks. The main drive began April 10 at Paoching, which served as their headquarters and supply funnel. They moved west along the highway to Chihkiang, and much of the fighting took place along this route. In the south, the Japanese took Sinning, then split into three smaller forces moving north toward Chihkiang, utilizing three valley approaches to the base. The third advance was in the northern sector, where smaller forces from Paoching and Youngfeng moved toward Sinhwa. This was the weakest of the three advances, and it was stopped fifteen to twenty miles short of its objective.

The Japanese must have been surprised by the stiff opposition that was mounted by the Chinese troops. Spearheaded by the 73d Army, which was largely U.S.-trained and equipped, the Chinese were able to counter the characteristic Japanese tactics of infiltration and envelopment, and they got more than a little help from the CACW outfits at Chihkiang.

Although the Chinese forces fought with more determination and skill in the Battle of Chihkiang (as it became known) than ever before against the Japanese, it was air power that finally swung the outcome their way. The Battle of Chihkiang marked the maturation of air-ground liaison tactics in China, as nine ground radio teams spread out in a ring around the base with the Chinese advance units to direct air strikes by the CACW fighters and bombers. Never before had the CACW been able to strike with such accuracy and immediacy against the Japanese. No fewer than seventy-one missions directed by the ground radio teams were flown in one seven-day period late in the month.

Typical of these missions was one on April 15. The main Japanese drive from Paoching had been proceeding steadily toward Chihkiang for the past four days before it finally ran up against stiff opposition from units of the 73d Army. On this day Captain Everest was leading five P-51s when they were directed to attack Japanese positions about sixteen miles southeast of Sinhwa.

Everest found the Japanese in a wooded area, where they had erected tents and staked out horses. The P-51s dove to the attack and dropped their bombs on the area, then came back to strafe what was left. As they came in on the strafing runs, the pilots could see men and horses running in panic. They took advantage of the fact that there was minimal ground fire from the running Japanese and thoroughly strafed the area. Subsequent reports from advancing Chinese troops indicated that some 500 Japanese soldiers and another 500 horses had been killed in that single attack.

Despite devastating attacks like this one, the Japanese kept coming. Missions were flown day and night, with the 4th B.S. using its B-25s to strike storage points, truck columns, and troop concentrations. By the end of the month, gasoline supplies were so low at Chihkiang that the 75th F.S. was moved out because there was only enough fuel left to fly for two more days.

Firebombing using napalm was found quite effective against the advance, especially when concentrations of troops were found. A typical mission was flown on April 29 by Capt. Bill Johnson and Lt. Liu L.C. of the 26th F.S. in their new Mustangs. Flying east out of Chihkiang, they made contact with the liaison team code-named "Scalding," who directed them to a small village near Fantung that the Japanese were in the process of occupying. Each pilot picked half the village, and they dropped their napalm directly onto the buildings. Many fires were started, and the village was soon covered by a thick cloud of black smoke. The P-51 pilots then came back over the town on four strafing runs and gunned down still more Japanese troops.

The seriousness of the threat to Chihkiang was brought home to the CACW personnel there April 20–21, when it was reported that the Japanese snipers had reached the base. The following report was filed:

"That the Japs were using plainclothesmen in their intent to take Chihkiang was evidenced by two incidents which took place the night of 20 April, 1945, and the following morning. On the night of the 20th at approximately 2230 hours, gunfire was heard coming from the hills overlooking the American hostel area at Chihkiang Air Base. The shooting at first was ignored, the belief prevailing that American personnel were shooting their carbines. The shooting continued to increase, and several bursts, as if from a machine gun, were heard. At times pieces of tile from the roof were hit and fell rattling to the floors of the hostel rooms. Some tents occupied by enlisted personnel were perforated by gunfire.

"A one-ball alert was called, and defense squads assembled by Colonel Dunning patrolled the hills adjacent to the hostel area. After several shots were fired by American personnel toward the gun flashes, the fire on the barracks ceased. It is estimated that the enemy gunfire was maintained for thirty to forty minutes. It is not known how many snipers were involved.

"At 0915 on 21 April, Capt. Stan Kelly, operations officer of the 26th F.S., was shot in the back by an unknown assailant while sitting at the northeast corner of the alert shack at the north end of the runway. The bullet entered his back on the left side near the base of his lungs. Medical officers administered first aid to Captain Kelly speedily as possible. He was flown to Kunming that same day for treatment and from last reports seems to be out of the danger stage."[6]

Kelly, in fact, survived the shooting, and he was sent home a month later. He had just joined the 26th when the shooting occurred, having been transferred from the 75th F.S. He had flown an earlier tour with the Royal Air Force in North Africa.

By the end of April the Japanese had advanced far enough to seriously threaten the base at Chihkiang. Nevertheless, there were signs that the base might be held. The 73d, 74th, and 28th Chinese armies were fighting well, and the Chinese high command was bringing in other forces to back them up. These support troops included two divisions of the 6th Army, which had fought under General Stilwell in Burma. They were brought in by air transport and trucked to Chihkiang to defend the base.

In addition to this, the air attacks were taking a heavy toll on the Japanese. The 27th F.S., for example, flew thirty-two missions between April 25 and 30, including ten each on the 27th and 28th. It was found that the two-plane formations worked best when under the direction of the ground radio crews, and because the distances to the targets were so short, the missions usually lasted only forty-five minutes to an hour. During the month of April, the 27th dropped 79,415 pounds of bombs and fired 165,870 rounds of .50-caliber ammunition.

Command changes continued in the squadrons of the 5th F.G. as more pilots finished their tours. In the 17th F.S., Maj. Glyn Ramsey was relieved on the 21st by Capt. Frank Stevens, who had just transferred from the 29th. Ramsey had flown eighty-six missions totaling 210 combat hours when he went home. Over in the 27th, Maj. Buck Erickson was replaced by Maj. Winton "Slick" Matthews. Capt. Charles Souch became operations officer of the 27th.

In the 1st B.G., Lt. Col. Bill Dick was moved to group headquarters from the 4th B.S. at Chihkiang, and his place was taken by Maj. Henry Stanley.

If April had been exciting at Chihkiang, May would be downright exhausting, especially the first three weeks. During the first ten days of May it became clear that the defense of Chihkiang had held. This was the first time since the beginning of the Sino-Japanese War in 1937 that the Japanese had been denied an objective in China.

The fighters and bombers flew night and day, attacking Japanese troop and cavalry concentrations, gun positions, ammunition and supply dumps, convoys, and anything else that flew the flag of the rising sun. The 5th F.G. lost six aircraft in action during May, and another five were destroyed in accidents. In all, the group flew an amazing 732 missions in the month.

Two pilots in the 27th F.S. experienced double doses of bad luck on single days during May. On May 17, Lt. Yu Y.H. made a belly landing at Chihkiang after his P-40 was hit seventeen times by ground fire on his first mission of the day. Yu was unhurt and took off in another P-40 for a second mission that afternoon. This time Yu's fighter was damaged so severely by ground fire that he was forced to bail out. He was unhurt again, and returned to Chihkiang on foot. On May 27, Lt. Yao C.Y. had his engine conk out on takeoff from Chihkiang. He was able to belly-land the P-40, but it was washed out. Unhurt, Yao was assigned another P-40 to fly that afternoon. He got his P-40 off the ground, but the engine overheated en route to the target and he bailed out. Like Yu, he returned to base unharmed. Lt. Chuang F.S. of the 27th wasn't so lucky. His P-40 was hit while he was strafing troops near Paoching on May 19, and he was killed when the plane crashed

One of the first good missions of May was flown by two pilots of the 27th F.S. on May 3. After making contact with a ground radio team, they were directed to a wooded hilltop in the Chiangkow area. They blanketed the target with fragmentation bombs and napalm, then thoroughly strafed the target before turning for home. The liaison team reported that the napalm had caused considerable secondary explosions, indicating that ammunition dumps were probably hit. The frags and strafing were also effective, for a mortar position was knocked out, and Chinese troops were able to move up to more advanced positions.

On May 8 three P-51s escorted three B-25s of the 4th B.S. to Youngfeng. There was no opposition, and after the bombers had hit their target, the formation flew to Fantung and made contact with the "Scalding" liaison team, who instructed them to bomb and strafe a group of supply caches about a mile east of Fantung. Many direct hits were scored on this target, and then another team, "Scurvy," gave them another target. This time they caught a group of 500 to 600 enemy troops in a wooded area and killed about a fifth of them through bombing and strafing.

Lt. Robert Qualman of the 26th F.S. led a particularly daring mission on May 12. He was leading four P-51s off late in the day when a last-minute change was made in the primary target after a returning flight reported seeing a large convoy between Sinshih and Changsha. Qualman radioed the change to his flight, which consisted of Lieutenants Liu, Shieh, and Ma, as they circled the field. Then he led them off on the longer mission, which would require them returning some 200 miles in the dark.

The flight began its search for the convoy just south of Sinshih by following the highway toward Changsha. Soon they found their prey, which consisted of twenty to thirty trucks, more than 100 large horse-drawn carts (all camouflaged and apparently loaded with ammunition), more than 300 horses, and a number of soldiers. Qualman's Mustangs followed the standard formula: first napalm, then frag, followed up by strafing. The napalm was dropped onto massed groups of the carts and caused a tremendous fire, one heavy explosion, and then many secondary explosions that continued after the P-51s had used up their ammunition and headed for home. It was estimated that seventy of the carts and all their contents were burned or blown up, and that three trucks were destroyed and seven damaged. The troops and horses had scattered in all directions when the attack began, and the pilots estimated thirty-five men and sixty-five horses were killed. After the attack was complete and the P-51s were ten miles away from the target, the pilots saw a tremendous explosion behind them in the target area.

One pilot in the 27th F.S. stood out during the month, a young lieutenant named John Demorest who had joined the squadron in March. During the week of May 8 Demorest emerged as the champion "bridge buster" by destroying five of the six he attacked in the squadron's creaking P-40s.

Part of the success of the 5th F.G. during the Battle of Chihkiang can be attributed to the high experience level of the pilots, as was noted by Captain Carran of the 26th F.S. in his monthly historical report. He wrote that in the 26th, most American pilots had between forty and sixty-five missions behind them, and many of the Chinese had even more. They were "experienced with Japanese methods of camouflage and had learned the technique of seeking out and properly attacking enemy convoys, motor pools, river-shipping, and supply depots. . . . Each mission seemed to develop new targets; many convoys of trucks, horses, and munitions were hit hit repeatedly . . . while facing in most cases Japanese antiaircraft fire exceeding in intensity anything encountered in this or the campaign of 1944."

The last confirmed aerial victory scored by the 5th F.G. was made on May 14 by Lt. Julian Robinson of the 29th F.S. While flying lead with another pilot in P-51s, Robinson had glide-bombed and strafed a target near Yangchi when the "Safety" liaison team directed him toward a Japanese aircraft that had been seen dropping leaflets to retreating enemy troops nearby. The "Val" dive-bomber (again, most likely an Army Ki-51 Sonia) was sighted about three miles south of Yangchi flying at about 100 feet altitude.

Robinson took after it and gave the enemy aircraft a short burst of fire that caused it to begin smoking. Then the Japanese plane was lost in the haze, and Robinson turned his attention to the troops the aircraft had been leafletting in a valley below. The two P-51s bombed and strafed the Japanese soldiers, then returned to Chihkiang. In the meantime, the "Safety" crew members saw the stricken Japanese plane drop out of the haze and crash near their position, so they radioed confirmation of the kill to Chihkiang.

On May 28, Lt. Liu L.C. of the 26th F.S. caught a Ki-43 Oscar on the runway at Wuchang and destroyed it in a strafing attack to claim the only other kill of the month.

It is difficult to determine the precise beginning and end of a military campaign, but May 15 is generally accepted as the last day of the Battle of Chihkiang. By this date the Japanese were in full retreat, with the Chinese, especially the 18th Army at Sinhwa, hot on their heels. By month's end Chinese troops were only ten to fifteen miles from Paoching, and practically all Japanese forces had withdrawn to the positions from which their original attack had been launched.

For their major contribution to the Battle of Chihkiang, the 5th F.G. and 4th B.S. were awarded a unit citation. It read, in part:

"These units waged a brilliant battle which was principally responsible for the first major Allied land victory in China. In thwarting the enemy, this small combination aerial force wrote a classic in employment of tactical air power against ground forces. . . . In these thirty-six days they killed more than one-fourth of the enemy troops, slashed their supply lines so thoroughly, and destroyed such quantities of supplies that the enemy drive was completely paralyzed. Ill-equipped Chinese forces, heartened by this aerial support, began their own offensive and rolled the enemy back to Paoching. Flying 920 missions in both day and night attacks, the pilots braved vicious barrages of antiaircraft and small-arms fire to hit the enemy. The relentless attacks left 6,024 enemy troops killed, 1,491 cavalry and packhorses killed, and thirty-seven gun positions destroyed. Supply lines disintegrated under attacks that destroyed and damaged 1,639 small riverboats and knocked out 304 vehicles. Thirty-nine river vessels of longer than 100 feet were sunk or damaged, while forty-eight bridges on supporting rail and road arteries were destroyed or damaged. Immense quantities of enemy supplies and equipment were lost in the 4,006 buildings destroyed by fighters and bombers. . . . This rampage of devastation cost the cited units eighteen aircraft and two pilots lost. . . ."

Perhaps fittingly, Maj. Fred Ploetz was relieved of command of the 29th F.S. on May 15. Ploetz was the last of the original American flight leaders to serve in the 5th F.G. (After Ploetz went home the only original pilot left was Colonel Dunning.) Ploetz, who had flown a tour on Guadalcanal with Major Hull before coming to China, had taken part in every major campaign flown by the group. He was replaced by Capt. Frank Everest, but Everest held the post for only thirteen days before being shot down and captured on May 28. An account of Everest's experiences in the CACW and in captivity is contained in his autobiography, *The Fastest Man Alive*, which also chronicles his service as a test pilot after the war. Command of the 29th must have been jinxed during the weeks after Ploetz departed, for Everest's replacement, Capt. Dick Turner, was killed flying an F-6 recon Mustang back from a mission on June 18 when he crashed during a storm. Capt. Byron McKenzie, who had been in the 5th F.G. for a year and was at the end of his tour, took command until Maj. Henry Lawrence arrived on July 1. Then Lawrence was shot up on July 23 and had to bail out, putting the squadron back under McKenzie's command until Lawrence returned to Chihkiang in early August, just before the war ended.

12

With the knowledge that the war was over in Europe, the summer of 1945 loomed ahead for the men of the CACW like a big question mark. Though the Japanese advance in China had been halted at last, bases like Chihkiang, Ankang, Peishiyi, and Hanchung were still a long way from Tokyo. The Allied advance in the Pacific was encouraging, as was the prospect of getting reinforcements from the units in Europe, but in June 1945 none could guess that two mushroom clouds rising over Japanese cities in early August would bring the war to an end before fall.

The CACW's twin nemeses, weather and supplies, continued to hound the combat units in June, particularly those at Ankang and Hanchung. The 1st B.S. watched the mercury rise to over 100 degrees at Hanchung and feared the wind would blow the top layer of crushed rock right off the runway. Then unclean conditions in the mess hall led to an outbreak of dysentery that the men called, with no affection, the "Yellow River Rapids." Finally, Capt. Allen Sweeney, the squadron's intelligence officer, took charge of the food situation and got the mess cleaned up.

June also saw the last original flight crew member of the 1st B.S. depart. Capt. Emory Smith, the squadron lead bombardier, had trained crews in India and been among those who flew out of Kweilin in the early days. When he boarded a B-25 flown by the squadron commander, Capt. Dick Varney, to leave for Peishiyi on the first leg of his trip home, the entire squadron turned out to say good-bye. Other original squadron members leaving in June were M. Sgt. "Pappy" Sage, the line chief, and T. Sgt. David Johnson, the tech inspector.

In all, the squadron was able to fly eight missions in June, primarily against the Japanese forces that were pulling out of the Yellow River "Great Bend" area to the north. Strikes were flown against the railroad west of Loyang, the Yellow River Bridge at Chungmow, and the railroad yards at Sinsiang. In the Sinsiang strike, Captains Varney and Smith led all twelve of the 1st B.S. Mitchells in two flights to the target. The first element hit about 100 railroad cars and two locomotives, starting five big fires that sent smoke 4,000 feet high. The next element came in fifteen minutes later but missed the yards. About sixty percent of their bombs hit nearby warehouses and other buildings, however. Leaflets also were dropped by the B-25s.

The 4th B.S. at Chihkiang also was busy during the month, catching several big Japanese convoys on night missions in the Hankow-Kweilin corridor. The original commander of the 4th, Lt. Col. Bill Dick, finally went home during June. He had spent nearly two years in action and received a DFC for having flown 200 hours of combat, finishing his tour in the CACW as operations officer of the 1st B.G. at Liangshan.

The base at Liangshan was probably the quietest in the CACW during June, with the 2d and 3d bomb squadrons getting very little flying time because of bad weather and a shortage of gas. In all, the group flew 108 sorties and dropped 160.3 tons of bombs during June.

The 3d F.G. at Ankang spent an uncomfortable month that was first hot, then wet, then short on gas. The rest of the war would be little different. The group had largely given over the job of harassing the nearby targets on the Yellow River and Peking-Hankow railroad to the shorter-range P-47s of the 312th Fighter Wing at Hsian by this time, using the long-legged Mustangs mostly for "ass buster" missions against distant targets on the Yangtze River. River sweeps and B-25 escorts were the order of the day, plus, for good measure, a few attacks on ground targets near Suichwan with the few P-40s left. A particularly effective mission was flown on June 24, when the 32d F.S.'s two-seat P-51B, "Black Maria," was flown with an observer contacting a ground liaison team to direct four P-40s in a strike against a radio station at Suichwan.

The group flew just twenty-four missions during June, and morale dipped with the drop in operations. The rainy weather fouled up the baseball and volleyball schedules, and then a number of tents and mud huts on the base began to give way under the pressure of the summer rainstorms. Finally, some of the "permanent" structures had to be propped up with poles to prevent them from capsizing.

With the low level of operations, only one 3d F.G. pilot failed to return from a mission during the month. Lt. Morris Pitts of the 28th F.S. was shot up June 9 in his P-51K and bailed out, returning to the squadron later. The 7th F.S. lost two of its outstanding pilots when Captains J. T. Moore and Ed Mulholland got their orders to return home. Mulholland, son of a Navy doctor, had been with the squadron for a year and flown through all the toughest campaigns, scoring two confirmed aerial kills along the way. Moore's combat history went all the way back to the Tunisia campaign, when he had flown P-39s with the 350th F.G. He later took part in the air coverage of the Anzio invasion before coming to China with the 81st F.G. in 1944. Moore was particularly successful during the flying at Laohokow and scored seventeen ground kills, second only to Tom Reynolds in the entire 14th Air Force.

The 3d F.G. was able to fly only three offensive missions during the last week of June, because of the shortage of gas. This was partly due to a command decision at higher levels to concentrate the supplies farther south in China with units that could strike at the main Japanese retreat. Another problem was the supply route that led to Ankang. The gas had to be flown over the Hump from India to Luhsien on the Yangtze River 100 miles southwest of Chungking. Then it was floated on barges downriver to Wanhsien, about forty miles northeast of Liangshan. From there the drums of gasoline were carried by truck to Liangshan, where they were loaded back on transports and flown up to Ankang. With a crooked mile like that to cover, it's a wonder there was enough gas for the 3d F.G. to fly as much as it did.

Supplies of gas—and most everything else—were better at Chihkiang, and it remained this way for the rest of the war. Even the airfield itself was getting some attention. A force of 18,000 coolies descended on the base to begin lengthening the runway to 6,500 feet, which would greatly enhance the pilots' margin for error. There was also an infusion of new blood as a number of new pilots arrived, both from the United States and from up north in the 3d F.G.

The last hurrah for the 5th F.G.'s P-40s was flown, ironically, not at Chihkiang but at Enshih, the former home of the 28th F.S. during Mission A. The base had been used only for staging in recent months, and word was received that a stock of 25,000 gallons of gas was there for the using. The 27th F.S. took ten of its P-40s up to the empty base on the last day of May to begin hitting targets east of Hankow that hadn't felt the 5th's sting for a number of months.

The first day at Enshih was less than encouraging, for not only did Major Matthews and his troops find less gas than they expected, but they also lost two P-40s right off the bat. One of the P-40s, flown by Lt. Llewelyn Thomas, was wrecked when it lost power just after takeoff and crashed in a river three miles from base. The plane landed in about six feet of water and sank, but Thomas floated free, unhurt. Then he remembered that his baggage was still stored in the compartment behind the cockpit, so he dove back down to retrieve it. Everything was ruined, however. As the squadron historian noted, Thomas "caught a ride on a truck to Enshih, where he arrived in good condition but in a bad temper. He then bummed a dry cigarette and settled down to work at Enshih."

"Work" at Enshih consisted of nine missions—forty-two sorties—before the squadron returned to Chihkiang June 9. One of the pilots who remembers his stay at Enshih is J. W. Fetzer, who was operations officer of the 27th at the time. He recalls the mission of June 7:

"The mission that was outstanding occurred on a warm summer afternoon and was a flight of four P-40s led by Capt. Louis A. Phillips. While the mission was out, the rest of us occupied ourselves by swimming in the river that ran along the side of the runway, or sunning on the gravel bar. Suddenly a Chinese staff car escorted by a couple of Jeeps came storming onto the field with flags flying and a couple of Chinese army colonels demanding to know who was in charge.

"As I was operations officer for the squadron, I accepted the brunt of their anger. They demanded to know why our planes were destroying Chinese army supplies in the area of I-ch'ang. I had to wait until Phillips and the flight returned about an hour later. They landed very excited and elated about an extremely successful mission. They described in great detail how they had found a large number of riverboats loaded with gasoline drums—the fires they had made would make great pictures.

"About that time the telex machine started clattering, and in came a wire from General Wedemeyer's headquarters demanding to know what the hell was going on down there. After a little discussion with Phillips and the Chinese colonels it became apparent that we were getting a snow job from the Chinese. They claimed that these supplies that had been destroyed were to be used by a Chinese armored division that none of us had ever seen or heard of.

"I prepared an answer for General Wedemeyer describing the location of the destroyed boats and asked if anyone could explain what the Chinese were doing with our gasoline that far downriver, which happened to be the dividing line between Chinese and Japanese-held territories. Needless to say we never heard any more about this mission."[1]

The next day another of the pilots, Capt. Ransom Rideout, had quite a thrill. He flew through an eight-strand high-tension wire during a strafing run and tore it down. He also brought back a 200-foot long souvenir in the form of high-tension wire wrapped around the propeller and fuselage of his P-40.

The 27th had one more high point during the month, on June 8 at Chihkiang. That was the day Lieutenant Demorest returned from India leading ten brand-new P-51D-25s bound for the squadron. This was the latest version of the Mustang, and all ten were concentrated in the 27th to ease maintenance problems. When the P-40s returned from Enshih the next day they were parceled out among the other squadrons at Chihkiang, with two kept on in the 27th, one N-20 and one N-25 model.

The only 5th F.G. pilot killed during June was Capt. Dick Turner, the new commander of the 29th, who crashed in a storm while returning from a mission on the 18th. Three pilots in the 17th F.S., Capt. James Russell and Lieutenants John Pensyl and Glen Hesler, were shot down in June, but all three returned safely to Chihkiang. In the 26th, two Chinese pilots of long experience added to their lists of being shot down. Lt. Kuo K.C. was forced to bail out for the third time on the 24th, and Lt. Leng P.S., it could be said, became a Japanese ace on the 26th when he lost his fifth aircraft in combat. Each time he had reached friendly forces when he went down and returned to Chihkiang to fight again.

The most successful mission of June came on the first day of the month for the 5th F.G., when eighteen P-51s were sent out to firebomb a concentration of river craft in Yochow Harbor and north and south of the city. The Mustangs swept in low to drop their napalm bombs on the closely docked junks, and they got excellent results. Some fifty-three junks, which were probably loaded with oil, to judge by the thick, black smoke that belched from them when they were hit, were destroyed, and 114 were damaged.

The Mustangs then swept up the northwest fork of the Yangtze River and attacked twelve warehouses and a 100-foot motor barge, all of which were destroyed. One flight split off then and followed a railroad line northeast to Sienning, destroying eight boxcars along the way. Heading home the P-51s strafed two machine-gun positions near Changsha, knocking out both of them.

For all the action in the air, June was also marked by an important event in headquarters of the 5th F.G., for this was the month that the CACW would bid farewell to Col. John Dunning. On the morning of June 16, a review and awards ceremony was conducted just to the west of the main runway at Chihkiang. As the sun flashed through scattered clouds above, the twin flags of the United States and Nationalist China flew overhead while the officers and enlisted men marched in formation. Colonel Dunning presented a number of awards, then gave an inspirational farewell talk to the men with whom he had served for the past eighteen months. It was described as "a ceremony to stir one's deepest emotion."

On June 21, Dunning turned over command of the group to Lt. Col. Charles C. Wilder, Jr., and Maj. Bill Hull, just back from a rest in the United States, took Wilder's place as group operations officer. Wilder, twenty-eight years old, had 103 combat missions behind him. He had come a long way since being pulled out of that wrecked Tomahawk at Malir nearly two years earlier during the CACW's infancy. Wilder commanded the group until July 6, when his replacement arrived and he could begin his well-earned trip home to the United States.

Wilder's replacement was Col. Howard M. Means. This thirty-year-old career officer had nine years' service behind him. He served in the Pentagon during the early part of the war, then was transferred to 10th A.F. headquarters in India in September 1943. He was eager to see combat and came to China in July 1944 as plans officer at 14th Air Force headquarters in Kunming. Upon finally getting his combat assignment with the 5th F.G. he immediately began to make up for lost time, flying fourteen missions in his first month at Chihkiang. Means was still flying on the last day of the war.

July was a busy month for everyone at Chihkiang, as the mission total climbed to 212 from the previous month's 137. By this time the Japanese were moving back up the Hsiang Valley corridor through Kweilin and Hengyang, headed east toward Shanghai. From there the Japanese forces could be shipped back to the home islands to prepare for the final offensive against them or be used to defend Shanghai and Manchuria from Allied landings there. Quite a few of the Japanese and much of their equipment wouldn't be seeing their homeland again, however, thanks to the heavy attacks mounted by the 5th F.G. and 1st B.G. units at Chihkiang.

The Chihkiang aircraft concentrated their attention on a force of about 30,000 Japanese who were moving out of Central China overland to Kanchow and Nanchang. There they were to meet rail transportation that would take them on to Shanghai. Another Japanese force moving eastward out of the Changsha-Liling area also got the attention of Chihkiang's fighters and bombers. A month later it was estimated that these forces had been cut by approximately a third because of the aerial pounding, harassment from pursuing Chinese ground forces, and the normal sickness and accidents suffered by all armies. At the same time, revitalized Chinese forces in South China were pushing the Japanese completely out of that area. First Nanning was regained, and by the end of July Kweilin was back in the hands of the Allies.

This action was not without cost for the 5th F.G. On July 3, Lt. Chang S.T. of the 26th F.S. was returning from a mission when he attempted to land his P-51 without dropping the flaps. It was thought that his hydraulic system, which operates the flaps, had been damaged during the mission. Lt. Bill Thayer of the same squadron had just landed and was turning onto the taxi strip at the south end of the field when Lieutenant Chang touched down. Chang's Mustang raced down the field out of control and smashed into Thayer's, both aircraft bursting into flames. Thayer was pulled from the wreck badly burned and taken to the base hospital. He died the next day. Lieutenant Chang was not seriously injured.

Late in the month Maj. Frank Stevens took six of his 17th F.S. Mustangs to a small advanced field at Yuankisu. They flew seventy-one sorties in support of Chinese forces in the Suichwan area by the end of the month. One of the new pilots who had joined the squadron only a few weeks previously, Lt. Jack Hammel, was killed on the 25th while flying from Yuankisu.

In addition to the new pilots arriving at Chihkiang, some familiar faces returned in July. Capt. Bill Bonneaux, one of the most popular and successful pilots in the 17th F.S., returned from a rest in the United States. A similar figure in the 27th, Capt. Buck Joyner, also came back. Within eight days, Joyner was shot up on a mission and forced to bail out for the second time in China. He again returned safely to Chihkiang and resumed flying combat.

The 29th F.S.'s new commander, Maj. Henry Lawrence, took over on July 1 and went down on the 23d during a river sweep. He bailed out over Hutien and returned to the squadron some two weeks later. The 29th also got a new Chinese commander in July when Capt. Chang C.M. arrived from the 28th F.S. at Ankang. He was a seasoned veteran with three confirmed kills scored in 1944.

Two missions on July 18 were representative of the pounding given the withdrawing Japanese during the month. On the first mission, four P-51s were able to work effectively with a ground liaison team at Suichwan, receiving instructions to bomb and strafe a group of buildings reportedly housing Japanese troops about a mile east of the city. Two of the buildings were destroyed by the napalm bombings, and three were damaged. Then the Mustangs returned in strafing runs, and the radio team "Cal" reported heavy damage when they finished. Eleven days later word was received through U.S. intelligence channels that 600 Japanese had been killed in the attack.

Later that day Colonel Means led three 26th F.S. pilots—Lieutenants John Allen (newly transferred from the 3d F.G.), Bill King, and Liu L.C.—to the same area. Radio contact with "Cal" was poor, but the formation found an entrenched Japanese position on a hill overlooking the airfield at Suichwan with help from ground panels laid out by Chinese troops. The Mustangs swept down to attack and worked over the position. Word was received later that seventy-five Japanese and fifteen horses had been killed.

July also was a good month for the 4th B.S. at Chihkiang—so good, in fact, that the 2d and 3d bomb squadrons sent crews down from Liangshan in their B-25s to share the plentiful gas and ammunition and get some combat missions in.

Also moving to Chihkiang during July was the CACW headquarters. The move pushed the 5th F.G. out of its headquarters building as the wing personnel set up shop there. With the end of the threat to Chihkiang and the rapid movement of the Japanese eastward, it had been decided to move the wing headquarters closer to the action. At the same time, a new base was being prepared at Hsupu, some eighty miles northwest of Chihkiang. It was planned that the 3d F.G. and 1st B.G. would move in there, since action had diminished to such a degree in their areas up north.

During July those forces up north, the 3d F.G. and 1st B.G., were very quiet. Bad weather and a lack of gasoline combined to limit operations at Ankang and give the troops there another dent in their morale. Some thirty five years later 28th F.S. commander Don Campbell described the summer of 1945 like this:

"The war effort was at low ebb at the time, and while there were a couple of interesting missions, it is questionable if any but one or two were worth the gas."

At this time the 3d F.G. had thirty-five P-51s, two P-40s, and one L-5 liaison aircraft. Most stayed on the ground until July 20, when the weather broke and supplies of gasoline arrived. The rest of the month was busy with river sweeps and escort missions. One new technique developed during July was for bomb-carrying P-51s to pull in close behind B-25s and drop their loads with the bomber. This was used on short missions when the Mustangs could carry two 500-pound bombs on their wing racks and was only possible because Japanese aerial opposition had been completely eliminated from northern China.

Two events stood out in July for the 3d F.G. One was the CACW's second anniversary reunion, which was attended by the few remaining original members of the wing. Col. Gene Strickland and four others at Ankang flew to Peishiyi on July 22 for the celebration, as did three majors and a captain from the 1st B.G. at Liangshan.

The other event of significance in the 3d F.G. was the farewell to Colonel Strickland. In a ceremony rivaling the one at Chihkiang for Colonel Dunning the previous month, Strickland turned over command of the group he had served for almost two years to Lt. Col. William

Yancey. Strickland remained in the Air Force following his return to the United States, and he retired as a brigadier general after a distinguished career.

Strickland's departure at the end of July was the last bit of excitement for the 3d F.G., for the war ended some two weeks later, with hardly any missions flown during the interim. Those few were mostly escort of C-47s into the secret airfields in the "pocket" east of the Peking-Hankow rail line. The last one was flown on August 14 to Valley Field. The last wartime command change in the 3d occurred on August 11, when Maj. Ross Bachley replaced Capt. Bert Welch as 7th F.S. commander.

The gas supply had improved at Liangshan as well late in July, allowing the 2d and 3d bomb squadrons to resume operations there. Nevertheless, the B-25 pilots often shut down one of their engines during the return flight from their targets to save gas and reduce wear on their engines' reconditioned spark plugs.

For the 1st B.G. headquarters, there was plenty to do in early August. The men were busy packing for the first few days, then boarded transports bound for their new base at Hsupu. The headquarters contingent was all moved in by the 10th, but the various squadrons stayed put at Liangshan, Hanchung, and Chihkiang. The 3d F.G. also was preparing to move down to Hsupu, but the end of the war canceled those plans. The big base at Hsupu seemed oddly empty and quiet for its few inhabitants when news of the cease-fire arrived.

Throughout the stay in North China, one target had continued to hound the 1st B.G.: the railroad bridge over the Yellow River just north of Chenghsien. This target was hit time after time, but the construction of the long span was such that the Japanese always were able to repair it quickly and resume rail traffic on the Peking-Hankow line. In early August the decision was made by the 14th A.F. to knock the bridge out once and for all. This planned mission is vividly recalled by Allen Sweeney, who was intelligence officer in the 1st B.S. at Hanchung. His story:

"We did not have too much success [attacking the Yellow River Bridge] until after a briefing by Bishop Thomas Meaghan, formerly the prelate of the Shanghai diocese. After being forced to flee for his life and with no assignment from the church, he became A-2 for Chiang Kai-shek. On our initial raids we had dropped bombs fused with a delay fuse, but these, even when they made direct hits, went bouncing off into the wild blue yonder. Even bombs equipped with nose spikes for piercing bridge ties went astray. The bishop told us that the bridge deck between the rails and from the rails to the outer edges of the bridge were covered with 1¼-inch boilerplate steel, and the only way to damage the bridge was to use a slanting approach and attempt to skip the bombs under the bridge using delayed fuses.

"Such missions knocked out one to four spans. The Japs had them rebuilt in twenty-four to ninety-six hours. They, however, got tired of such bombings and installed AA on the flats on the north bank of the river, AA on the mesa on the south bank, which was several hundred feet above the river, and also dug caves in this mesa that were equipped with AA and large-caliber machine guns so that any low-level bombing attempt was surely a suicide mission. Subsequent missions were assigned to the B-24s and B-29s at high altitude out of range from any AA fire, but these were not too successful. The bridge's total length was [five or seven] miles.

"Several weeks before V-J day all the American commanders, operations officers, and intelligence officers were ordered into the 14th A.F. headquarters for a briefing by Col. Jack Chennault [Gen. Claire Chennault's son, who commanded the 311th F.G. at Hsian]. He started the briefing by stating that nothing that he was about to say was to be discussed with any other members of the respective units. His next statement was [about] the target, the Yellow River Bridge, and [the fact] that previous attempts to destroy it had been like trying to kill a fly with a toothpick. The B-24s and -29s were assigned to knock out the AA emplacement on the north and south banks by high-level saturation bombing. Certain fighter units were assigned the task of laying down a smoke screen in front of the caves on the south bank and renewing the screens every five minutes or so to make the use of the weapons in the caves impossible.

"The four B-25 squadrons, using twelve airplanes each, were then to come in from the north side of the bridge, fly south over the bridge, two on each side, and drop their bombs on the best angle they could. They would attack in units of four, and if the first four destroyed the south end, the next four would not go any farther south than needed to hit the remaining part of the bridge, and so on until all forty-eight aircraft had dropped their bombs. In this way probably the entire bridge could be wiped out at once.

"The mission was assigned the code name 'Butcher,' and the weather had to be just right for it to succeed. It must be clear, with the wind not exceeding 4 mph out of the north or northwest so that the smoke screen would actually blow into the caves and not dissipate too quickly. Chennault himself would be at an altitude out of range of the AA and would coordinate the attack from his position above the bridge. Bombs were to be fused with four to five seconds' delay, and timing between each section of B-25s was fifteen or twenty seconds.

"Weather reports were to be from naval mobile units behind the Jap lines and would be transmitted every morning over the radio network. When the weather was not OK, the report would be 'Butcher is on hold.' When it was to be run, the message 'Butcher on green' would be sent. All personnel at the meeting were sent back to their home bases to assign crews to the aircraft and make doubly sure all aircraft were ready to go, including having bombs loaded but not fused. Tight security was taken around all aircraft. Chennault expressed a desire that the mission could be accomplished within a week, but the weather would not cooperate.

"I was scheduled to go on the 'Butcher' mission as a navigator-bombardier with our operations officer [Capt. Gail A. Smith]. Since the B-25 did not have a copilot seat, he took me up several times to make sure I could land the '25 or at least get to where we could bail out if we were shot up. Although General Chennault had grounded all IOs [intelligence officers] from combat, I volunteered for the mission since there was no one left after the first eleven crews were picked.

"Of course, the rumors at each base were rampant, and when orders came in at 0400, briefing was set for 0500 and takeoff at 0600. The 1st Bomb Squadron had everything right on schedule and was all of twenty minutes en route to the assigned area when over the radio to each aircraft came the message: 'Butcher mission is canceled. Return to your base and get ready to go home. The war is over.' So ends the last mission."[2]

Soon thereafter, the 1st B.G. historical officer, Capt. Robert Eisner, wrote of his feelings on V-J day:

"The operations of the 1st Bomb Group, which were spread over almost two years of combat in China, can speak for themselves. When these are analyzed, consideration must be given to the obstacles that had to be overcome in jointly operating with the Chinese Air Force—differences in language, methods of doing things, and ways of thinking. In this time, with an enviable record of destruction behind us, we can look back proudly. And as we do so, we can hold in memory the men of the six American crews lost in action."[3]

If the war ended anticlimactically for the 3d F.G. and 1st B.G., this was much less the case at Chihkiang. There, the 5th F.G. and 4th B.S. kept up steady operations against the withdrawing Japanese, right up to the last day. A total of 101 missions were flown in the first fourteen days of August by the 5th alone.

The month started off with a thrill for Lt. Bill Hill of the 29th F.S. This aggressive pilot, who three decades later would be the driving force behind creation of the 5th Fighter Group Association, flew sixty-four missions with the 17th and 29th squadrons. On August 1, he was making a dive-bombing attack in a P-51C-11 when the canopy suddenly tore away from the aircraft and fell to earth. Hill was able to recover from his dive and head for home, getting a taste of the old wind-in-the-face days of open cockpit flying as he made his way back to Chihkiang.

The August 1 mission was one of the better flown during the month. In all, eleven Mustangs from the 17th, 26th, and 29th squadrons were sent out to attack a railroad bridge across the Miu Shiu River near Kweiyi. Four planes carried eight M-64 500-pound demolition bombs with T-3 parachute attachments, and seven of these were dropped within a few feet of the 1,150-foot beam span. Capt. Liang T.S., of the 26th F.S., made a direct hit just south of the center section that left a thirty-foot gap in the span. The attack, which had been led by Lt. Max Dixon of the 26th, definitely knocked out this important railroad link to the east. The Mustangs then swept the rail line and strafed four boxcars, several buildings, and three antiaircraft gun positions.

In the 27th F.S., Major Matthews was sent to India to ferry new P-51s back to China, leaving Capt. Buck Joyner in command of the squadron. Matthews didn't get back to Chihkiang until the end of the month, so Joyner was the last wartime commander of the squadron. In this capacity, Joyner continued to fly missions, and on August 8 he flew what must have been one of the last P-40 combat sorties ever flown by an American pilot. He considered the P-40 an excellent aircraft for the ground-attack work that was the mainstay of the 5th F.G., citing its load-carrying ability and its maneuverability. "I loved it," he said simply of the Curtiss fighter.

Also on August 8, Lt. John Demorest of the 27th became the envy of the 5th F.G. when he was scrambled from Chihkiang to check out a report of a Japanese fighter flying near Hengyang and returned to claim the last aerial kill scored over China during World War II. This was particularly unusual because the last previous kill claim had been filed nearly three months earlier.

At about 1600 on that day, the radio station at Chihkiang picked up a report from a C-47 pilot that he was being attacked by a Japanese fighter about forty miles southwest of Hengyang. Lieutenant Demorest took off in a 26th F.S. P-51 immediately and made contact with the C-47 pilot by radio en route to the area where the Japanese fighter had been reported. The transport pilot said he had evaded the fighter by ducking into some clouds, and that he had last seen the enemy aircraft heading north.

Demorest scouted the area, then headed directly for Hengyang. As he approached the airfield there, he spotted his quarry, which he identified as a white "Jack" fighter (a short-coupled Navy interceptor introduced late in the war). The enemy fighter was preparing to land, so Demorest dove from 8,000 feet, encountering 20- and 40mm antiaircraft fire. Demorest opened fire while he was still out of range, and the enemy pilot began to make an S-turn in front of him. As the Japanese plane turned, Demorest put a long burst from his guns into its right wing, and the aircraft began to leave a trail of white smoke behind it. Then it went into a spin, crashed, and exploded about midway between the center and south end of the airfield.

This kill was not recorded in the 27th F.S. history and may never have been confirmed by the 14th A.F. The account of the combat was found in the squadron history of the 26th F.S. (with Demorest's name misspelled). The 5th F.G. monthly combat totals show an increase of one aerial kill from July to August, however, and this certainly is supportive of the theory that Demorest scored the last victory of the war in China. Unfortunately, the author was not able to locate John Demorest for his own story of this interesting encounter.

The CACW lost its last pilot in action on August 9, when Lt. Max Dixon of the 26th F.S. went down near Yochow. Dixon, one of the squadron's most popular officers and most capable pilots, crashed while making a low-level pass against a concentration of Japanese troops at an embarkation point on the bank of the Yangtze River. He was either hit by antiaircraft fire or simply mushed into the water before he could release his bombs, and his aircraft exploded on impact with the water.

The 5th kept up its relentless attacks on the withdrawing Japanese until the last day of operations, August 14. One of the missions flown that day was a recon of the airfields at Nanking by the 27th F.S. and was led by Colonel Means. On the way to Nanking the weather closed in, so Means led the formation over Changsha to test the Japanese antiaircraft defenses there and then headed back to Chihkiang.

On that same morning, Capt. Walter Griffin led four Mustangs of the 17th F.S. on a bombing and strafing mission to Liling. The strike was very successful, leaving twelve buildings destroyed. A similar mission was flown to Hsiangtan by the 26th F.S., with Capt. Ed McMillan leading.

The last mission of the war for the 5th F.G. was, fittingly, a joint Chinese-American effort. Lieutenants James Bower and Shen C.T. took off at 1310 in two P-51s on a weather recon of Paoching and the surrounding area. They found the cloud cover generally broken with heavy thundershowers over the mountains and returned to Chihkiang with their report. It was the final mission of the day, and the next morning word was received that hostilities had ceased.

Upon receiving the news of the Japanese surrender on the 15th, Colonel Means called the personnel of the 5th F.G. together for a memorial service to honor the men of the unit who had lost their lives fighting in China. The 27th F.S. historian noted:

"As the chaplain's solemn words engulfed us all, we remembered squadron losses and resolved in our minds to live up to the memory of those fine and brave fellows by doing our small bit to keep the world fit for their memory."

That same day, General Bennett ordered all U.S. personnel in the wing with twenty-four months' foreign service or eighty-five points toward rotation to travel to Yangkai on the first leg of their trip home. The rest of the men were to be reassigned to other 14th Air Force units or to the liaison team being set up to aid the Chinese Air Force in adjusting to operating on its own. This liaison team was supposed to help set up systems of operations, maintenance, and supply so the Chinese could put to use all the American equipment that was to be turned over to them. Most of these men would return to the United States by January 1946.

In the 5th F.G., all aircraft were turned over to the CAF, and one B-25 was assigned to the group for the use of the U.S. personnel. The historian noted that in the weeks that followed the cease-fire, all supplies and equipment were turned over to the CAF through Lend-Lease, then "books were balanced and stored for shipment to central records depot."

Since Colonel Means was one of those who qualified to leave China immediately, he was relieved of his command on August 26. His replacement was no newcomer to the CACW. Lt. Col. Bill Turner, who had been serving with General Bennett in wing headquarters since returning from the United States, was named the new 5th F.G. commander. Thus he became the only man to command both fighter groups of the CACW.

While an immediate quiet settled over most bases in China after the war ended, one day of excitement remained for the men at Chihkiang. On August 22 a Japanese Topsy transport, escorted by 5th F.G. P-51s that a short week earlier would have been lining up to put a burst of gunfire into it, circled the runway at Chihkiang and then glided in for a landing. The escorting pilots, led by Maj. Frank Stevens of the 17th F.S., were glad to let this one get away, however.

U.S. and Chinese personnel lined the runway as the Japanese plane came in, then watched as its occupants were loaded on Jeeps with excruciating slowness and paraded past the men to preliminary surrender ceremonies with the Chinese at the base hospital. These men of the CACW had seen the very end of their war in a way few soldiers are lucky enough to do. Now they were ready to go home.

On September 19, 1945, orders were issued to the now depleted units of the CACW that they were being disbanded. The wing itself was dissolved, and the tactical units were transferred to Chinese Air Force control. This was the official end of the Chinese-American Composite Wing, a grand experiment in the mixing of cultures under special pressures of war that had proved more successful than any of its founders could have hoped.

Capt. Richard Mallon, adjutant of the 1st B.G., probably best captured the spirit of the American members of the CACW that day:

"In conclusion, let it be said that while most of the personnel . . . are not exactly anxious to return to China by the first boat, they have definitely had experiences which will be good for numerous drinks in their neighborhood saloons and with which they can regale their grandchildren for years to come. The air raids, lost comrades in arms who went down fighting, rice wine, water buffalo meat . . . lack of mail and Post Exchange supplies, and lack of sufficient supplies with which to conduct the war, will not be easily forgotten. GOMBAY!!"[4]

Afterword

The banquet will, perhaps, more subdued than the ones they had shared in Kweilin, Liangshan, or Hanchung. After all, there were ladies present. . . . It was July 21, 1982, the opening night of the thirty-fifth annual convention of the 14th Air Force Association. In a private dining room of Trader Vic's in Seattle, about forty Chinese and American veterans of the 3d Fighter Group were getting reacquainted after a lapse of thirty-seven years.

Over at a corner table sat Maj. Gen. T. Alan Bennett, with his wife, Ellie, on one side and Gen. Loh Ying-Teh on the other. Bennett, now sporting a silver mustache but otherwise looking just as formidable as he had when he commanded the CACW, was busy catching up with Loh, who had risen to vice-commander in chief of the CAF before becoming his nation's ambassador to Korea. The two had served together in wing headquarters during 1945. Also at the table were two of Bennett's most able subordinates in the 3d Fighter Group, J. T. Bull and Tom Summers, both looking every bit as fit as their old boss.

At other tables were Major Generals Cheng Sung-Ting, Hsu Chi Hsiang, Liu Shiao-yao, and Kuan Chen-min, all of whom have shown up in the preceding pages. In total, some twenty-five Chinese pilots were on hand, far outnumbering their American comrades. They were mostly in their sixties and retired from the CAF, but many were busy in second careers.

The toasts began after the meal, though the deadly Chinese rice wine that had shot down so many brave young Americans at similar gatherings during the war was nowhere to be seen. Perhaps it was their age—more likely their experience—but no one shattered the dignity or decorum of the occasion with outbursts of intoxication. At least for the moment, these men and their families were taking their common past very seriously.

"We Americans made some of the best friends we ever made while we were in China—and they were Chinese," said General Bennett. "It was an experience that only the CACW could have afforded anyone."

General Loh returned the toast: "I believe the image of the 14th Air Force and especially the CACW is very deeply into the hearts of the Chinese people. I can tell you this: the Chinese people are always your friends."

Then Wilbur Walton stood up. Walton, who was operations officer of the 7th F.S. during the summer of 1944, had been principally responsible for arranging the banquet, along with 32d F.S. pilot Yu Wei in Taipei. Walton read a letter from Gen. Kuo Ju-Lin, commander in chief of the Chinese Air Force and a 28th F.S. pilot during the war. General Kuo's letter caught the spirit of the moment, even though he had been forced by his duties to miss the occasion. It said, in part:

"I remember vividly the 1943 period when the Japanese warlords were invading my country and endangering the lives of my countrymen, to the point of complete annihilation. It was during this very trying span of time that you gentlemen left your sweet homeland and came to our assistance, at the cost of many personal sacrifices, to fight the common enemy on our side for the sake of international justice and world peace. Your shining combat records won for yourselves the deepest admiration and respect from my people, and your sacrifices and support rendered to us during this dark page in Chinese history will be cherished forever by liberty-loving Chinese the world over."

What had happened after that "dark page in Chinese history" was turned in August 1945? For the Americans, the answer is predictable.

American personnel in the CACW were sent home as quickly as possible when the war ended. Those assigned to the liaison team that was supposed to help the CACW units convert to all-Chinese operation waited longest. They spent four to five months sitting on their hands with nothing to do, for the dual command of the CACW meant that

Chinese were already in place and doing everything that needed to be done.

Once home, the Americans scattered to the four winds like all citizen-soldiers before and since. Most, of course, left the military and spent their civilian lives experiencing the full range of triumphs and tragedies.

A considerable number of the American pilots chose to make the military a career. Some of these men would fight again, like Phil Colman of the 5th Fighter Group, who shot down four MiGs over Korea.

The story was different for the Chinese members of the CACW, for they were far from finished fighting. Now, however, their enemies were fellow Chinese.

The sudden capitulation of the Japanese following the atomic bombings left the Kuomintang in a bad position in late 1945. Repressive and exploitive, Chiang Kai-shek's government was unready and unable to take control of the vast armies of China surrendered by the Japanese. Moreover, the Nationalist government had competition: Mao Tse-tung's Communists. The bitter rivalry between the two organizations that had been put on hold by the war against Japan now was rekindled and burst into the flames of revolution.

With off-again, on-again cease-fires and half-hearted attempts to form a coalition government, the struggle between the Nationalists and Communists grew steadily more intense. Early in 1946 it appeared that U.S. mediator Gen. George Marshall had made some progress toward settling the dispute, but by April the Communists were on the move in Manchuria while Chiang struck at the Red guerrillas in North China. Angered, the U.S. government cut off aid to Chiang for the next eight months.

In the meantime, the island of Formosa, now called Taiwan, had been returned to Chinese control after its long period under the Japanese. At first, the island was inundated with corrupt Kuomintang officials and profiteering Chinese merchants. By February 1947 the exploitation had caused such unrest among Formosans that the Communists were able to incite serious rioting. In one of his wiser moves, Chiang cleaned house and started over to make Taiwan a "model colony." He installed some of his most trusted generals and his own son to run the island, setting the stage for later events.

Throughout this period, and indeed until the end of the civil war, the units of what had been the CACW were in action. The CAF leadership, however, apparently was unable to employ the hitting power of these outfits with anything like the effectiveness that the 14th Air Force had. Perhaps all the years of hoarding and holding back had left the CAF unprepared to go on the offensive.

Chiang's control of the army was slipping away, and early in 1948 the soldiers began to mutiny in Manchuria. By August much of the remaining army had been cut off by the Communists in Manchuria and was under seige. Thousands more were killed and the remainder were evacuated south in October. Control in North China also evaporated at this time, the Communists taking Nanking and the Yangtze Valley in December 1948, then Peking and Tientsin in January 1949.

A peace conference followed in April 1949, but the Nationalists were unwilling to accept Mao's demands. On April 20, 1949, the Communists attacked south across the Yangtze River. By this time Chiang had moved to Taiwan, and the remnants of the Nationalist government were on the south coast at Canton. The Communists marched south practically unopposed. When Canton was taken in October, the Nationalists moved west to Kunming, with the Communists hot on their heels. On October 10, 1949, Mao proclaimed the formation of the Chinese People's Republic. Chiang flew to Chungking to try to mount a last-ditch counterattack, but it was far too late. He left the mainland for the last time on December 10, 1949.

With the Nationalists now driven from the mainland, the Communists began massing their forces on the southwest coast for a final assault on Taiwan via the offshore islands of Quemoy and Matsu. Instead, the Korean War broke out in June 1950, and the Communists diverted their attention to the more pressing matter. While an invasion across the Taiwan Straits would have been very difficult for the Communists, lacking air power as they did, it is nevertheless probable that the Korean conflict was all that saved Chiang's government from extinction in the early 1950s.

General Kuo recalled, in a letter to the author: "After the removal of the CACW in 1945, all the units engaged themselves actively in combat to subjugate the rebellion of Chicom and fought in every theater of war on the mainland, obtaining fruitful combat results. In 1949, those units retreated one after another from the mainland to Taiwan, performing the mission of blockading the coastal areas of the mainland so as to ensure air superiority over the Taiwan Straits."

At the end of World War II, the highest-ranking CAF officers in the CACW were lieutenant colonels, too young and without enough rank to exert much influence, despite their experience and proven ability in combat. Time remedied that situation eventually, and the CACW veterans were to provide the Chinese Air Force with a solid core of leadership with which to enter the jet age.

In 1953, the jet age arrived on Taiwan, when the CAF began to reequip with North American F-86 Sabrejet fighters. Many of the Sabres had been flown by USAF squadrons in Korea before the fighting ended there in late July 1953.

Eugene Strickland recalls that period:

"In 1953 while on Okinawa I visited Taiwan and talked at length about the effectiveness of the Chinese Air Force on Taiwan. At that time the Chinese Air Force had wholly adopted the supply and maintenance procedures developed in the CACW, and this experience with the CACW had made the job much easier.

"In my squadron, all pilots except one chose to go to Taiwan. This squadron [the 28th] had the highest number of officers of any Chinese unit to make general officer."

The passage of time had done its job: the CACW veterans were now in control of the CAF. Gen. Hsu Huan-Hsien, the second vice-commander of the CACW, became the commander in chief of the CAF. As a young officer in 1938, Hsu had flown the first raid of World War II over Japan, leading two Martin B-10s on a leaflet-dropping mission to Nagasaki and Fukuoka.

Five years of preparation and training left the CAF in a high state of readiness in 1958 when the Communists again began making noises about invading Taiwan. In a series of air battles over the Taiwan Straits during September 1958 the CAF clearly established its superiority over the Communists' MiGs. In fact, on September 24, 1958, the CAF became the first air force in history to use heat-seeking air-to-air missiles in combat, when fourteen Sabres took on twenty Migs over the straits and destroyed ten of the Communist fighters, with no losses. Four of the kills were made with American-built Sidewinder missiles.

The CAF has remained one of the most potent air forces in Asia, and the spirit of the CACW continues to have a heavy influence. All of the CACW units remain in existence: the 1st Bomb Group has become a fighter-bomber unit and was flying F-5As in 1979, the 3d Fighter Group converted from F-86Fs to F-5Es in 1979, and the 5th Fighter Group was flying F-104G interceptors in 1979.

General Kuo summed up the state of the CAF in 1982 this way:

"Today, all the CAF units . . . glorify their traditional spirit of loyalty and bravery and the adventurous morale shown in the period of the CACW, and they stick firmly to the democratic camp to curb the expansion of Communism."

CACW Unit Commanders, 1943–45

USAAF

Wing HQ
Winslow C. Morse, October '43
T. Alan Bennett, December '44

1st Bomb Group
John A. Hilger, August '43
Irving L. Branch, September '43
David J. Munson, September '44
Austin Russell, December '44
  1st B.S.
  John H. Washington, October '43
  Raymond L. Hodges, September '44
  Richard Varney, May '45
2d B.S.
Thomas F. Foley, August '43
Winston S. Churchill, April '44
William P. Carson, June '44
Lawson Horner, September '44

CAF

Vice-Wing Commander
Chiang I-Fu, March '44
Hsu Huan-Hsien, January '45

Li Hsuch-Yen, December '43
Wang Yu-ken, August '44

Lee Yien-Luo, October '43
Wang Chih-Lung, March '44
Huang Ho-Sheng, December '44

Hu Chao-Tung, November '43
Song Shou-Ch'un, February '44
Yang Leu-shyang, July '45

3d B.S.
Chester M. Conrad, March '44
Mark Seacrest, February '45
——Hamilton, April '45
4th B.S.
William H. Dick, January '44
Henry Stanley, April '45

Wu Ch'ao-chern, July '44
Mao Shang-chien, July '45

Chang Tyng-Chieh, March '44
Tung Kai-Shyuan, September '44

3d Fighter Group
T. Alan Bennett, August '43
William N. Reed, December '44
William L. Turner, December '44
J. Gilpin Bright, January '45
Eugene L. Strickland, March '45
William Yancey, July '45
  7th F.S.
  William N. Reed, October '43
  Armit W. Lewis, December '44
  Thomas A. Reynolds, January '45
  Bert Welch, May '45
  Ross Bachley, July '45
  8th F.S.
  Howard Cords, October '43
  Harvey Davis, April '44
  James T. Bull, September '44
  Frank Klump, December '44
  Eugene H. Mueller, February '45
  28th F.S.
  Eugene L. Strickland, August '43
  Keith Lindell, December '44
  Robert Ferguson, May '45
  Donald Campbell, June '45
  32d F.S.
  William L. Turner, August '43
  Raymond L. Callaway,
    September '44
  Herman Byrd, December '44
  Jesse Harris, May '45

Yuan Chin-Han, October '43
Yang Ku-Fan, August '45

Hsu Chi-Hsiang, October '43
Yieh Won-Fie, November '44
Wang Kuang-Fu, March '45

Liu Meng-Jinn, March '44
Tsang Hsi-Lan, June '44
Niu Tseng-Sheng, September '44

Tseng Pei-Fu, August '43
Cheng Sung-Ting, September '43
Yang Yun Kuang, December '44

Hung Chi-Wei, August '43

5th Fighter Group

Frank E. Rouse, January '44

John A. Dunning, November '44

Charles C. Wilder, June '45

Howard M. Means, July '45

17th F.S.

Charles C. Wilder, March '44

Glyn W. Ramsey, November '44

Frank W. Stevens, April '45

26th F.S.

Robert L. Van Ausdall, January '44

William J. Johnson, March '45

27th F.S.

James A. Dale, March '44

Irving A. Erickson, January '45

Winton E., Matthews, April '45

William H. Joyner, August '45

29th F.S.

William T. Hull, January '44

Frederick F. Ploetz, February '45

Frank K. Everest, May '45

Richard Turner, May '45

Byron E. McKenzie, June '45

Henry W. Lawrence, July '45

Shiang Kuan-Cheng, January '44

Chang Tang-Tien, September '44

Chiang Hsiu-Hui, March '44

Hsiang Shih-Tuan, June '44

Yao Jei, January '44

Chu Fu-Hua, July '44

Wei Hsien-Ko, February '45

Li Chao-Chyuan, March '44

Liao Kuang-Chia, November '44

Ho H.H., January '44

Chang C.M., July '45

Fighter Aces of the CACW

The following list of fighter pilots who claimed five or more aerial victories is based on the authors' study of available records. It should be noted that these tallies agree with the research published by Dr. Frank J. Olynyk in 1986. One other ace flew briefly with the 3d Fighter Group, Lt. Col. Gil Bright. However, all his victories were scored prior to his service in the CACW.

William N. Reed, 7th F.S.	9	(Includes three victories scored with AVG, 1942)
William L. Turner, 32d F.S.	8	(Includes three victories scored in the Southwest Pacific, 1942)
Heyward A. Paxton, Jr., 7th F.S.	6.5	
Wang Kuang-Fu, 7th F.S.	6.5	
Raymond L. Callaway, 8th F.S.	6	(Later served in 32d F.S.)
Philip E. Colman, 26th F.S.	6	
Tsang Hsi-Lan, 8th F.S.	6	(Includes one victory scored with 75th F.S., 1943)
Tan Kun, 7th and 32d F.S.	5	

In addition, four CACW pilots were credited with four aerial victories: William K. Bonneaux, 17th F.S.; Chung Han Fei, 32d F.S.; Leng Pei-Su, 29th F.S.; Thomas A. Reynolds, Jr., 17th and 7th fighter squadrons, who also was credited with thirty-eight Japanese aircraft destroyed on the ground.

CACW Aircraft Markings

3d Fighter Group P-40s:

The four squadrons of the 3d each were equipped initially with ten new P-40Ns, which they received at the end of their training at Malir and flew over the Hump into China.

The first two squadrons, the 28th and 32d, got their fighters, all N-5 models, in October 1943. By the time the 7th and 8th squadrons got their aircraft in December 1943, P-40N-15s were available for them. All were painted in standard USAAF camouflage of olive drab over neutral gray, and some displayed leading/trailing edge dappling in medium green.

All P-40s flown by the 3d F.G. carried Chinese Air Force markings, though they varied a little. Generally, the twelve-pointed Kuomintang star in white on blue roundel was painted on the fuselage and on the bottom of both wings. Some fighters, however, didn't have the fuselage star. Most fighters also carried the 12 blue-and-white rudder stripes that were standard CAF marking. The blue in all these Chinese markings was considerably lighter than USAAF insignia blue, but it varied somewhat from plane to plane.

And, of course, there were the shark mouths. Hardly a single P-40 flew in the 3d without its teeth bared in a fearsome grin. The shapes of these markings varied, but each squadron seemed to have its own style and placement for the shark's eye.

A complicated system of unit markings also was worked out in the 3d, and it was further confused by the fact that aircraft often were swapped among squadrons and flown by pilots of other squadrons. The basic marking was a three-digit number painted in white or yellow about ten inches high on the fin. In the spring of 1944, each squadron also was allotted a block of four letters, one of which was applied with a single-digit number eighteen inches high in white behind the fuselage roundel. Apparently, only the numbers 1, 2, 3, and 4 were used on the fuselage. Finally, the CAF serial number was applied on the fin of some fighters below the aircraft number, again in yellow or white, but in very small figures. All Chinese serials began with "P" on fighters, followed by five digits.

All squadrons displayed kill markings on their P-40s, though not all fighters displayed their pilots' names.

Individual squadron markings were as follows:

7th F.S.—Tail numbers generally were 660–670, though some strays slipped in during the summer of 1944, when losses were heavy. The fuselage letters assigned were I-J-K-L. The squadron had a distinct shark mouth that turned up in a sinister grin on many of its fighters, though some P-40s that were obtained from the 5th F.G. retained their more rounded mouths. Some of the assignments during the summer of 1944 were: Bill Reed, 660, then 461 ("Boss's Hoss"); Wang Kuang-Fu, 663; A. W. Lewis, 664 ("Mouse House"); Don Burch, 665 ("Ruth-Less"); Ed Mulholland, 666 ("Pal Jim").

8th F.S.—Tail numbers were 678–689, again with strays. Fuselage letters were M-N-O-P, and shark mouths varied widely. Assignments included: Ray Callaway, 681 ("Shirley II"); Coyd Yost, 684; Tsang Hsi-lan, 610.

28th F.S.—Numbers were 631–639, plus a series from the 5th F.G. in the 700 range. Fuselage letters were E-F-G-H. Individual assignments: Eugene Strickland, 631, then 633 ("Porcupine II and III"); Richard Daggett, 638 ("Peep and Weep"); James Bush, 632, ("Corky"); James Sagmiller, 632, 633, and 640 (one of them was "Nana"); Cheng Sung-Ting, 637, then 731.

32d F.S.—Tail numbers were 640–657; fuselage letters were A-B-C-D. Known aircraft assignments were: Bill Turner, 646 (he had two of them); Tom Maloney, 648 ("Bad Tom").

The P-40s were modified in a number of ways to fit their fighter-bomber roles. Most, if not all, carried a DF loop atop the fuselage behind the canopy. They all were equipped with makeshift bomb racks under their wings (factory equipment on N-20 and later models), and some had fittings for rocket tubes outboard of the bomb racks. A few were equipped with cameras for recon work.

3d Fighter Group P-51s:

The group's first P-51s were C-models that came to Laohokow in January 1945 with a detachment of the 16th F.S., 51st F.G. These mostly natural metal fighters carried USAAF markings, three-digit tail numbers in the 300s, and many had shark mouths. Later detachments from the 25th and 26th fighter squadrons or the 51st would bring P-51Ds and -Ks to Laohokow, and all these 51st fighters were turned over to the 3d when the detachments rejoined their squadrons in South China.

In the spring of 1945 more P-51s became available in China, and the 3d F.G. started getting new D- and K-models, as well as a few F-6 recon Mustangs. These fighters mostly carried CAF markings. It is unknown, however, if the 3d's fuselage-marking system survived the transition to P-51s. Another item to note about the CAF-marked P-51s is that they did not carry a shark mouth marking unless they were former 51st F.G. aircraft that had been repainted into CAF markings.

5th Fighter Group P-40s:

The 5th F.G. also flew P-40Ns almost exclusively until they were replaced by P-51s in 1945. The first two squadrons, the 26th and 29th, originally were equipped with a mixed group of P-40N-15s, -20s, and -25s. These were the most distinctive of all CACW P-40s because of special markings applied to them at Malir. A supply of experimental "haze" camouflage paint had been obtained from Eglin Field, Florida, and this whitish color was applied liberally to the P-40s. The paint's reflective qualities made surfaces painted with it nearly invisible under certain light conditions, so it was applied to the spinners, leading edges of the wings, and the wingtips, plus areas of the tail surfaces.

The haze scheme was short-lived on most of the fighters. Upon their joining combat in China, it was found that the paint was so effective at changing the appearance of the P-40s that they were attacked several times by friendly fighters. The haze paint was ordered covere4 up, but at least one of the P-40s retained the scheme, Col. John Dunning's "Sam." Insult was added to injury in late April 1944, when half of these special fighters were turned over to 3d F.G. squadrons—primarily the 7th and 28th—for use during Mission A.

In any case, the white spinner marking of the early P-40s was retained on subsequent 5th F.G. P-40s, and it is a fairly reliable way of distinguishing P-40s of the two CACW fighter groups if tail numbers aren't known.

Like the 3d F.G., the 5th used a series of three-digit tail numbers as plane-in-group markings. These were about ten inches tall and were painted in black on most fighters. Neither Chinese nor USAAF serials were visible on the tails, though squadron forms referred to the aircraft by their U.S. serials. The numbers were in the 700 range and appear to have been allotted to the squadrons as follows: 17th, 760–770; 26th, 730–740; 27th, 770–784; 29th, 750–760. Headquarters aircraft may have been numbered in the 720s.

Many 5th F.G. P-40s carried names, some in Chinese characters and others in English. A number of them apparently carried kill markings, and the inevitable shark mouth was applied almost universally. There were many aircraft, however, that did not have an eye for the shark. It should be kept in mind that the numbers and other markings in the 5th were very fluid because of the shortages of fighters. It also appears that the 5th received more hand-me-down P-40s from other 14th A.F. units than did the 3d.

Aside from the original twenty-four P-40s, the 5th's -Ns carried the standard CAF fuselage and underwing stars and blue-and-white rudder stripes as described for the 3d (those twenty-four did not have the rudder stripes). As might be imagined, the fighters were camouflaged in the standard USAAF scheme, and the finishes rapidly became faded, stained, and chipped under the harsh conditions at Chihkiang.

5th Fighter Group P-51s:

The 5th F.G. began to get P-51s during the last week of February 1945 and gradually replaced its P-40s throughout the following spring. The squadrons received P-51Cs, -Ds, and -Ks, plus some F-6s. Almost all were natural metal in color, though the first few P-51Cs were olive drab over neutral gray.

The Mustangs retained the three-digit numbering system used on the 5th's P-40s, but they were a mixed batch of U.S. and Chinese national markings. One crew chief recalled that the U.S. markings were painted out with white paint as time allowed, and CAF roundel decals were applied over the painted-out U.S. stars. In all cases, the blue-and-white rudder stripes were eliminated, as was the shark mouth.

The 17th F.S. Mustangs appeared to carry a standard marking of two light blue bands around the top of the fin and rudder, plus a dark color on the rudder tab. Some later 17th P-51s had their entire noses painted a dark color, carried a two-digit tail number, and were in U.S. markings; these may have been hand-me-downs from the 74th F.S., USAAF. The 26th F.S. painted the front of the spinner and top of the fin and rudder black on its P-51s, and the 29th may have painted the tail number in white on a dark horizontal band around the fin and rudder. Markings of the 27th F.S. were polka dots on the fin and rudder. Again, personal markings were common on the Mustangs.

1st Bomb Group B-25s:

The first CACW aircraft to see action were the B-25Ds that the 2d B.S. took to China in October 1943. These were perhaps the ugliest aircraft flown by the wing. They were painted olive drab over neutral gray, but the U.S. markings applied at the factory were roughly painted out and replaced only with small CAF serials on the fins in yellow and Kuomintang stars under the wings.

Early in 1944 the 1st B.G. began getting new B-25Hs, and the 2d B.S. applied tail numbers 601–611 to its ships. When the 1st B.S. arrived at Kweilin in February 1944, its B-25s were numbered in the 700s, but these may have been changed to the 610s and 620s as the 1st and 2d squadrons began to fly together. Markings of the 4th B.S. are unknown. The 3d B.S. carried its squadron badge and aircraft numbers in the 710s and 720s on the noses of its bombers.

The four squadrons were never all up to strength at once until October 1944. By that time a few B-25Js were being received, and many of the H- and J-model Mitchells were in natural metal with CAF stars applied to the fuselage and undersides of the wings. Others carried U.S. insignia. Some B-25s at Chihkiang in 1945, probably of the 4th B.S., carried the CAF rudder stripes and no tail numbers at all.

Personal markings were common on 1st B.G. Mitchells, especially later in the war, with aircraft names, crew names, suqadron crests, and mission markers all in vogue.

Notes

Chapter 1

1. Chinese place names are listed in this book by the traditional spellings, which were in use during the life of the CACW, rather than the Pinyin spellings used today.
2. CACW headquarters unit history.
3. CACW headquarters unit history.
4. Letter from Henry C.Y. Lee to Molesworth, June 26, 1980.
5. Lee letter.
6. CACW headquarters unit history.
7. In Chinese, the person's surname is listed first. This book uses full names where possible; however, in many cases initials must stand for the pilots' given names, as they were listed in this fashion on most combat reports.
8. 3d Fighter Group unit history.
9. CACW headquarters unit history.

Chapter 2

1. Clinton D. Vincent and Glenn McClure, *Fire and Fall Back*. San Antonio: Barnes Press, 1975: page 132.
2. 28th Fighter Squadron unit history.

Chapter 3

1. Tape from Glyn Ramsey to Moseley, December 14, 1981.

2. "A Brief Outline of Events as They Happened During My Period of Overseas Service," an unpublished account by Robert D. Kruidenier, Fall 1945.
3. "The Real Thing," an unpublished article by Marvin A. Marx, 1974.
4. Interview with Charles Lovett, September 12, 1981, Portland, Oregon.

Chapter 4

1. Letter from William E. McCullough to Molesworth, March 24, 1980.
2. Ramsey tape.
3. 26th Fighter Squadron unit history.
4. Kruidenier account. A ground loop occurs when a moving aircraft twirls on its wheels at high speed, usually during the landing roll.
5. Ramsey tape.
6. Ramsey tape.
7. Letter from Glenn Burnham to Moseley, December 30, 1980.

Chapter 5

1. Letter from John Henderson to Molesworth, March 8, 1982.
2. Letter from Raymond L. Callaway to Molesworth, October 7, 1980.
3. CACW headquarters unit history.
4. Letter from Richard C. Daggett to Molesworth, February 7, 1986.
5. Letter from Armit W. Lewis to Molesworth, July 8, 1985.
6. Lewis letter. "Recce" was a slang term for a reconnaissance mission.

Chapter 6

1. Kruidenier account.
2. 26th Fighter Squadron unit history.
3. Kruidenier account.
4. Tape recording by James W. Bennie, January 1981.
5. Bennie tape.
6. Letter from Clifford L. Condit, February 9, 1981.
7. Ramsey tape.

Chapter 7

1. 28th Fighter Squadron unit history.

Chapter 8

1. Letter from William King to Molesworth, October 26, 1981.
2. King letter.
3. Ramsey tape.
4. Ramsey tape.

Chapter 9

1. Letter from James R. Silver to Molesworth, September 6, 1982.
2. Silver letter.
3. Lovett interview.
4. *Cedar Rapids Gazette,* approximately September 4, 1942.
5. 32d Fighter Squadron unit history.

Chapter 10

1. Letter from Thomas A. Reynolds, Jr., to Molesworth, August 30, 1981.
2. CACW headquarters unit history.
3. Letter from Joe L. Page to Molesworth, July 14, 1982.
4. Letter from Robert L. Gardner to Molesworth, August 8, 1980.
5. Letter from Burr Shafer to Molesworth, March 21, 1980.

Chapter 11

1. Interview with Glyn W. Ramsey, October 1981, Garland, Texas.
2. "Big John Dunning—A Texan in the Air Force," by Robert E. Hays, Jr., *Texas Military History,* Winter 1964.
3. Ramsey interview.
4. Letter from Glyn Ramsey to Molesworth, October 6, 1981.
5. 26th Fighter Squadron unit history.
6. "The Chihkiang Campaign, A Study of Air-Ground Teamwork," prepared by the 24th Statistical Control Unit, 14th Air Force, 1945.

Chapter 12

1. Letter from J. W. Fetzer to Moseley, February 25, 1981.
2. Letter from Allen H. Sweeney to Molesworth, March 16, 1982.
3. 1st Bomb Group unit history.
4. 1st Bomb Group unit history.

Bibliography

Books

Byrd, Martha. *Chennault—Giving Wings to the Tiger.* Tuscaloosa: University of Alabama Press, 1987.

Cornelius, Wanda, and Short, Thayne. *Ding Hao—America's Air War in China.* Gretna, La.: Pelican Publishing Co., 1980.

Craven, W. F., and Crate, J. L. *The Army Air Forces in World War II,* vols. IV and V. University of Chicago Press, 1950.

Heiferman, Ron. *Flying Tigers—Chennault in China.* New York: Ballantine Books, Inc., 1971.

Hess, William. *The American Aces of World War II and Korea.* New York: Arco Publishing Co., 1968.

Little, Wallace H. *Tiger Sharks.* Memphis, Tenn.: Castle Books, 1986.

Liu, F. F. *A Military History of Modern China, 1924–1949.* Princeton, N.J.: Princeton University Press, 1956.

Lopez, Donald S. *Into the Teeth of the Tiger.* New York: Bantam Books, 1986.

Rosholt, Malcolm. *Days of the Ching Pao.* Amherst, Wis.: Palmer Publications Inc., 1978.

Rosholt, Malcolm. *Flight in the China Air Space, 1910–1950.* Rosholt, Wis.: Rosholt House, 1984.

Rust, Kenn C., and Muth, Steve. *Fourteenth Air Force Story.* Temple City, Calif.: Historical Aviation Album, 1977.

Schultz, Duane. *The Maverick War—Chennault and the Flying Tigers.* New York: St. Martin's Press, 1987.

Vincent, Clinton D., and McClure, Glenn. *Fire and Fall Back.* San Antonio: Barnes Press, 1975.

Periodicals

Air Force magazine, "The Chinese-American Composite Wing," Lt. Col. Kenneth Kay, USAF ret., February 1976.

Cedar Rapids Gazette, "Bill Reed's Bag Grows to 16½ Planes," Clyde Farnsworth, approximately December 16, 1944.

Ibid., "AVG Flyers Rest in India on Way Home," Associated Press, July 25, 1942.

Jing Bao Journal, "Tragedy in the Mediterranean," Roland Smith, February 1978.

Ibid., "The Birth of the CACW," Malcolm Rosholt, October 1977.

Journal of the American Aviation Historical Society, "CACW—An American Ace in the Chinese-American Composite Wing," Hugh Stephens Moseley, M.D., Winter 1973.

Marion Sentinel, "Flying Tiger Bill Reed Lost in China," January 4, 1945.

Texas Military History, "Big John Dunning—A Texan in the Air Force," Robert E. Hays, Jr., Winter 1964.

Unpublished Unit Histories

Chinese-American Composite Wing headquarters; 1st Bomb Group; 3d and 5th fighter groups; 7th, 8th, 17th, 26th, 27th, 28th, 29th, and 32d fighter squadrons, CACW.

16th Fighter Squadron, 51st Fighter Group, USAAF.

Index